CONRAD: THE LATER FICTION

CONRAD: THE LATER FICTION

Daniel R. Schwarz

Professor of English
Cornell University

MACMILLAN PRESS
LONDON

First edition 1982
Reprinted 1983

Published by
THE MACMILLAN PRESS LTD
London and Basingstoke
Companies and representatives
throughout the world

ISBN 0 333 28308 2

Printed in Great Britain
by Anthony Rowe Ltd,
Chippenham

For my sons, David and Jeffrey

Contents

Acknowledgements

I am indebted to my colleagues in the Cornell English Department for advice and encouragement, and to my students for their perceptive responses to Conrad's works.

The Henry W. and Albert A. Berg Collection of the New York Public Library and the Astor, Lenox and Tilden Foundations have permitted me to quote from the Conrad material in the Berg Collection. An earlier version of my discussion of *The Shadow-Line* appeared in *Renascence* 29 (Spring 1977). I appreciate the generous support of the Cornell Faculty Humanities Research fund and the Cornell English Department grant-in-aid fund.

My greatest debt, as always, is to my wife Marcia.

Cornell University   DANIEL R. SCHWARZ
Ithaca, New York
January 1980

Abbreviations and a Note on the Text

I have used the following abbreviations for editions of the letters:

Garnett—Edward Garnett, *Letters from Joseph Conrad 1895–1924* (Indianapolis: Bobbs-Merrill, 1928).

LL, i or ii—G. Jean-Aubry, *Joseph Conrad: Life and Letters*, 2 vols (Garden City, NY: Doubleday, Page, 1927).

NLL—Joseph Conrad, *Notes on Life and Letters* (Garden City, NY: Doubleday, 1926).

Mme Poradowska—John A. Gee and Paul J. Sturm, *Letters of Joseph Conrad to Marguerite Poradowska, 1890–1920* (New Haven, Conn.: Yale University Press, 1940).

I have used the Kent edition of Conrad's works (Garden City, NY: Doubleday, 1926). For the shorter fiction, page numbers in parentheses refer to the collected edition in which the tale appears:

'Twixt Land and Sea: 'The Secret Sharer', 'A Smile of Fortune', 'Freya of the Seven Isles'.

Within the Tides: 'The Partner', 'The Inn of the Two Witches', 'The Planter of Malata', 'Because of the Dollars'.

Tales of Hearsay: 'The Black Mate', 'Prince Roman', 'The Warrior's Soul', 'The Tale'.

Occasionally Conrad did not publish his works in the order he wrote them. Within the text, dates in parentheses refer to the year the work was first published in periodical or book form. The appendix provides the date that each work of fiction was completed.

Introduction

Conrad: The Later Fiction continues the critical consideration of the entire canon of Conrad's fiction that I began in *Conrad: 'Almayer's Folly' to 'Under Western Eyes'*. Like my prior study, this book is concerned less with arguing a particular thesis than with examining each work according to its intellectual and aesthetic assumptions. Once again, I shall demonstrate that Conrad's characteristic themes and techniques derive in large part from his struggle to define his own character and values. In this work I take issue with a widely held assumption that, after 'The Secret Sharer' (1910) and *Under Western Eyes* (1911), most of Conrad's work from 1910 until his death in 1924 is not worth serious critical attention. I also differ with the two most influential critics of Conrad's later work, Thomas Moser and John A. Palmer. By showing the continuity of Conrad's art, this book questions both Palmer's argument in his *Joseph Conrad's Fiction* (1968) that Conrad writes symbolic and allegorical works in his later years, and Moser's contention in *Joseph Conrad: Achievement and Decline* (1957) that Conrad falters when he deals with the uncongenial subject of heterosexual love.

I believe that Conrad's later writing is best understood as an evolution and development of his prior methods, themes and values. He still demonstrates that each man's epistemology is peculiarly his own, the function of his psyche and experience, and he still regards man's moral behaviour as resulting from psychological needs that are often dimly understood or barely acknowledged. Conrad's letters provide evidence for the continuity of his work. For example, the following passage from a 1918 letter could have been written to Edward Garnett twenty years earlier:

> That is the tragedy—the inner anguish—the bitterness of lost
> lives, of unsettled consciences and of spiritual perplexities.
> Courage, endurance, enthusiasm, the hardest idealism itself,

have their limits. And beyond those limits what is there? The
eternal ignorance of mankind, the fateful darkness in which
only vague forms can be seen which themselves may be no
more than illusions.[1]

In a 1913 letter to Francis Warrington Dawson, he echoes the
language of the Preface to The Nigger of the 'Narcissus' (1897) when
describing the artist's lonely, agonising struggle to create: 'Suffering is
an attribute almost a condition of greatness, of devotion, of an
altogether self-forgetful sacrifice to that remorseless fidelity to the
truth of his own sensations at whatever [sic] cost of pain or contumely
which for me is the whole Credo of the artist.'[2] Conrad is still a
sceptical humanist who believes that man's best hope rests in personal
relationships. Conrad resented those who neglected his humanism
and implicitly accused him of 'brutality' and 'lack of delicacy';[3] he
always insisted that, as he wrote to Arthur Symons, 'I have always
approached my task in the spirit of love for mankind' (Aug 1908, LL,
ii, p. 73). Of course, despite the considerable continuity of his career,
Conrad still sought the appropriate form and style for each subject
and never ceased in his search for new subjects.

II

In 1910 Conrad was in his fifty-third year. He had lived and written
in England for sixteen years, and was very conscious that he was
ageing. While he had become recognised as an important novelist, he
had not achieved financial success. He was regarded as an oddity even
by his admirers, an outsider who wrote in English but whose
temperament and values were not quite English. His self-image
oscillated between, on the one hand, pride in his achievement and
artistic integrity and, on the other hand, disgust with his difficulties in
completing his work and despair about his severe financial problems.
He suffered from lack of public recognition and was still plagued by
personal and artistic self-doubt. As always, writing was extremely
trying for Conrad. He feared that he would leave both Chance (1912)
and The Rescue (1919) unfinished and that he would not reach the
goal of twenty volumes that he set for himself.[4] His relations with
Ford Madox Ford and his agent James Pinker were strained, and he
was beset by anxiety, hypochondria and gout. In this frame of mind
he suffered a nervous breakdown.

Bernard Meyer has written that after the 1910 breakdown Conrad 'could no longer afford these introspective journeys into the self'.[5] But this ignores the introspective journeys of *The Shadow-Line* (1916), *The Arrow of Gold* (1919) and *The Rover* (1923). One cannot agree with Meyer that 'the doubting, troubled men, like Marlow of *Heart of Darkness*, and hapless souls Jim or Decoud, caught in a neurotic web of their own creation, gave way to simple innocent creatures who, as pawns of fate, struggle with indifferent success against external influence, external accidents, and external malevolence'.[6] The later fiction, like the prior work, shows that man is ineffectual in his effort to shape permanently the larger rhythm of historical events, but is able to form personal ties and sometimes to act boldly in his own or others' interest. In 'The Secret Sharer', *The Shadow-Line* and *The Rover*, temporary personal victories give life meaning. And the act of telling in 'The Secret Sharer', *The Shadow-Line* and *The Arrow of Gold* is a kind of affirmation; by using assertive, energetic first-person narrators to structure important aspects of his own past, Conrad becomes, as he had been in the 1898–1900 Marlow tales, an active presence within his works. In the later works, passionate love and deep feeling temporarily rescue life from meaninglessness, even if they only provide fragments to shore against one's ruins.

Indeed, in the years that followed the breakdown, Conrad began to achieve financial stability and some measure of personal security. Selling manuscripts to John Quinn helped alleviate his debts. On occasion, Conrad would compromise his artistic integrity by writing potboilers for *Metropolitan Magazine*. Finally, beginning with *Chance*, his books began to sell. Gradually he began to create a public mask. In particular, he was concerned not only with marketing his works, but also with how he should appear as a literary presence. He developed a public personality for interviews and dialogues with critics, and adopted surrogate sons such as Richard Curle, Jean-Aubry, Gide and Warrington Dawson, all of whom propagated his reputation in the world of letters and in the market-place. He became more of an urbane Englishman and cultivated a stance of moderation and worldliness. Although, in his last years, he was somewhat shunted aside by the surge of the next generation of literary modernism, represented by the works of Joyce, Pound, Eliot, Lawrence and Woolf, he occupied a prominent place in the world of letters until his death in 1924.

III

Since I discussed *Under Western Eyes* in my prior study, *Conrad: The Later Fiction* begins with a consideration of the last two volumes of short fiction that were published in Conrad's lifetime. While 'The Secret Sharer' is one of Conrad's masterpieces, many of these short stories were artistic laboratories for the kind of fiction he wrote after *Under Western Eyes* (1911). After 'The Secret Sharer', Conrad was for the most part interested in his novels rather than his short stories. Although Conrad rarely used the romance element in the novels without including a component of realism, these stories, often written for the popular imagination, taught him to use the kind of simplified plot that provided the framework for the later novels.

We can divide Conrad's career after 1910 into three distinct phases. In the first, Conrad wanted to demonstrate that he was an English novelist, not a Slav writing in English, as some reviewers implied. The diffident, self-effacing narrator of *Under Western Eyes* owes something to this impulse. In a sense, *Under Western Eyes*, *Chance* and *Victory* (1915) are Conrad's English trilogy. Thus *Chance* and *Victory* focus explicitly on personal relationships and manners, and allude to contemporary issues in England. He had to prove to his audience and perhaps to himself that he had become an English writer. *Chance* and *Victory* represent Conrad's attempt to write English novels of manners and to explore the intricacies of personal relationships in the context of contemporary customs and values. He regarded *Victory* as a 'strictly proper' work 'meant for cultured people'[7] and he thought that 'The Secret Sharer' was English 'in moral atmosphere, feeling and even in detail'.[8]

In *Chance* and *Victory*, Conrad's subject matter is less his own life than the external world. The form and narrative technique stress his detachment and withdrawal. Even when he revives Marlow in *Chance*, that figure is no longer a surrogate who echoes his own anxieties and doubts. Although we certainly see important resemblances between Conrad and his characters Heyst and Captain Anthony, he is not primarily writing about fictional versions of himself.

The second phase of Conrad's later career derives more from a personal impulse. After *Chance* and *Victory*, he returns from contemporary issues to his own memories. *The Shadow-Line* and *The Arrow of Gold*, like 'The Secret Sharer' and 'A Smile of Fortune'

(1911), are expressive of Conrad's emotions and passions, but in these works, unlike the Marlow tales, Conrad recreates emotions of the past more than he objectifies his present inner turmoil. As Conrad aged, he sought subjects in his personal and literary past, and his fiction less frequently addresses his immediate personal problems or current public issues. *The Shadow-Line* and *The Arrow of Gold* reached back into his personal past, while *The Rescue* was completed primarily to settle his long standing anxiety about a work that had been stalled for two decades. *The Rescue* returns to the romance world of Malay which provided the setting of his first two novels, *Almayer's Folly* and *An Outcast of the Islands*, as well as such early tales as 'Karain' and 'The Lagoon'. It is a nostalgic look at his personal and literary past and provides something of an escape from Conrad's present anxieties and harsher memories.

In the final phase, he looks back in *The Rover* and the incomplete *Suspense* to the Napoleonic period and creates large historical canvases that recall the great political novels. While we do not know what he would have done in *Suspense*, his real concern in *The Rover* is coming to terms with his own approaching death. In that novel, the Napoleonic era provides the occasion for a moving lyrical novel about the possibility of facing death heroically. The principal character, an ageing seaman and an outsider, is a fictional counterpart of Conrad.

NOTES

1. From a letter of 6 Feb 1918 to John Quinn, quoted in Frederick Karl, *Joseph Conrad: The Three Lives* (New York: Farrar, Straus and Giroux, 1979), pp. 807–8. I am indebted to Karl's account of Conrad's later years.
2. Quoted ibid., p. 730, from a letter of 20 June 1913 to Warrington Dawson.
3. For example, see letter of 28 Aug 1908 to Garnett; quoted ibid., p. 650n.
4. See ibid., p. 639.
5. Bernard C. Meyer, *Joseph Conrad: A Psychoanalytic Biography* (Princeton, NJ: Princeton University Press, 1967), p. 243.
6. Ibid., p. 221.
7. From a letter of 7 Oct 1912 to Pinker; quoted in Karl, *Conrad: The Three Lives*, p. 717.
8. From a letter of 8 Dec 1912 to Edith Wharton; quoted and paraphrased ibid., p. 725.

1 'Twixt Land and Sea

'Twixt Land and Sea (1912) contains three long stories written for magazines in the 1909–11 period. 'The Secret Sharer' is one of the great tales in the English language, but, although not major works, the others—'Freya of the Seven Isles' and 'A Smile of Fortune'— deserve to be read more than they are. All three tales explore a young captain under stress. Although in this period of renewed personal and financial turmoil Conrad's imagination turns nostalgically to life at sea, the sea is no longer the simplified world of 'Typhoon' or 'The End of the Tether', where moral distinctions are clear. In these 1909–11 tales, a young captain is faced with circumstances and emotional traumas for which neither the maritime code nor his experience has prepared him. Both 'Freya of the Seven Isles' and 'A Smile of Fortune' provide evidence that Conrad is interested in the hetero-sexual relationships of inexperienced young adults. In each case an ingenuous and imperceptive male figure ceases to function effectively in his career because of his passionate involvement with an immature young woman. 'A Smile of Fortune' is the most autobiographical and the most revealing; in fact, it may suffer from Conrad's inability to separate himself from the captain--narrator. But 'The Secret Sharer' is personal in the way great lyrical poetry is personal, drawing from experience that is at once individual (Conrad's assuming the captaincy of the Otago in 1888) and representative of the deepest strains of human experience: fear and self-doubt in the face of challenge.[1]

II. 'THE SECRET SHARER' (1910)

The failure to concentrate on the narrator has been responsible for some rather bizarre interpretations of 'The Secret Sharer'. The captain--narrator recounts a tale of initiation in which he successfully overcame debilitating emotional insecurity to command his ship. The significance of the events for the sensitive and intelligent captain is that he discovered within himself the *ability to act* decisively that he had lacked. As a younger man, the captain doubted himself, felt a 'stranger' to the community to which he belonged, and wondered if he should 'turn out faithful to that ideal conception of one's personality every man sets up for himself secretly' (p. 94). His concern now is to present the issues in terms of what Leggatt meant to him. Although he certainly knows that harbouring an escaped murderer represents a threat to maritime civilisation and a violation of his own legal and moral commitment, his retelling ignores this.

The captain–narrator, separated by a 'distance of years' from the meeting with Leggatt, delivers a retrospective monologue. But, despite the past tense, the reader often forgets that the events have already occurred; as Albert J. Guerard has written, 'The nominal narrative past is, actually, a harrowing present which the reader too must explore and survive.'[2] Perhaps we can draw upon Louis L. Martz's conception of a meditative poem to clarify what is happening. The intense reflective process in which the speaker's past comes alive in his memory and offers a moment of illumination by which he can order his life, recalls Martz's definition of the meditative process: 'The mind grasps firmly a problem or situation deliberately evoked by the memory, brings it forward toward the full light of consciousness, and concludes with a moment of illumination, where the speaker's self has, for a time, found an answer to his conflicts.'[3] A meditative poem, such as Herbert's 'The Collar', recollects a vital episode in which the speaker experiences spiritual growth by conquering the secular demands of his ego. In both 'The Collar' and 'The Secret Sharer', the recollection is informed by insight that was lacking when the original event took place. That the captain can give meaning and structure to an experience which includes neurotic immobilisation demonstrates his emotional and moral development and his present psychic health.

As I argued in *Conrad: 'Almayer's Folly' to 'Under Western Eyes'*, one of Conrad's recurring themes is that each man interprets events according to his moral and emotional needs. Because one's version of events reflects an interaction between, on the one hand, experience and perception, and, on the other, memories and psychic needs, interpretation always has a subjective element. The captain's interpretation of his experience dramatises the process of his coming to terms with what Leggatt symbolises. In reductive terms, Leggatt is a man of unrestrained id and underdeveloped superego. The captain, an example of hyperconscious modern man who fastidiously thinks of the consequences of every action to the point where he cannot *do* anything, is his opposite. Self-doubt and anxiety create an illogical identification with Leggatt as his 'double'. He risks his future to hide the man he regards as his 'other self'. To avoid discovery, he begins to act desperately and instinctively without conscious examination of the consequences of each action. Leggatt's presence creates situations where the luxury of introspection is no longer possible. Symbolically, the captain completes himself. He finds within himself the potential to act instinctively and boldly that his 'double' exemplifies. It can be said that his adult ego is created by appeasing the contradictory demands of the id and superego. Listening to the narrator, we tentatively suspend our moral perspective and fail to condemn him for giving refuge to a suspected murderer. This is because, as his words engage us and as we become implicated as his confessor, we come partially to share his perspective.

I believe Conrad wishes us to perceive Leggatt and the captain as representatives of a split in modern man between his mind and his instinct. Leggatt's predecessors are Falk and Kurtz, while the captain recalls the narrators of 'Il Conde', 'The Informer' and 'An Anarchist', and anticipates the language-teacher of *Under Western Eyes*, to which Conrad returned after finishing 'The Secret Sharer'. The effect of Leggatt's presence is to disrupt the ship's community and to raise further doubts in the minds of the captain's officers about his own self-control and sanity. The captain becomes more neurotic because he has to consider whether his every sentence and every word might reveal his secret. He now has twin loyalties, mutually exclusive, to the man he is harbouring and with whom he identifies, and to his ship. Paradoxically, the desperation of his paranoia, of his belief that he is constantly being scrutinised by his subordinates, leads him to give his 'first particular order'. When threatened, he 'felt the need of asserting myself'. The pressure of circumstances makes it increasingly difficult for him to distinguish between himself and Leggatt:

> all the time the dual working of my mind distracted me
> almost to the point of insanity. I was constantly watching
> myself, my secret self, as dependent on my actions as my own
> personality, sleeping in that bed, behind the door which faced
> me as I sat at the head of the table. It was very much like
> being mad only it was worse because one was aware of
> it. (pp. 113–14)

His distinction between self and other threatens to collapse; he had the 'mental feeling of being in two places at once [which] affected me physically as if the mood of secrecy had penetrated my very soul' (p. 125). Like Prufrock and Gabriel Conroy, the integrity of the captain's personality is threatened by a disbelief in the authenticity of self. If R. D. Laing's *The Divided Self* aptly describes a phenomenon of modern literature, it is because the terms in which existential psychology describes schizoid conditions are directly related to the crisis of identity which Eliot, Joyce and Conrad analyse:

> If one experiences the other as a free agent, one is open to the possibility of experiencing oneself as an *object* of his experience and thereby of feeling one's own subjectivity drained away. One is threatened with the possibility of becoming no more than a thing in the world of the other, without any life for oneself, without any being for oneself . . . . One may find oneself enlivened and the sense of one's own being enhanced by the other, or one may experience the other as deadening and impoverishing.[4]

Retrospectively it is clear that the captain has been 'enlivened' by his experience of Leggatt, although at first Leggatt's appearance—like the presence of the threatening first mate, whose whiskers and manner intimidate him—has the effect of 'deadening' the captain.

The captain's creation of Leggatt is a major part of the original experience. Before Leggatt's appearance, the captain is immobilised by self-consciousness and self-doubt: 'My position was that of the only *stranger* on board. I mention this because it has some bearing on what is to follow. But what I felt most was my being a *stranger* to the ship; and if all the truth must be told, I was somewhat a *stranger* to myself' (p. 93, emphasis added). That 'stranger' carries the meaning of 'alien' and 'outside' from the French word *étranger* is an instance of how the richness of Conrad's language is occasionally increased by his appropriating French definitions for similarly spelt English words.

The character of Leggatt is a function of the captain's need for someone to share the burdens of loneliness and anxiety. When he hears of Leggatt's alternatives (to keep swimming until he drowns or is welcomed on board the captain's ship) he responds, 'I felt this was no mere formula of desperate speech, but a real alternative in the view of a strong soul. . . . A mysterious communication was established already between us two—in the face of that silent, darkened tropical

sea' (p. 99). The captain recalls that 'the voice was calm and resolute.
A *good* voice. The *self-possession* of that man had somehow induced a
corresponding state in myself' (ibid., emphasis added). But this
contrasts with his original response of seconds before: 'He seemed to
struggle with himself, for I heard something like the low, bitter
murmur of doubt. "What's the good?" His next words come out
with a hesitating effort' (p. 99). Jumping from one assertion to
another without empirical data, the captain continues to convince
himself of Leggatt's resemblance to him on such flimsy grounds as
that they are both 'young'. Although he tells us that they looked
identical, he later admits that Leggatt 'was not a bit like me, really' (p.
105). His original, flattering description of Leggatt is continually
modified until it is almost contradicted. Before Leggatt even begins to
explain how he killed a man, the captain has excused him: ' "Fit of
temper," I suggested, confidently' (p. 101). Insisting upon the value of
his second self enables the captain to discover himself morally and
psychologically. But the process of idealising his 'double', his 'other
self', into a model of self-control, self-confidence and sanity is
arbitrary and non-cognitive. Perhaps we better understand the extent
of the narrator's surrender of self if we recall Laing's analysis of a man
who suffered what he calls 'ontological insecurity': 'In contrast to his
own belittlement of and uncertainty about himself, he was always on
the brink of being overawed and crushed by the formidable reality
that other people contained. In contrast to his own . . . uncertainty,
and insubstantiality, *they* were solid, decisive, emphatic, and substantial.'[5] Despite the evidence that Leggatt murdered another man in a fit
of passion, he holds to a belief in Leggatt's control and sanity and
insists that the killing was an act of duty. But the reader does not
forget that Leggatt commits a horribly immoral act which *he does not
regret.*

Conrad emphasises how the destructive relationship between the
doubting crew and the insecure captain creates the captain's attitude
to Leggatt. He never criticises Leggatt, despite his penchant for
criticising everybody else, from the ratiocinative first mate to the
'impudent second mate' and 'unintelligent' Captain Archbold,
because, believing himself a stranger and an alien on the ship, he
desperately needs an ally against self-doubt and the hostility of the
crew. He identifies with Leggatt not as a criminal, but as an outcast: 'I
felt that it would take very little to make me a suspect person in the
eyes of the ship's company' (p. 110). Because in *the captain's own mind*
Leggatt is the picture of resolute self-confidence, he becomes in some

respects an ideal to be studied: 'And yet, haggard as he *appeared*, he *looked* always perfectly self-controlled, more than calm—almost invulnerable' (p. 127, emphasis added). The foetal position which Leggatt assumes as he hides in the cabin hardly suggests invulnerability. The now-mature captain *believes* he learned from this second self qualities of courage, self-confidence and psychological wholeness which became his means of achieving maturity.

Paradoxically, Leggatt disrupts the captain's psychic health, and hence the order of the ship, at the same time as he is a catalyst for a more efficient integration of both the captain's personality and his fitness to command. As we have seen, the captain projects on Leggatt a confidence he himself lacks and an ability he does not yet possess to face crises. Yet Leggatt's struggle with the crewman came when he was himself highly excited, and he shows considerable emotion several times in discussions with the captain.

The captain is as much Leggatt's secret sharer as Leggatt is the captain's. Indeed, each of the two men has a partial understanding of the other, but each *believes* the other's partial understanding to be complete. In this sense, too, Leggatt is the captain's double. Leggatt says, 'As long as I know that you understand', and then adds, 'But of course you do', because he too needs to believe he is understood (p. 132). Leggatt desperately reaches out for someone to share his psychic burden. He likes to be looked at and spoken to, and even stammers when recalling their first meeting. At one point he says, 'I wanted to be seen, to talk with somebody, before I went on' (p. 111). As R. W. Stallman says, 'it is this mutual, sympathetic understanding of what the other's plight means to him that bolsters and morally fortifies their spiritual being'.[6] They both create a buffer to protect themselves from their feelings of excruciating loneliness in a hostile world. In each other, they find the intimacy of a captain–mate relationship that both pathetically lack in their professional capacities. For the first mate's suspicion of the captain echoes Leggatt's opinion of *his* captain. And Archbold, or, at least, Leggatt's and the captain's version of him, is the very type of captain that the narrator might have become if he had not engaged in this process of self-development.

While experiencing Leggatt's objective world, the captain adopts Leggatt's perspective. Therefore he has no hesitation or ambiguity in his attitude to Archbold. Not only does he compare the man, who stands, however poignantly, as an upholder of the moral order, to a criminal, but, in addition, he describes him as 'a tenacious beast'. Speaking of an exchange with Archbold, the captain recalled, 'I had been too frightened not to feel *vengeful*; I felt I had him on the run, and I meant to keep him on the run. My polite insistence must have had something menacing in it because he gave in suddenly' (p. 121, emphasis added). However, the reader knows that the captain's judgement of Archbold is really Leggatt's and cannot exclude the possibility that Archbold is everything *he* says he is.

Nor can we accept the distinctions so essential to the captain that Leggatt deserves the allegorical identity of Truth, and Captain Archbold that of Falsehood. His recollection of Leggatt's captain is consistent with his present myth-making. Although he does not remember his name, he assigns a pejorative name that we realise would be far more appropriate to Leggatt: 'He mumbled to me as if he were ashamed of what he was saying; gave his name (it was something like Archbold—but at the distance of years I hardly am sure), his ship's name, and a few other particulars of that sort, in the manner of a criminal making a reluctant and doleful confession' (p. 116). Although he is certain that the captain suspects him, he offers no real evidence to support this notion; after all, he has told us how *different* from Leggatt he looked: 'I had become so connected in thoughts and impressions with the secret sharer of my cabin that I felt as if I, personally, were given to understand that I, too, was not the sort that would have done for the chief mate of a ship like the *Sephora*. I had no doubt of it in my mind' (p. 119). Conrad hardly expected his readers to believe the captain's assertion that he suggested Leggatt to Archbold.

Following our insistence that 'The Secret Sharer' be regarded as a drama about the problems and interrelationships of people we must ask why Leggatt requests to be abandoned. Does he sense that the captain cannot continue to operate as a split personality? Probably, but Leggatt also needs to assert his own independence, to accept the role of exiled wanderer which his impulsive act had defined for him. The narrator, of course, puts the best possible interpretation on Leggatt's behaviour and implicitly invites us to do the same. Certainly, when the character with whom we identify and whose judgement is practically beyond reproach enlists our sympathy, it is not surprising that our first response is to accept *his evaluation*. He admires Leggatt both as a man of self-control who can accept the consequences of his actions and as a man whose instinctive behaviour saved the *Sephora*. For him, Leggatt is not a mutineer, but an effective officer.

The captain's final view of Leggatt is significant: 'I was in time to catch an evanescent glimpse of my white hat left behind to mark the spot where the secret sharer of my cabin and of my thoughts, as though he were my second self, had lowered himself into the water to take his punishment: a *free* man, a *proud* swimmer striking out for a new destiny' (p. 143, emphasis added). The only way to satisfy his conscience, now that he had cast him from his boat, is to create the myth of a triumphant departure, for even retrospectively he cannot admit that he might have sacrificed Leggatt in order to preserve his own position. Yet, for the reader, Leggatt is a tragic, lonesome figure, branded not only by the standards of civilisation, but by the captain himself as an outsider destined to wander the earth.

It is the teller who has fulfilled the implied prophecy of a new destiny. He had lived up to an ideal conception of himself by proving his ability to command and by establishing his hierarchical position as captain. And Leggatt, abandoned to a world where the captain's epistemology is irrelevant, no longer exists within the civilised community except as part of the captain's consciousness. As soon as Leggatt departed, the captain 'hardly thought of my other self, now gone from the ship, to be hidden forever from all friendly faces, to be a fugitive and a vagabond on the earth, with no brand of the curse on his sane forehead to stay a slaying hand . . . too proud to explain' (p. 142). It is almost as if the captain can now cast aside the man who once threatened his identity, although the telling shows that he regards the experience as crucial to his personal development. Retrospectively it seems that Leggatt represents his own potential for evil, which must be expurgated before he can become morally, as well as psychologically, whole. The narrator clearly knows that he has behaved quite differently from the man he regarded as a double when confronted with a similar situation. As Louis H. Leiter perceptively argues,

> Leggatt seizes the man by the throat at the climax of his archetypal trial by storm and kills him in a fit of uncontrolled passion; the narrator also seizes the Chief Mate under similar circumstances, his archetypal trial by silence, but by controlling himself, controlling the frightened, disbelieving man, he controls the ship and consequently saves her from destruction, while saving his reputation and winning the respect of his crew.[7]

He found within himself the confidence to act entirely without the paralytic self-consciousness that previously interfered with his ability to command the ship.

Leggatt is flippantly conscious of the possible analogy between Cain and himself: 'The "brand of Cain" business, don't you see. That's all right. I was ready enough to go off wandering on the face of the earth—and that was price enough to pay for an Abel of that sort' (p. 107). [8] Ironically, although Leggatt proclaims indifference to legal and religious standards, he cannot avoid responding to them:

> You don't suppose I am afraid of what can be done to me? . . . You don't see me coming back to explain such things to an old fellow in a wig and twelve respectable tradesmen, do you? What can they know whether I am guilty or not—or of *what* I am guilty, either? That's my affair. What does the Bible say? 'Driven off the face of the earth!' Very well. I am off the face of the earth now.   (pp. 131–2, Conrad's emphasis)

It disturbs the conventional morality of the captain to be on the side of Cain; but for a time he becomes an Abel figure in protecting his double: 'The very trust in Providence was, I suppose, denied to his guilt. Shall I confess that this thought cast me down very much?' (p. 123). Yet it is soon clear that both men contain Cain and Abel elements. Leggatt plays the role of Abel when he willingly leaves the ship and thus helps the captain through the crisis. The captain's Cain identity derives from our realisation that, to fulfil his own aspirations, he must abandon Leggatt.

The captain's use of Leggatt has its analogy in the creative process of art. Leggatt comes into his experience as a fact of the objective world; he transforms him into a fiction partially congruent with the objective data; and then he releases him back into the objective world. [9] Unwilling to risk his future, the captain *sacrifices* Leggatt for the unity of his own personality, just as the artist may sacrifice moral engagement for his artistic purposes. Conrad believed that all men have a Cain aspect in their personalities in the sense that physical and psychic survival is dependent on conscious and unconscious decisions that jeopardise the best interests of others. And the artist is a radical example because the creative process is a kind of withdrawal into the imagination at the expense of immediate participation in the community. The persistent allusions to the Cain–Abel myth suggest that each man must continually confront an unresolvable conflict between self-fulfilment and commitment to others. In an early letter

to Mme Poradowska Conrad had written, 'Charity . . . is a gift
straight from the Eternal to the elect. . . . For Charity is eternal
and universal Love, the divine virtue, the sole manifestation of the
Almighty which may in some manner justify the act of creation.' But
later in the same letter he wrote:

> Abnegation carried to an extreme . . . becomes not a fault but
> a crime, and to return good for evil is not only profoundly
> immoral but dangerous, in that it sharpens the appetite for evil
> in the malevolent and develops (perhaps unconsciously) that
> latent human tendency towards hypocrisy in the . . . let us say,
> benevolent.   (5 Mar 1892, *Mme Poradowska*, p. 42)

The captain understands that it would be a 'sham sentiment'—what
Conrad called 'abnegation carried to an extreme'—to sacrifice his
future by indefinitely harbouring Leggatt.

III. 'A SMILE OF FORTUNE' (1911)

Completed in September 1910, 'A Smile of Fortune' has not received
the kind of substantive discussion that it merits. Specifically, no critic
has satisfactorily come to terms with the elusive narrator – protagonist, who, despite his apparently disarming honesty, does not
understand his aberrant behaviour or the consequences of it upon the
severely disturbed woman whose affections he has aroused. Jocelyn
Baines expresses a typical reaction to the tale's narrator – protagonist:
'There is something very distasteful about the way in which the
captain goads, and rather lubriciously, flirts with Alice; by rousing her
feelings he may well have done irreparable harm to her.'[10] But what
Baines does not realise is that Conrad expected us to see the captain –
narrator's psychosexual shortcomings. I believe we should view the
tale as a dramatic monologue in which the speaker's tormented
conscience gradually reveals a far different version of events from that
he believes he is telling, despite his conscious and semiconscious
efforts to evade the implications of his relationship with Alice.
Viewing the tale in this way makes irrelevant Guerard's indictment of
Conrad for 'the forms of clumsiness and evasion displayed in
approaching the subject of sexual attraction' and his complaint that
'the evasion of the sexual subject now and then leads . . . to a major
vulgarity'.[11] We might recall Conrad's surprise at reviewers' calling

Alice a 'sensual animal'; he claimed that he had 'tried to make her pathetic' (*LL*, ii, p. 144). [12] Apparently, Conrad expected his readers to see Alice as the helpless victim of a sexually inept man who, if unable to understand his aberrant behaviour, nevertheless poignantly feels his failure to fulfil his self-created role as rescuer. However awkward the later Conrad may be in treating romantic and sexual material, his consistent awareness of obsessive voyeurism can be demonstrated by his treatment of Falk's attraction to Hermann's niece, of Heemskirk's peeping-Tomism in 'Freya of the Seven Isles', and of George's attraction to Rita in *The Arrow of Gold*. Certainly, Conrad's controlled handling of this sexually inept narrator and of Captain Anthony's passion in the next novel, *Chance*, questions the accepted view that sexuality is such an uncongenial subject for him that it often undermines the later work.

The narration of 'A Smile of Fortune' is retrospective. Telling becomes the making of the pattern and is as much a quest for values as the experience on which it is based. Not only is narration in the past tense, but the conversational tone and informality of the opening paragraph give us reason to suppose that the narrator is recalling a past experience for the benefit of an imagined audience: 'Well, let us call it the "Pearl." It's a good name. A pearl distilling much sweetness upon the world. . . . This is only a way of telling you that first-rate sugarcane is grown there. All the population of the Pearl lives for it and by it' (p. 3). The captain's tone of ennui and melancholy pessimism throughout the narration is best explained by our imagining the captain's having a foreknowledge of recently completed events. His cynical meditations concerning man's ability to control his own destiny and his emotions are apparently motivated more by his own sense of inadequacy and self-disgust than by sympathetic grief for the bereaved captain. Inappropriate to the immediate situation, such remarks as 'In the instability of his emotions man resembles deplorably a monkey' must be regarded as interpolated by the narrator into a retelling rather than as part of the captain's original responses (p. 16). Finally, by having his narrator introduce a variety of seemingly unrelated anecdotes which, as we shall see, do serve an important structural function, Conrad dramatises the narrator's excruciating difficulty in recalling his humiliating experience.

Caught between the pressures of commercial life and his own self-doubt, the captain sought a refuge in his relationship with the ingenuous girl. He had been given a command that 'was like a foot in the stirrup for a young man' but his abilities 'appeared to [him] no bigger than a pinhead' (pp. 88, 4). In a world marked by commercial morality and social hypocrisy, he found a sense of order and certainty in his patronising feelings toward Alice. But, as the captain probed from the shore toward the centre of the island, he moved further away from the values he respected.

From the outset, the captain's monologue demonstrates his romantic nature and his inability to deal with his responsibilities. His resentment of commercial interests derives from a belief, or, rather, a rationalisation, that business affairs interfere with emotions and instincts. Wistfully, the captain, like Conrad himself in 1910–11, looks to a simpler world that is not blemished by commerce. When he heard of Alice's plight, he cast himself in the romantic roles of a potential Prince Charming who would rescue Cinderella – Alice, and of a potential Pygmalion who would transform the statue-like Alice into a living person. His tendency to explain ordinary events with supernatural explanations and to find omens in almost every action clearly distinguishes him from the men who possess the pragmatism and self-control that Conrad believed were essential for a captain.

Conrad believed that a captain must have consummate faith in himself if he is to carry out his responsibilities. The captain – narrator allowed himself to be distracted from complete dedication to his ship. He became involved in a relationship that undermined the self-confidence and devotion to duty upon which the benign autocracy of a ship depends. As his account of a visit to aristocratic acquaintances reveals, the narrator is pathologically terrified of women. And this is consistent with the captain's sexual ambivalence which had been made clear by Jacobus's 'floral tribute'. While Conrad's limiting the perspective to the captain makes it impossible to be certain of Jacobus's motives, it seems likely that Jacobus's pointed insistence that the captain smell the flowers that he had brought aboard constituted his way of testing whether the captain is a homosexual or a potential suitor for his socially ostracised bastard daughter. The captain's 'jocular' assurance that 'he made me feel as if I were a pretty girl, and that he mustn't be surprised if I blushed' certainly makes the reader suspect the captain's pretensions as Prince Charming and Pygmalion (pp. 22–3). We recall Jacobus's suspicions about the captain's sexual proclivities when the captain indicates that he was attracted as much by Alice's masculinity and resemblance to her father as by anything else: 'I marvelled at the girl's resemblance to this man. . . . All the rest of the face, the design and the modelling, the rounded chin, the very lips—all that was Jacobus, fined down, more finished, more expressive' (p. 71).

That Alice is ostracised by the community *attracts* the captain to her. Resentful of the island's morality that condones Ernest Jacobus's sexual misconduct and savage behaviour while condemning Alfred's indiscretions, the narrator wanted to associate with those estranged from society. Success in business, according to the Pearl culture, justifies brutality and bad manners; furthermore, moral judgements do not apply to relations between a white man and a native. Once the captain recoiled from Ernest's barbaric manners and abusive behaviour towards his illegitimate mullato son, he reflexively sought refuge in Alfred's apparent delicacy. He is one of Conrad's many young protagonists who, like Conrad himself, search for a surrogate father; he chose Alfred rather than Ernest Jacobus as his guide because Alfred's hospitality and observation of the amenities appealed to him. Once he became an intimate of the despised Alfred, he was ostracised as alien to the community standards.

As soon as he heard of Alfred's perverse relationship and consequent social exile, the captain began to imagine himself as heroic rescuer and chivalric lover. (If we recall Marlow's scepticism in *Chance* of Captain Anthony's tendency to see himself as a rescuer and chivalric lover of a helpless victim, we are less likely to think that Conrad does not understand the psychosexual complexity of the captain in 'A Smile of Fortune'.) Characteristically, he romanticised the ship-chandler and his lonely daughter into 'a lonely pair of castaways on a desert island . . . like two shipwrecked people who always hope for some rescuer to bring them back . . . into touch with the rest of mankind' (p. 39). Because of her vulnerability as a scapegoat of Pearl society, the captain was not intimidated by Alice. In his first meetings with her, he thought of himself as a master figure, a figure of strength dealing with a helpless creature who was more like a pet than another human being. Yet, though he recalls her as if she were a small animal, it is clear that her appearance also carried the semi-conscious suggestion of sexuality: she sat 'as if crouching for a spring' and she looked as if she would '[bound] away'; he spoke to her with 'a gentle caressing intonation as one talks to soothe a startled wild animal' (p. 44).

It is soon transparently clear to the reader, but not the captain, that he has been attracted to an emotionally disturbed young woman. Whatever the cause—the companionship of her lunatic aunt or the social ostracism or both—Alice has severe withdrawal symptoms.

But the captain's psychic needs prevent his noticing that she is anything but a pathetic and helpless creature who needs his compassion. As soon as the captain recalls his first visit to Jacobus's home, it is obvious that he was not only emotionally and morally defective when the events took place, but that *now at the time of the narration he still does not understand how his behaviour was defective*. Throughout his circumlocutory discussion of Alice's attire and his reaction to it, the captain feels the need to explain and excuse his behaviour. He cannot restrain his exultation when he describes his awareness of her flimsy clothing: 'I felt it actually embarrassing at first; but that sort of embarrassment is got over easily by a mind not enslaved by narrow prejudices' (pp. 44–5). We should not let his glibness make us forget that this is the same man who has been emphasising the refinement of his feelings and the rectitude of his conduct. (His supersensitivity to scandal, he tells us a few minutes later, made him feel 'moral discomfort' in that 'house lying under the ban of all "decent" people'—meaning, of course, Alfred Jacobus's house [p. 56].)

Telling is a painful experience when the narrative is a retrospective vision of one's own failure. The captain's reminiscence contains confused and partial understanding of his own motives and alternates between awareness and self-contempt. Self-consciously, he undertakes a precise examination of his own past conduct. But he continually drifts into rationalisation: 'My self-communion as I walked away from his door, trying to believe that this was for the last time, was not satisfactory. I was aware myself that I was not sincere in my reflections as to Jacobus's motives, and, of course, the very next day I went back again' (ibid.). We feel a narrator trying to come to grips with his past conduct, yet subconsciously using bland and comfortable words such as 'satisfactory' and 'sincere' to avoid the complexities of his behaviour. He does not understand the reasons why he was compulsively attracted to Alice and seeks to rationalise his continued visits by universalising his behaviour: 'How weak, irrational and absurd *we* are! How easily carried away whenever *our* awakened imagination brings *us* the irritating hint of a desire!' (ibid., emphasis added).

Self-doubt fed by the difficulty of finding his cargo-bags and by his disillusionment with the island's morals increased the captain's vulnerability. Even in retelling, the captain desperately seeks to justify his voyeuristic visits to Alfred Jacobus's home. At times he tries to raise Alice's pathetic plight to the tragic level and by implication give his own role some dignity. Typically, he insists that Alice's sullenness had an 'obscurely tragic flavour'. During his monologue, the captain's self-image fluctuates radically. At one moment he sees himself as a seducer, then as a rescuer of castaways, and shortly thereafter as an indignant moralist. But the reader can see that his obsession with Alice has completely changed his original determination to eschew involvement with women: 'I would have given up the society of the whole town, for the sake of sitting near that girl, snarling and superb and barely clad in that flimsy, dingy, amber wrapper, open low at the throat' (p. 58).

One of Marlow's comments in *Chance* helps us understand Conrad's attitude to the captain's conduct:

> And I know also that a passion, dominating or tyrannical, invading the whole man and subjugating all his faculties to its own unique end, may conduct him whom it spurs and drives, into all sorts of adventures, to the brink of unfathomable dangers, to the limit of folly, and madness, and death. (p. 329)

Belying his statements of indifference to his having been ignored by Alice, the captain admits that he continued to return to his voyeuristic activities even after he had learned that he would receive the loading bags. In an unusually honest moment, the captain realises that it was not 'mere gratitude' that made him stay, for 'Mere gratitude does not gnaw at one's interior economy in that particular way. Hunger might, but I was not feeling particularly hungry for Jacobus's food' (p. 53). In this awkward and even pathetically crude comment, the captain demonstrates his awareness that his particular kind of sexual frustration was a principal reason for his having wanted to watch Alice. To look at Alice, he had been willing to submit to the insane aunt's abuse and Jacobus's scrutiny: 'I loved to *watch* her slow changes of pose, to *look* at her long immobilities composed in the graceful lines of her body, to *observe* the mysterious narrow stare of her splendid black eyes . . .' (pp. 58–9, emphasis added). But this is only a surface self-awareness, distinct from an understanding of why he found solace in Alice's presence.

What bothered him most after he had announced his departure was her indifference coupled with the realisation that her interest in him seemed to be largely derived from a fear of being kidnapped. Exhibiting symptoms of paranoia, he believed that she was 'revelling contemptuously in a sense of relief' and speaks of her 'ingratitude doubled with treachery' (p. 69). He realised that his voyeuristic activities were at an end, that he could no longer, as he puts it so paradoxically and ambiguously, 'taste perversely the flavour of contempt in her indolent poses, drink in the provocation of her scornful looks, and listen to the curt, insolent remarks uttered in that harsh and seductive voice' (p. 65). His repressed and frustrated impulses finally exploded in violence, and he forced his affections upon her. With masochistic relish, he seems to enjoy retelling what could have developed into a rape or worse, even though his incredible candour displays him in a grotesque light. During the struggle which he describes, she simultaneously attracted and repelled him; at the same time as he felt 'a fierce desire never to let her go any more', he squeezed her 'as if she were my mortal enemy' (p. 70). And the extent of his love – hate dichotomy is revealed when, recalling her exit, he avows that he didn't know 'whether to shake my fist . . . or blow a kiss' (p. 70). Assuredly, we are listening to the confessions of a disturbed young man who had become obsessed with an even more disturbed young woman.

The events have deeply affected the captain's self-conception. The speaker feels guilty because he has deserted the girl whom he had managed to arouse, and yet he cannot help enjoying the recollection of his voyeurism. Even in the retelling, he never sees her as the pathetic victim of his sensuality. When he does question his own behaviour, it is primarily for the wrong reason. His real offence is not breaking his promise to himself to avoid trade, but exploiting the girl for selfish pleasure. Getting involved in the potato trade is only a symbol of the captain's failure to follow through as Alice's rescuer after he has succeeded in arousing her from her 'immobility'. He finds a comfortable position in his contempt for Jacobus, specifically in his defensive assertion that nothing he could do would equal the 'characteristic Jacobus impudence'. While judging Jacobus's conduct as 'unrelenting' and 'rapacious', he will not admit that his voyeuristic obsession got him into trade. He accepted Jacobus's offer only because this was a way that he could order Jacobus to the wharf and see Alice again. Despite his hatred of business ('Horrid thoughts of business interfered with my enjoyment of an accomplished passage' [pp. 3 – 4]) he entered into a sordid agreement which appeared to be valueless to him. By meeting Alfred Jacobus's terms, the captain could partially assuage his conscience. After all, he has paid *something* for his voyeuristic pleasures and his inability to fulfil his promised role as Prince Charming.

Let us take a closer look at the captain's climactic parting from Alice. Once he had experienced the excitement of his abortive sexual encounter, he demurred from further involvement with Alice. Because he did not take Jacobus's offer of the slipper, an action symbolic of his refusal to take possession of the girl, he felt that he had a moral obligation to take the potatoes. Jacobus knowingly used the slipper as a threat to the captain, who had tried to possess his daughter without paying the price of marriage, and the captain knows full well that he had been intimidated by Jacobus's manipulation of the 'fascinating object'. Putting the slipper back on Alice's 'inanimate foot' represents his refusal to take her off Jacobus's hands. After the captain had been intimidated by Jacobus's 'commanding gesture' with the 'fatal shoe' into agreeing to trade, it is clear that he did not want a warm response from Alice. His fears of emotional and sexual involvement prevail over his desire to fulfil his imagined roles of lover and rescuer. Even Alice's touching offer of affection, her 'hasty, awkward kiss', did not stir the captain from his resolve to abandon her.

The melancholy and ennui that pervade the entire monologue indicate how the speaker has been affected by his experience with Alice. His guilt-wracked conscience responded to what he knows was a callous rejection of Alice. Because the cargo of potatoes reminded him of his sordid behaviour to her, the narrator's last voyage lacks what he calls the 'blessed forgetfulness of sailors' (p. 82). For a while the very word 'garden' evoked a 'vision of gorgeous colour, of sweet scents, of a girlish figure crouching in a chair' (p. 84). After his commercial coup, his dreams were haunted by the girl that he, too, finally consigned to the role of scapegoat: 'That night I dreamt of a pile of gold in the form of a grave in which a girl was buried, and woke up callous with greed' (p. 84). By resigning his command, the captain avoided any further confrontations with Alice and her father. While his refusal to return to the Pearl assuages his conscience as regards Alice's feeling, it is obvious that his fear of further humiliation and his desire to protect the remnants of his self-esteem played an important role in a resignation that endangers his future.

Paul Kirschner has noticed that 'A Smile of Fortune' resembles Maupassant's 'Les Soeurs Rondoli'.[13] Yet, given the probable influence of Maupassant's tale, it is the *difference* in treatment of the sexual motif which strikes the reader. Despite the narrator's disenchantment with life, Maupassant's speaker can enter into a casual, sexual relationship without the burden of guilt. When we compare

the captain's obsessive behaviour with the basically normal behaviour
of Maupassant's narrator, we can see how Conrad reshaped the man's
encounter with the reluctant woman to show a relationship between
an abnormal couple. The captain's romantic conceptions of himself as
rescuer, courtly lover, and as a chivalric Edwardian renouncing the
opportunity to exploit Alice, contradict the actuality of his voyeuristic and narcisstic activities. Conrad exposes his narrator as an
emotionally and sexually inept suitor of a pathetic female. We see
through the captain's rationalisations, and we realise the extent to
which his monologue indicts him as emotionally and morally
defective. While Maupassant's speaker is candid about his sexual
desires, Conrad's narrator does not understand how his avowed
distaste for marriage conceals his fear of heterosexual relationships.
Kirschner accurately speaks of the captain's 'erotic obsession' and his
'tormented half-conscious flirtation'. But he overlooks the emotionally disturbed female's role in the relationship, and the important fact
that the frustrated and repressed captain *chooses* a bastard, a scapegoat
of society, because he *needs* to cast himself in the dominant role. If
Conrad did indeed have 'Les Soeurs Rondoli' in mind, perhaps he is
saying that the vague uneasiness felt by Maupassant's nearly amoral
protagonist is a luxurious emotion when compared with his captain's
psychosexual difficulties.

IV. 'FREYA OF THE SEVEN ISLES' (1912)

Combining the genre of romance with the subject of heterosexual
love, 'Freya of the Seven Isles', which was completed early in 1911,
serves as an artistic laboratory for the next two full-length novels,
Victory and *Chance*. Conrad does not depart entirely from realistic
characters, but the pervasive allusions to epic and romance materials
are part of a not entirely successful effort to place the characters in an
inflated context and to expand their significance into representative
figures.

It is instructive to compare 'A Smile of Fortune' with 'Freya of the
Seven Isles'. These stories, written within six months of each other,
have a great deal in common. In both tales, the captain—protagonist
becomes enamoured of an eccentric father's only daughter and
imagines himself as a potential rescuer of a captive daughter. But in
each case there is something inherently defective in the quality of the
captain's passion: Jasper's faith in human love and his hyperbolic

idealisation of Freya disarm his defences, while making him a prey to the invidious Heemskirk. Both Freya and Alice have a voyeuristic admirer whose repressed passions overflow into violence. Of course, the major formal difference between the two tales lies in the division of the lover – voyeur – narrator of 'A Smile of Fortune' into the separate characters of Jasper, Heemskirk, and the narrator.

Jasper Allen allows his romantic interest to undermine his judgement. He continually defers to Freya's wishes even when good sense dictates otherwise, and he does not take the precautions to safeguard his brig. The title, which recalls a saint's name (such as Mary of the Fountains), has its ironic aspect, for Captain Jasper thinks of Freya as if she were a saint with the power to guard his especial interests. If Jasper had been less under Freya's power as a worshipping servant, as an anachronistic courtly lover, he could have successfully persuaded her to elope. For Jasper, she is the image of peace and serenity whose warnings to act cautiously are unquestioningly obeyed. Despite her exterior of independent aloofness, she becomes more and more reluctant to accede to her father's whims by placating Heemskirk.

Despite her apparent strength and independence, Freya allows her filial commitment to a paranoid father to take precedence over the promise of a fulfilling love relationship; she thus anticipates Flora in *Chance*. Her tendency to substitute abstractions for inductive, pragmatic responses to the demands of the situations that confront her is perhaps the major reason for the tragedy. Freya is the catalyst for Jasper's fantasies and enjoys inhabiting his make-believe world. Fearful of sex, she fantasises that not Jasper but the brig 'will carry [her] off'. She enjoys being worshipped by males and enjoys her role as a Lady of the Isles playing music in harmony with the thunderstorm, as if she imagined herself to be in tune with the natural elements. Controlling situations and people is as important to her as feeling that Jasper needs her. Freya relishes manipulating emotions. She not only carefully stages her hypothetical elopement but she transforms it into a game with its own complex ground rules. She enjoys belittling Jasper to a third party, the narrator, even while savouring her beloved's irresponsibility, because the concept that she has 'tamed' him is a significant aspect of her self-image. Yet making Jasper more cautious is, ironically, what causes his undoing. In the ruthless masculine world in which he lives, circumspect behaviour has little place.

Freya partly brings about Jasper's and her disaster. She enjoys

articulating effusions of love in Heemskirk's presence as retribution
for Heemskirk's humiliating assault. The narrator emphasises the
shallowness of Freya's gloating, self-indulgent triumph when she
plays the piano as Heemskirk departs after she had aroused his ire and
voyeuristic impulses: 'She was excited, she tingled all over, she had
tasted blood! He *must* be made to understand that she had been aware
of having been watched; he *must know* that he had been seen slinking
off shamefully' (p. 205, emphasis added). She lacks the perception to
see that Heemskirk's potential for violence and his hurt pride must be
treated gingerly. Her deliberately ostentatious show of affection
triggers Heemskirk's malice towards Jasper. He is a neurotic with no
defences and a man who thinks in black and white. When he sees
Freya with Jasper, his first inclination is to imagine that she is a whore
available to everyone's advances. And Jasper makes the crucial error
of not taking Heemskirk seriously. He fails to see the meaning of
Heemskirk's animosity when the latter knocks over his beacons. The
result is that he foolishly lets his ship and himself be captured. Because
he was warned by Freya to be 'guarded and cautious' (p. 211), he is
unmanned and deliberately shows 'neither annoyance, nor even
surprise' at Heemskirk's request to come aboard. Conditioned by
Freya's influence, his response is pathetically incongruous to the
threat.

   Jasper seeks refuge in his twin fictions that his brig is indestructible
and that romantic love can transform his life:

> Nothing, nothing could happen to the brig, he cried, as if the
> flame of his heart could light up the dark nights of uncharted
> seas, and the image of Freya serve for an unerring beacon
> among hidden shoals; as if the winds had to wait on his future,
> the stars fight for it in their courses; as if the magic of his
> passion had the power to float a ship on a drop of dew or sail
> her through the eye of a needle . . . .   (p. 168)

The narcissism of the above passage indicates Jasper's immaturity and
his tendency to live in his imaginative world. Since in his own mind
the boat is a symbol for both Freya and his expected happiness, his
entire world collapses when he loses the brig. Like Jim in *Lord Jim* and
Jukes in 'Typhoon', Jasper is another version of the imaginative man
whose fantasy interferes with his ability to cope with events.

   The narrator of 'Freya' is a minor character who is peripherally involved in the action, but he engages Conrad's interest. The alternately reductive comic perspective and expansive operatic perspective indicate that the narrator is groping for an epistemology with which to understand Jasper's tragedy. The changes Conrad made in the story when preparing the magazine version for the volume *'Twixt Land and Sea* indicate that he wanted to increase the emphasis on the characterisation of the narrator. He probably sensed that the tale needed another focus of interest, but the changes only marginally improved the tale. In the later version, he stressed the narrator's interest in pedestrian detail. Conrad adds the prolix discussion of moving the piano and the foolishly chatty 'to be sure, to be sure' to make the narrator a tediously loquacious Pandarus figure. Somewhat self-conscious about his aging, he enjoys his self-appointed role as confidant for the lovers. He tacitly arranges the flirtations of Jasper and Freya, and he enjoys such obvious sexual innuendoes as the puns on Jasper's 'soaring love' and on Jasper's being 'elevated' 'in the true sense of the word'. Trying to justify his own role, he speaks of how he tried to keep the lovers alert to danger. If there is one place where the narrator *could* have made a difference, it is when Jasper invited him to criticise his having hired Schultz as a crew member. Although Jasper's behaviour suggests a little child who knows he has behaved naughtily and wants to be told so, the narrator refused to chastise Jasper, preferring the pleasure of momentarily reversing Jasper's expectations of a scolding. (The narrator says, Jasper 'so evidently expected me to scold that I took especial pleasure in exaggerating the calmness of my attitude' [p. 169].)

The narrator's attempt to place the tale in a comic perspective is unconvincing in the face of his own personal interest in the outcome. Not only does he persist in using the word, 'comic', but, in addition, he assigns the characters roles from Italian comedy: Antonia is the faithful 'comedy camarista' and Nelson is the gullible old 'comic father'. Repeating the epithet 'black beetle' for Heemskirk enables the narrator, who, like Jasper, longs for a simpler world, to understand Heemskirk as ludicrous and grotesque rather than as perverse and psychotic. Often the narrator seeks refuge in formulaic similes and one-dimensional character analyses. Thus, for the narrator, Heemskirk becomes, within the romance world he has created, a kind of devil infiltrating into the innocent existence of Jasper and Freya. Indeed, Conrad's subtitle, 'A Story of Shallow Waters', may indicate his own misgivings about a tale which depends upon a lack of moral and artistic depth.

NOTES

1. In December 1909 Conrad interrupted his work on *Under Western Eyes* to write 'The Secret Sharer'. Commenting on Conrad's original plan to call the story either 'The Second Self', 'The Secret Self' or 'The Other Self', Karl writes in *Joseph Conrad: The Three Lives* (pp. 675–6), 'His psychological need to share his situation with those close to him is a personal manifestation of what he had just been writing. . . . He displayed now his familiar pattern of dependency, seeking supports as he was being deserted, first by Ford, then by Pinker.'

2. Albert J. Guerard, *Conrad the Novelist* (Cambridge, Mass.: Harvard University Press, 1958), p. 27 (see also pp. 21–8).

3. Louis L. Martz, *The Poetry of Meditation*, 2nd edn (New Haven, Conn.: Yale University Press, 1962), p. 330.

4. R. D. Laing, *The Divided Self: An Existential Study in Sanity and Madness* (Baltimore: Penguin Books, 1965), p. 47.

5. Ibid., p. 48.

6. Robert W. Stallman, 'Conrad and "The Secret Sharer" ', in *The Art of Joseph Conrad: A Critical Symposium* (East Lansing, Mich.: Michigan State University Press, 1960), pp. 275–88; repr. in Bruce Harkness (ed.), *Conrad's 'The Secret Sharer' and The Critics* (Belmont, Calif.: Wadsworth, 1962), pp. 94–109 (see in particular, p. 99).

7. Louis H. Leiter, 'Echo Structures: Conrad's "The Secret Sharer" ', *Twentieth Century Literature*, vol. 5 (Jan 1960), pp. 159–75; repr. in Harkness, '*Secret Sharer*', pp. 133–50 (see p. 142).

8. See Leiter's suggestive comments on the Cain–Abel archetype, ibid., pp. 142–50.

9. See Stallman for an allegorical reading of the captain as artist, ibid., pp. 103–5.

10. Jocelyn Baines, *Joseph Conrad: A Critical Biography* (New York: McGraw-Hill, 1960), p. 375.

11. Guerard, *Conrad the Novelist*, pp. 51, 52.

12. For discussion of the autobiographical element in 'A Smile of Fortune', see Meyer, *Conrad: A Psychoanalytic Biography*, pp. 79–85, and Karl, *Conrad: The Three Lives*, pp. 254–60. I am arguing that, at the distance of years, Conrad was able to understand his youthful sexual immaturity.

13. Paul Kirschner, 'Conrad and Maupassant: Moral Solitude and "A Smile of Fortune" ', *Review of English Literature*, vol. 7 (1966), pp. 62–77.

2 The short story as romance

I

Economic exigencies, combined with an interest in experimenting with new forms, motivated Conrad to write a number of short stories for popular consumption in which he eschews moral and psychological subtlety. The tales published in *Within the Tides* (1915)—'The Inn of the Two Witches: A Find', 'The Partner', 'The Planter of Malata' and 'Because of the Dollars'—possess the quality neither of Conrad's great short stories nor even of the lesser novels of the later phase. Written in the 1910–14 period, their emphasis is on *plot*, and to an extent *theme*, but not character analysis. Characters within the narrative do not develop gradually as they interact with circumstances or other persons; rather, they remain fixed or are manipulated into sudden change at the conclusion of hectic adventures.

In *The Nature of Narrative*, Scholes and Kellogg distinguish between 'empirical' narrative, and narrative that is 'fictional' such as romance. Rather than imitate reality, either by reference to 'truth of fact and to the actual past' or by reference to 'truth of sensation and environment, depending on observation of the present', the world of romance is 'the ideal world in which poetic justice prevails and all the arts and adornments of language are used to embellish the narrative'.[1] Romance often combines with the other kind of 'fictional' narrative, the '*fable*, a form which is ruled by an intellectual and moral impulse as romance is ruled by an esthetic one'.[2] Conrad's work always had a romance component, but it played a less significant role in the major political novels. Rightly or wrongly, Conrad felt that romance elements had popular appeal. Writing of *Romance* (1903), his collaboration with Ford, Conrad stressed both the economic and aesthetic motives: 'L'idée que nous avions était purement esthétique: rendre quelques scènes, quelques situations, d'une façon convenable. Puis il ne nous déplaisait pas de montrer que nous pouvions faire

23

quelque chose dans le genre fort en vogue avec le public en ce moment-ci' (8 Nov 1903).[3]

In *Within the Tides*, Conrad uses the melodramatic episodic plot of romance to demonstrate the kind of transparent moral scheme that he believed would have appeal for the periodical audience of magazines such as the *Metropolitan*. These tales are potboilers, deriving from Conrad's desire to write a kind of fiction that would sell and be widely read. They begin with a realistic framework, but details are not very important, stock epithets often convey the essence of a character's significance, and the plots demonstrate a thinly disguised didactic lesson. The polarisation between the forces of good and evil often leads to oversimplification and sentimentalism.

In a 1913 letter, Carl Hovey, an editor of *Metropolitan*, speaks of wanting Conrad to write 'things which are simple and direct, in which the element of suspense is fairly obvious and is not too fine and psychological for [the public] to grasp' (unpublished letter, 16 Dec 1913, Berg Collection, New York Public Library).[4] Although Conrad objected to Hovey's advice, he did begin to publish in the *Metropolitan* stories in which he used one-dimensional narrators who are rarely prone to self-analysis and who present reductive and exaggerated versions of events. These speakers focus the reader's attention on very obvious conflicts between exploiters and victims, between those concerned with others and those motivated by egoism and greed. That Conrad was conscious of a new emphasis on artifice may be implied by his epigraph to *Within the Tides*: 'Go, make you ready', Hamlet's instructions to the visiting players to prepare to perform for the king. Like the play within the play in *Hamlet*, these stories are 'performed' for a particular purpose and rely on simplified action to make their didactic point. Moreover, the epigraph may contain an element of self-mockery at his becoming a performer who plays the part of a popular writer to meet the demands of the *Metropolitan* audience.

II. THE FAILURE OF IMAGINATION: 'THE PARTNER' (1911), 'THE INN OF THE TWO WITCHES: A FIND' (1913) AND 'BECAUSE OF THE DOLLARS' (1914)

'The Partner', 'The Inn of the Two Witches: A Find' and 'Because of the Dollars' suffer from Conrad's belief that he could make his potboilers into significant works of art simply by insisting within the texts that their sensational plots had allegorical meaning. In these tales, Conrad dramatises a relatively unintelligent and insensitive narrator in the process of allegorising melodramatic material. He tries to have it both ways. While he patronises the intellectual accomplishments of his principal speakers, he endorses the simplified and reductive versions they present. He does this in part by the use of a frame device: a nominal narrator overhears or peruses the original version and retells it to the reader. Conrad wishes to show how quite ordinary people seek to discover patterns of moral significance in events that they experience or learn about. In these tales, Conrad is interested not in dramatising the subtleties of individual consciousness, but in examining the interpretations of speakers who are confident of their judgements. The tales fail in part because Conrad's principal speakers interpret the events they present in terms of stereotypic images that polarise the characters into incarnations of Good and Evil.

'The Partner' is an undistinguished story about a plot to wreck a ship for insurance money. Cloete, the villain, typifies for Conrad the moral anarchy of the modern city. Like the characters of *The Secret Agent*, he has a double identity. Underneath the exterior of a respectable businessman, Cloete is a confidence man. The very sound of his name is unpleasant, suggesting such words as 'low', 'bloat' and 'gloat'. He not only lacks scruples, but also actively recruits others to his immoral enterprises. He tempts George to 'tomahawk' the *Sagamore*, which is commanded by Captain Harry, and enlists Stafford to be the active arm of his plot. Yet Cloete is not unappealing to the stevedore and the writer as the story's most vital personality. He is a sort of Mephistophelean figure who has a good deal of wit and even a touch of humanity in his energetic opportunism. Obviously he did not intend his plot to result in Harry's death or subsequently cause Harry's wife to go mad.

Much of the story's interest depends upon the relationship between the blunt, straightforward and even occasionally coarse stevedore and the 'writer of stories' who provides his audience. The idiomatic, colloquial former stevedore barely knows any characters other than the opportunistic Cloete, with whom he is superficially acquainted and who serves as his principal source. In 'The Partner', Conrad's technical experiment with a rather bland if not stupid speaker contains the ingredients of its own failure. The stevedore's crude sensibility and lack of intelligence ensure that his interpretation of events will be primitive and myopic. His rugged delivery and discursive method of presentation are pointedly contrasted with the writer's detached tone, occasional lyricism, and references to a broader experience of the world. The two men speak at cross-purposes without communicating because their interests, life-styles and attitudes to language are completely incompatible.

Without much subtlety, Conrad explores the process of myth-making within the stevedore's mediocre intellect. His ingenuous way of imposing meaning is to place the tale on a vertical axis between heaven and hell and to separate the characters into those of the devil's party and those of God's. Thus Captain Harry's idyllic life on the *Sagamore* is ruined when he takes on board Stafford, a character whom the stevedore thinks of as a 'devil'. The stevedore insists that Harry could face his maker and thus would never be a suicide, and wants to believe that Harry endures misfortune with a stoic attitude.

One should not assume that Conrad's sympathies are totally with the writer. For the latter's aesthetic standards are questionable. Apparently he will turn any gossip into pulp literature; nor is he above ill-mannered derision of the taste of his intended audience. Conrad knows that the writer, who apologises for offending his audience's over-delicate sensibilities, should be apologising for his failure to transform 'fact' into imaginative literature. Rather than distil the stevedore's crude tale into more sophisticated fiction, he says, 'it would have been too much trouble to cook it for the consumption of magazine readers' (p. 128). Probably Conrad became so embarrassed by the tale's fundamental lack of quality that, rather coyly, he attributed it to an insipid writer's failure to make the necessary effort.

Since it would be difficult to imagine a writer more interested in problems of perspective and methods of narration than Conrad, it is hardly surprising that the convention of the discovered manuscript should provide the basis for 'The Inn of the Two Witches: A Find'. The editor uses the present tense to re-create the experience of encountering the manuscript: 'next we come upon the panegyric' and 'we discover then'. He universalises his personal reaction to certain parts of the manuscript: 'There is something touching in the warm pleasure [Byrne, the protagonist] remembers and records at this meeting with the professional mentor of his boyhood' (p. 134). By means of his relaxed, informal tone, the editor establishes the congenial familiarity of a bibliophile sharing his discovery.

The tension of the gothic narrative is all the more overpowering because of the contrast with the relaxed beginning. For a time, the editor reminds us of the manuscript by quoting Byrne, its protagonist and author, but very soon the pedestrian world of the fastidious scholar is left behind. Conrad suddenly takes us into a romance world where people resemble fauns, dwarfs and witches, and where the supernatural experience of hearing a dead man's warning needs no naturalistic explanation. The bibliophile, presumably himself conversant with medieval and renaissance romances, allegorises Byrne's quest for Tom, his missing comrade. While we cannot be sure where Byrne's tale ends and the narrator's editing begins, it is clear that Conrad has tried to create a landscape that is archetypal rather than descriptive of any locale.

Byrne's quest engages the narrator's interest. The narrator stresses that Tom has symbolic value for Byrne: 'Tom . . . was becoming endowed with a compelling fascination, like a symbolic figure of loyalty appealing to [his] feelings and [his] conscience' (p. 143). As Byrne leaves the coast, we are told by the narrator (who now assumes the guise of a third-person privileged speaker) that he '*struggled* manfully to the west against wind and rain, on a barren dark upland, under a sky of ashes' (p. 145, emphasis added). Byrne's physical journey parallels a psychic and, especially, a moral quest in which he must test his courage, dedication, and loyalty. 'In *himself* he carried the impression of the desert solitudes he had been traversing for the last six hours—the oppressive sense of an uninhabited world' (p. 146, emphasis added). Like Browning's 'Childe Roland to the Dark Tower Came', 'The Inn of the Two Witches: A Find' is about the process of experiencing the unknown. Byrne sees a gleam of light, but it proves a false light when the house is found to contain an unholy trinity of murderesses.

Byrne thinks that these women must be 'affiliated to the devil'; within the romance world of the tale, Byrne's radical metaphor has a reality beyond that of a figure of speech. The 'Satanic girl', allegorically representing Sin, and possibly derived from that figure in *Paradise Lost*, combines sensuality and violence; she simultaneously attracts and repels him: 'Her eyes were a little oblique, her mouth rather thick, but admirably formed; her dark face had a wild beauty, voluptuous and untamed'; and she has a 'sensuously savage' gaze (p. 150). Although 'a tortured soul', he solves the mystery of the death of his friend who had fought with him and taught him how to defend himself. He overcomes the forces which threaten his mental and emotional balance. While Byrne does not save his friend, he proves his moral worth by persevering in his quest for Tom. In its stress on courage, judgement and the need for 'decorum and restraint' in a

difficult situation, the tale may be a tentative step towards the moral
ideal that, as we shall see, Conrad defines in *The Shadow-Line*. But
Byrne's struggle with Sin, from which he emerges victorious, albeit
'pale and weak', is arbitrarily and awkwardly superimposed on
material that does not sustain an allegorical level.

By the time he wrote 'Because of the Dollars', Conrad had few
illusions about the literary value of these efforts to create allegory out
of melodramatic plots and one-dimensional characters that are easily
accessible to an unsophisticated audience. He could hardly have
spoken more disparagingly of the story, considering it an instance of
'prostituting his intellect to please the *Metropolitan*' (unpublished
letter, 16 Dec 1913, Berg Collection, New York Public Library). As
in 'The Partner' and 'The Inn of the Two Witches', the principal
narrator tends to understand characters in terms of simple moral
differences rather than to make subtle psychological distinctions. In
'Because of the Dollars', Conrad has a new solution to the problem of
presenting an allegorised version of events. Because the nominal
narrator becomes an almost completely anonymous figure, the
version of Hollis, the major speaker, has an autonomy that the tale of
the stevedore in 'The Partner' lacks.

The unsophisticated Hollis reductively allegorises his tale into a
conflict between virtue and moral darkness. For Hollis, his friend
Davidson has become synonymous with virtue. In language suggesting the unleashing of the devil's forces, Hollis depicts the introduction
of evil into Davidson's idyllic world. The Frenchman, posing as a
'poor, harmless cripple', is referred to as a 'devil' and is the
inspirational source of evil. Hollis compares Davidson's home to a
'frozen hell' and intimates that his wife, despite her angelic profile,
proves that a 'stupid woman with a sense of grievance is worse than an
unchained devil' (p. 210). Underneath her sweetness and 'innocent
profile' is a self-interested, egocentric shrew, capable of malicious
fantasising and unwilling to trust her husband.

If Hollis overzealously praises Davidson's moral excellence, nevertheless it is Davidson's goodness which is the salient fact of the tale. He
not only plays the forgiving Christ to Anne's Magdalen, but also
refuses to believe ill of his wife or her motives, and he dismisses the
potential for evil of the Frenchman and his friends. That Anne failed
to conform to Victorian notions of chastity does not blind him to her
redeeming qualities. His more flexible and humane morality is
favourably contrasted to his wife's astigmatic, narrow puritanism.
Hollis's bitterness and sarcasm rise to a crescendo of resentment when

he remembers Mrs Davidson, and he implicitly contrasts her with Anne's pathetic groping for love and security. By making the loose woman the heroine and the traditionally passive wife the villain, Conrad is not only flouting conventions but also titillating the sensibilities of the *Metropolitan Magazine* audience.

The muddy landing-place with its 'impenetrable darkness' is a fitting place for Davidson to learn about the existence of human malice. On this primordial mud, Hollis gives us the image of the giant Frenchman as a savage Neanderthal, crushing skulls with his seven-pound stone. Certainly, his lack of hands is appropriate for a figure who is more animal than human in his conduct and motivation. The Frenchman is described in non-human terms and is referred to by the pronoun 'it' to indicate his lack of humanity. After Davidson discovers the plot and chases him away, the Frenchman stalks the forest like a predatory beast. In what is surely the tale's most interesting scene, Davidson discovers Anne's crushed skull and is so 'overcome by remorse' that he feels 'the impulse of creeping away from that pitiful corpse on his hands and knees to the refuge of the ship', and 'actually [begins] to do so' (p. 205). Once again, in Conrad, contact with savagery and barbarism threatens to undo the trappings of civilisation.

But Davidson's shame and guilt only momentarily deprive him of his self-respect. His conscience recalls him to the necessity of rescuing Tony, Anne's pathetic child, whose life he regards as a sacred trust. When he assumes 'an erect attitude' and bravely, despite the menace to his own life, walks towards the house to rescue the boy, he is fulfilling his metaphoric role as Christ-figure. But, more importantly, he is asserting his and, by implication, civilised man's refusal to be defeated by man's primitive instincts. Yet, as in 'Il Conde', a chance encounter with man's atavistic impulses has a permanent effect; Davidson's tainted smile reflects his having discovered the nature of fear and evil.

III. 'THE PLANTER OF MALATA' (1914)

Written between *Chance* and *Victory*, 'The Planter of Malata' vacillates between psychological study and allegorical romance. The opening tale and the most ambitious of the *Within the Tides* volume, it traces the downfall of Geóffrey Renouard, who lives on an island removed from society, pursuing his agricultural experiments. His

values conflict with the commercialism and banality of urban life. As
Jim does on Patusan, Renouard sees himself as the creator and master
of a place which he seeks to dominate by the force of his personality:
'Malata was himself. He and Malata were one' (p. 58). His efforts to
circumvent the processes of nature by producing vegetable silk are
related to his inability to accept mortality as a condition of life. While
aspiring to complete detachment from passionate relationships,
Renouard becomes captivated by the ironically named solipsist
Felicia Moorsom. A superficial, pretentious representative of fashionable urban life, she rejects him. (Just like the young female
revolutionary in 'The Informer', her life, as her father recognises,
is 'agitation in empty space' [p. 41].) As part of his effort to magnify Renouard, Conrad presents him as the symbolic heir to heroic
aristocrats: 'They stood on the naked soil, had traditions to be faithful
to, had their feet on this earth of passions and death which is not a
hothouse. . . . They had to lead, to suffer with, to understand the
commonest humanity' (p. 77). Within the tale's allegorical context,
Renouard is destroyed not by sexuality, but by 'the moral poison of
falsehood' represented by Felicia (p. 65). If taken realistically, Felicia's
assertion that she 'stands for truth', or Renouard's addressing her with
the apostrophe 'O Divinity', is absurd. But the persistent allusions to
myth, the inflated rhetoric of the later scenes, and the lack of specific
details with which to establish verisimilitude partially succeed in
removing the tale from durational time and naturalistic space.

Conrad's concern with the effects of isolation and repressed passion
anticipates his next novel, *Victory*. But no more than Axel Heyst can
Renouard withdraw from human relationships. Stimulated by sexual
attraction, he does not *perceive* Felicia's actual character, but *creates* it
in his imagination to fulfil his desire for a mirror image of himself.
Renouard myopically invests Felicia with value not sustained by
what the narrative reveals about her. Because he has repressed or
ignored his physical desires, he is especially vulnerable. He reacts to
Felicia as one might respond to an object in an art museum rather than
to a human being. Solitude has affected not only Renouard's mind
but even his sense organs. It is almost as if he has developed
hyperacuity of vision on his island. His response to her is usually in
terms of visual impressions. He is first struck by her 'wealth of hair',
the blackness of her eyes and the 'gleaming' splendour of her
shoulders and arms. And he never gets past superficial appearances. In
one notable scene, he dreams of Felicia on the schooner, and he
imagines her as a statue; in a proleptic image, while he stares at the

chiselled head, it crumbles 'into a handful of dust' which blows away (p.31). On the mythic level to which the tale aspires, he becomes a Pygmalion *manqué*, unable to transform his aesthetic object into life. Gradually, his metaphors comparing Felicia to the goddess Venus and to a work of sculpture become ironic. As we come to learn about her character, these comparisons accrete not to magnify her, but to reduce Felicia to an aesthetic object.

Part of the reason this frustrated Prospero commits suicide derives from his inability to include Felicia in the world he has created to escape reminders of mortality and mediocrity. The omniscient narrator stresses this when he compares the rejected Renouard's feelings with those of 'an explorer trying to penetrate the interior of an unknown country, the secret of which is too well defended by its cruel and barren nature' (p. 79). To some extent, Felicia becomes a new territory to be conquered and explored, and his failure to do so makes him give up for the first time in his life. His self-image, dependent upon a career of successful adventures, requires his imposing a kind of control over Felicia. Renouard is not comfortable with anyone whom he must treat on an equal footing, whether it be the worldly professor or the simplistic aunt, who reminds him of 'a wax flower under glass'. The only people with whom he communicates are the natives on his island, whom he can completely dominate and who obey his every whim.

As in the early story 'The Return', we are not always sure whether Conrad is debunking his protagonist or sympathising with him. If the narrator's values are elusive, if not incoherent, it is because Conrad alternately identifies with and undercuts Renouard's romantic quest. Conrad cannot seem to decide whether Renouard is a morbid neurotic or a solitary vessel of lost values. Because Conrad detests his female lead, Felicia, he *needs* to emphasise how she destroys Renouard. His narrator satirises Renouard's adolescent romanticism and exposes him as a sexually frustrated man who has fallen in love with Felicia, although she is the epitome of the life he despises. On the one hand, like Kurtz and Falk, Renouard has atavistic impulses; at one point, he imagines himself taking Felicia to some 'profound retreat as in the age of Cavern men' (p. 45). On the other, he is a man with splendid aspirations. In the climactic interview with Felicia, he overcomes his tendency for romantic excesses and speaks with high purpose.

To call this ambitious but finally unsatisfactory tale a 'masterpiece', as Edward Said has, is ostentatiously generous.[5] The legerdemain to

hide Renouard's knowledge about Arthur, Felicia's lost lover, for the
purpose of creating rather meretricious dramatic suspense occupies
Conrad's attention and deflects him from coming to terms with the
secret of Renouard's character, the tale's real subject. But, soon
suspecting why Renouard responds 'hastily' to the editor's inquiries,
we become rather tired of the supposed mystery. Not only does
Renouard's mind function in obscurity, but so also does Conrad's.
We learn little about Renouard's motives and feelings from his prolix
analysis. If Renouard is supposed to be a complex, psychological
study, his subtleties are never disclosed. We really do not know
whether he commits suicide because his illusions about Felicia are
destroyed or because he despairs of the quality of contemporary life.
His feeling of 'immense deception' is really self-deception. Conrad's
sympathy with Renouard's isolation, desire and consequent despair
may have interfered with his examination of his protagonist's egoism.
Possibly a dramatised first-person narrator would have enabled
Conrad better to define and control his own attitude.

NOTES

1. Robert Scholes and Robert Kellogg, *The Nature of Narrative* (London: Oxford
   University Press, 1966), pp. 13, 14.
2. Ibid., p. 14.
3. Letter to K. Waliszewski, 8 Nov 1903, quoted in Baines, *Conrad: A Critical
   Biography*, p. 275; his source is *Lettres françaises*, ed. G. Jean-Aubry (Paris:
   Gallimard, 1930), p. 54.
4. Lawrence Graver in *Conrad's Short Fiction* (Berkeley and Los Angeles, Calif.:
   University of California Press, 1969) has quoted from this letter (including the
   passages I quote); see pp. 168–9. Yet, in 1920, Conrad turned the story into a
   surprisingly lively two-act play entitled *Laughing Anne*.
5. Edward W. Said, *Joseph Conrad and the Fiction of Autobiography* (Cambridge,
   Mass.: Havard University Press, 1966), p. 162.

3 Conrad's later novels

In recent years, Conrad's later novels—*Chance* (1912), *Victory* (1915), *The Shadow-Line* (1916), *The Arrow of Gold* (1919), *The Rescue* (1919) and *The Rover* (1923)—have been discussed as symbolic tales and allegories, as if they belonged to a different genre from his previous work. Thematically, they have been seen as symptoms of Conrad's inability to deal with love and sexuality on a mature level. While not ignoring differences between these novels and his prior work, I shall stress the biographical, thematic and formal continuities with Conrad's previous work.

The later novels, like their predecessors, need to be understood as expressions of Conrad's psyche and imagination. They continue to test and explore ways of feeling and ways of knowing. To the last, Conrad was interested in dramatising states of consciousness, and the later Conrad novels, like his prior work, explore how men cope in an amoral cosmos more than they argue for a system of values. Conrad still shows that each person sees reality according to his own needs. For example, *Chance* depends on the elaborate presentation of multiple points of view. Conrad has the omniscient narrator of *Victory* give perspectives other than Heyst's to undermine ironically that apparently strong figure and to show the reader an alternative view of Heyst. *The Arrow of Gold* consists of an appealing, but imperceptive, speaker and a dramatic monologue between two notes provided by an editor. Conrad's later novels continue his interest in exploring heterosexual and family ties, often in the context of futile and morally bankrupt political activity. These novels are not divorced from the social and historical context in which the characters live, and they are usually as much concerned with psychological realism and social observation as his previous work. And, as in Conrad's prior work, his humanism is tempered by scepticism and tentativeness.

There is scant evidence either in the Author's Notes written in 1919–20, in his letters, or in his non-fiction, that in his later years Conrad thought he was writing drastically different kinds of fiction

or that his values had fundamentally changed. Yet, in his important
study *Joseph Conrad's Fiction*, John Palmer argues,

> [Conrad's later novels] are intellectually more complex than
> the earlier works, and more remote in tone. Partly because his
> own intellectual growth was reaching full fruition, and partly
> because the philosophic threats to his moral optimism
> demanded a strong analytic counterbalance, Conrad at times
> adopts a tone of cold intellectual conviction which tends to
> freeze the stream of ideas. . . . His later work is successful only
> where he succeeds in transmuting these convictions into
> allegorical or near-allegorical form. . . . The pleasure of
> reading a novel like *Victory* derives less from the recognition of
> acute psychological or social observation than from the
> recognition of subtleties in the dramatization of a set of ideas,
> and to insist on the first at the expense of the second would be
> to resist the creation of allegory at all.[1]

Had Conrad sought to write allegories, we should expect a writer as
self-conscious as he to comment upon that. Yet one only has to reread
his letters to understand the continuity of his subjects, themes, and art.
His letters and Author's Notes show that not only verisimilitude,
but also the factual origins of his work, were important to him. Of
The Shadow-Line he wrote, 'The whole thing is exact autobiography. . . . That experience is transposed into spiritual terms—in
art a perfectly legitimate thing to do, as long as one preserves the exact
truth enshrined therein' (27 Feb 1917, *LL*, ii, pp. 182– 3). And in
1917 Conrad contended that throughout his career 'all my concern
had been with the "ideal" value of things, events and
people. . . . Whatever dramatic and narrative gifts I may have are
always, instinctively, used with that object—to bring forth *les valeurs
ideals*' (8 Mar 1917, ibid., p. 185).
    Allegory depends upon the artist's wishing to create a fable to
illustrate a moral vision. Conrad's later novels do not dramatise an
ethical system. Throughout his career, Conrad's focus is on the
psychic needs, motives and eccentricities that separate one man
from another. The representative aspect of his novels derives not
from the situation but from the character's archetypal aspirations. Jim
wants to be a courageous hero and Razumov needs public recognition as an intellectual figure. Gould wishes to be a powerful
figure who uses material wealth in the service of progress. If there is a

difference in the later novels, it is that Conrad deals with obsessions and repressions that are peculiarly singular to one individual character. Because Heyst, George, Anthony, Lingard and Peyrol have their own unique psyche, they may at times be less representative of moral and cultural issues than Conrad's prior protagonists. Because his later protagonists have motives with which most readers identify, we are drawn to them; because their unacknowledged needs and obsessions are often eccentric (although eccentric in a way that to our discomfort suggests *our* repressed selves), we draw away to a distance that approximates the stance of the omniscient narrator, with whose emotional and moral standards of behaviour we as readers are more comfortable.

Any consideration of the later novels must take very seriously Thomas Moser's splendid *Joseph Conrad: Achievement and Decline* (1957), because Moser's arguments have shaped discussion of these novels since his book appeared.

(1) '*The heroes and heroines of the later Conrad are sinned against, themselves unsinning.*'[2] On the contrary, Heyst, George, Lingard, Réal, and even Peyrol act self-righteously and arrogantly as they respond to their own motives and needs. If one must choose between sinning and sinned against (an admittedly reductive polarity), one must choose the former. But I believe that in these works Conrad is more interested in the psychosexual needs of his characters and the situations those needs create than he is in moral categories. That he wishes us to understand that Peyrol, Lingard, Anthony and Heyst do not usually make moral decisions, but make psychological decisions disguised as moral ones, establishes continuity with his prior work.

(2) '*We are basically sound. When trouble comes to us, we are in no way responsible for it. The fault lies elsewhere, in other people.*'[3] Lingard, Heyst, Anthony, Réal, and George are shown to be people who on occasion behave illogically, irrationally, inadequately and ineptly; certainly their behaviour does not reveal them as fundamentally sound even if, like Jim, they *wish* to behave correctly. But, although they are not involved in situations where their conduct can be measured by rigid external standards of conduct, they must choose between basic values—such as loyalty to a comrade or a lover versus loyalty to oneself. Conrad continues to be concerned with the way in which man's passions, instincts and needs trigger behaviour that has unfortunate consequences. Because Conrad is obsessed with psycho-

sexual problems, he is more interested in particulars and *less* concerned with ideals and values than in his prior work. Yet, contrary to Moser's assertion, individual guilt does not disappear. Except for *The Shadow-Line*, some of the situations involving personal relations are puzzling to Conrad and, hence, his standards may be less explicit. Each novel depends on a character's recognising an ethical imperative in a difficult moral situation. Paradoxically, except for *The Shadow-Line*, the later novels are novels of manners, but without a *norm* of manners in which Conrad believes.

(3) '*The perceptive hero disappears.*'[4] But where is the perceptive hero in Conrad? As I argued in *Conrad: 'Almayer's Folly' to 'Under Western Eyes'*, even Marlow is rarely completely perceptive; in any case, his place is taken by an omniscient narrator, a surrogate Conrad, who is the perceptive figure even if he provides alternative behavioural standards to those of the major characters, standards which are not as lucid as they might be.

(4) '*By the end of 1913, Conrad's surrender to the association between love and death is fairly complete.*'[5] While Conrad's later protagonists face an external menace (like most of the earlier ones), and most of them (unlike in the earlier novels) are in love, this does not establish an unnatural relationship between love and death. While death is a frequent presence in Conrad's later plots, is the mortality rate of his major characters really any greater than in his earlier fiction? Heyst is the only central figure in the novels whose death is directly related to sexual love. The example Moser cites, Renouard in 'The Planter of Malata', is depicted as a pathological personality.

(5) *Conrad is a misogynist.* While there is some truth to Moser's contention, it is an hyperbole that has become an accepted critical shibboleth. The major evidence for misogyny is the views of Marlow in *Chance*; but Marlow, although an objectification of an aspect of Conrad, is, as he had been in the previous three works in which he appears, a dramatised character. Mrs Fyne's peculiar masculinity and lesbianism derive from her compensating for an exploitive tyrannical father; her brother, Captain Anthony, compensates in equally unusual ways—namely, by his inability to respond physically to Flora's need, because of over-fastidiousness and lack of self-regard. Surely Flora's idyllic relationship with Anthony and forthcoming marriage to Powell do not verify Moser's statement that 'the later

Conrad's hostility to feminine self-assertion results in the immediate destruction of his women as soon as they embark on a plan of action'.[6] Arlette's initiative does not destroy her but leads to her happy marriage to Réal. And Peyrol's heroic death is not the act of a misogynist. Lena's death derives not from her failure to obey Heyst or the inadequacy of her plan, but from the failure of Heyst to respond boldly and bravely when he is threatened and, in the climactic scene, from his failure to prevent the shooting.

(6) 'The productions of Conrad's last years [The Arrow of Gold, The Rover, the fragment Suspense and the later half of The Rescue] are virtually without a redeeming feature. They reveal that Conrad has exhausted his creative energy. He has no longer anything to write about and must rework old material.'[7] My chapters on these novels will argue that this ignores the psychological complexity of his last novels and the structural brilliance of The Rover.

As I indicated in my introduction, Conrad's later novels can be divided into three separate movements. At first, in Chance and Victory, Conrad wished to establish that he was an English novelist by writing novels that, notwithstanding their romance component, were concerned with manners, personal relationships and, at times, contemporary issues. In the next three novels, he turned to various strands of his personal past for his subject-matter. The Shadow-Line is a fictional memoir of his initiation into command, while The Arrow of Gold is a fictional version of initiation into sexual maturity. The Rescue enabled him to recapture his literary youth, the period of Almayer's Folly, An Outcast of the Islands and his favourite work, The Nigger of the 'Narcissus'. In the three later works he is, like Marlow in 'Youth', placing his back to the future and looking longingly into the past with the hope of recapturing lost feelings of energy, vitality, and success. Finally, in The Rover and in the long fragment Suspense, he sought an historical panorama in the Napoleonic period. While we do not know what he would have done with Suspense, the backward journey into the historical past in The Rover is an occasion for expressing deep personal concerns. The Napoleonic era provides the setting for Conrad to dramatise the heroic death of a seaman who is a fictional version of himself. Peyrol is an ageing former seaman who is, like himself, an outsider, an individualist and a man who has participated in historical events only to discover the importance of personal relationships.

Except for The Shadow-Line, Conrad's later novels usually have three not completely integrated organising principles: (1) a basic adventure tale, often a voyage, dominated by a self-sufficient, independent, single-minded male figure; (2) the heterosexual interaction between the protagonist and the woman whom he loves; and (3) the historical and social setting in which the events take place. These principles often stand in an uneasy relationship, particularly in the novels' second halves when the love relationship intensifies and often overwhelms the potential moral consequences of the males' behaviour in the adventure. In *Chance*, for example, from the time Flora and Captain Anthony elope, the structure revolves around their relationship and undermines the baroque narrative technique. Conrad's fundamental interest in the characters' psychosexuality reasserts itself in spite of the intervention of Marlow and the nameless narrator. In fact, Powell, the nominal source of the last phase, is subsumed into the love motif because of his passion for Flora. Again, in *Victory*, the external views of Heyst and the double narrator— Davidson and his anonymous listener—become less important after the elopement; the novel becomes concerned with the lovers' interaction. Peyrol undertakes his final mission less from commitment to a political cause than out of affection for Arlette and inability to face defeat for her hand.

In these novels, Conrad's conception of heterosexual love is often bourgeoise and conventionally Edwardian. Moments of passion and displays of physical affection are often depicted as extraordinary events that violate society's taboos. Conrad is ambivalent to those whose love takes place in remote settings and unusual situations and whose love thus challenges the validity of traditional manners and mores. Typical is Réal's sudden kissing of Arlette's hand, which he fastidiously interprets as a violation not only of decorum but also of morality. He excoriates himself for the kiss; a man of 'pedantic conscience', Réal thinks of that kiss as if it had been a rape. That so much is made of Rita's reputation and her illicit relationship with Henry Allègre, and that José Ortega and then Blunt become her nemesis as if in response to her passion for George, testify to the fastidious conscience of the author.[8] The editor's patronising view of George indicates Conrad's desire to separate himself from a protagonist who is a version of his passionate, impulsive younger self. The purpose of George's memoir is to discover 'a little sympathy . . . for his buried youth, as he lives it over again at the end of his significant course on this earth' (pp. 4–5). At times the reader feels Conrad's longing for absolute standards with which to judge the passions that constitute the major subject of his later work.

'The Secret Sharer' and *The Shadow-Line* rank with Conrad's masterpieces—*Nostromo*, 'Heart of Darkness', *Lord Jim* and *The Secret Agent*. Not so incidentally, in both works Conrad uses his characteristic technique of a meditative mind probing the significance of a crucial past experience. While *Victory* and *The Rover* are quite splendid, even they share the flaws that occasionally disrupt the later fiction. In the first place, often Conrad does not give himself to the narrative voice or to his other major characters; at times, his withholding of the full range of his psychic involvement is responsible for a more flaccid form. Secondly, as Conrad seeks a larger audience, he begins to use a more conventional chronology and abandons the non-chronological movement that depends upon the striking juxtaposition of incidents. His unique juxtaposition of events had enabled him to present the reader with a complex moral context for judging the actions of central characters. Thirdly, the later novels *focus* on fewer characters and fewer dramatic situations and lack the moral density of the prior works. Fourthly, Conrad does not always successfully integrate his protagonist's private life into the historical or social background. In its way, *The Rover* addresses the French Revolution, as 'Heart of Darkness' addresses imperialism, but its characters do not typify or epitomise their historical moment. *Nostromo* and 'Heart of Darkness' penetrate to our deepest levels because they are representative of their *Zeitgeist* in the same way that Odysseus's journey is of his. What makes Conrad's major novels so compelling are the tensions between public issues and private lives and between representative aspirations and idiosyncratic characters, and these tensions are often missing in the later works.

NOTES

1. John A. Palmer, *Joseph Conrad's Fiction: A Study in Literary Growth* (Ithaca, NY: Cornell University Press, 1968), pp. 168–9.
2. Thomas Moser, *Joseph Conrad: Achievement and Decline* (Cambridge, Mass.: Harvard University Press, 1957), p. 141.
3. Ibid., p. 140.
4. Ibid., p. 163.
5. See ibid., p. 144.
6. Ibid., p. 162.
7. Ibid., p. 180.
8. Bernard C. Meyer, in *Conrad: A Psychoanalytic Biography* (Princeton, NJ: Princeton University Press, 1967), p. 182, has written, 'The re-establishment of a blissful intimacy between mother and child seems to represent the deepest significance of the conception of love in many of Conrad's stories . . . .'

4 *Chance*: The novel of manners as psychosexual drama

I

When working upon *Chance* (1912), Conrad had the kind of writing block that he had had earlier in his career: '[I have been] absolutely unable to write even a letter. Better now' (27 Oct 1910, *LL*, ii, p. 119); 'In writing I wrestle painfully with that language which I feel I do not possess but which possesses me—alas!' (23 Jan 1911, ibid., p. 125). He had a severe breakdown in 1910 and a relapse in early 1911, as well as several episodes of hypochondria, before completing *Chance* in 1912. The cumbersome and idiosyncratic first chapter provides Conrad with a means of launching his narrative, although it was written in 1907 and really belonged to an earlier conception of the novel, which had occupied him intermittently since 1905. Since the stress in the puzzling first chapter is on beginning a career in the merchant marine, the chapter is related less to Conrad's formal plan than to his psychic need to recoil in times of writing difficulty to memories of his maritime past. As Jean-Aubry notes, 'Conrad has transferred to the young Powell his own experience' of passing his first examination (ibid., i, p. 57).

As he had done when faced with writer's block prior to *The Nigger of the 'Narcissus'*, Conrad uses the process of beginning a voyage as a means of beginning a novel. As with *The Nigger*, he speaks of *Chance* as a voyage to be completed: 'Having got a slant of fair wind with *Chance*' (May 1911, ibid., ii, p. 128). Again he relies upon his sea experience to overcome self-doubt as an author. Finishing *Chance* enabled him to recover his self-esteem; at one point it looked as if *Chance* would join *The Rescue* as a novel that he could not complete: 'My only objection [to finishing] the *Rescue* would be that it does not advance me very much whereas *Chance* would have been a long step'

(27 Aug 1910, ibid., p. 114). That he had signed a contract for *Chance* with the *New York Herald* gave him the sense of 'a black winged phantom' hovering over him (22 June 1911, ibid., p. 131): 'There are weeks, whole weeks, when I am utterly unable to write a single sentence. I struggle with my thoughts like a man stricken dumb suddenly . . .' (22 June 1911, ibid., p. 132). As if he were the Ancient Mariner in the grip of a restraining curse, he writes, 'I think that the evil spell is broken at last. I've just written 500 words of *Chance* in a couple of hours. It's about time. Over two months, indeed nearly three, without (practically) a line!' (15 Oct 1911, ibid., p. 136).

After concluding *Chance* in March 1912, he ceased writing for several weeks. His criticism of Dostoevsky may relate more to his own state of mind as he awaited the publication of *Chance* than to his reading of Dostoevsky: 'I don't know that he is too Russian for me. It sounds to me like fierce mouthings from prehistoric ages' (27 May 1912; ibid., p. 140). Since *Chance* is a unique effort to combine the novel of manners (the striking examples of which for Conrad were the novels of Henry James) with the adventure tale, it is not surprising that at this time he should have judged Dostoevsky's passionate energy severely. Yet it is precisely the kind of barely restrained energy which he finds in Dostoevsky that distinguishes Conrad's best work, including 'Heart of Darkness', *Lord Jim* and *Nostromo*.

As he had in 1898–1900, Conrad uses Marlow when he has difficulty writing, because he can transfer the problems of writing and understanding to an alter ego within the world he is trying to create. Like his creator, Marlow has retired from the sea but sustains himself with the possibility—surely a fiction in Conrad's case—that he might somehow return to that life. The following comment of the frame narrator, Conrad's other tentative alter ego in the novel, reflects Conrad's nagging feeling that he had left his 'true element' when he left the sea:

> From year to year he dwelt on land as a bird rests on the branch of a tree, so tense with the power of brusque flight into its true element that it is incomprehensible why it should sit still minute after minute. The sea is the sailor's true element, and Marlow, lingering on shore, was to me an object of incredulous commiseration like a bird, which, secretly, should have lost its faith in the high virtue of flying (pp. 33–4).

The subject-matter of *Chance* becomes a means whereby Conrad may

imaginatively escape the disappointments of land and the difficulties
of writing. Conrad has Marlow consistently allude to a land–sea
dichotomy in reductive terms. Criticism of the land is an aggressive if
childish response to the source of Conrad's frustrations in his personal
and professional life.

In *Chance*, Marlow becomes an unintentional caricature of his
former self. If we have any doubts that Marlow's richness as a
character in prior works depends upon his embodying Conrad's
psyche, we have only to look at what happens when he becomes
hardly more than a narrative instrument, a mere garrulous device to
tell a tale. He is a surrogate for Conrad's middle-age prejudices rather
than for his quest for values and for emotional stability. Conrad
returned to Marlow during a time of personal trial; based on the prior
Marlow tales, we expect Conrad to use him as a means of defining
himself. During this period his letters reveal the most serious neurosis
since the 1890s if not his life: 'I've lost all self-respect and have abandoned myself to a debauch of illness and laziness. . . . I am all of a
shake yet. I feel like a man returned from hell and look upon the very
world of the living with dread' (28 June 1910, *LL*, ii, p. 113). But he
seems to have deliberately avoided transferring his own doubts and
anxiety to his character. Much of the effectiveness of the prior
Marlow tales depends upon the reader's intuitive understanding that
Conrad's own psyche is a dramatised presence within his text. Conrad
tries to establish continuity with the early Marlow tales by giving him
his identity as a thoughtful seaman and by reviving his meditative
syntax. But his meditations are only tangential to the issues
dramatised by the narrative episodes. Unlike the earlier Marlow
tales, the past and present do not interact as he narrates; more
importantly, Marlow is fundamentally unaffected by his tale, as if it
were peripheral to his values and even, alas, to his imagination.

Recalling no doubt the grounds of Marlow's appeal to Jim and of
Marlow's own relationship to his audience in both *Lord Jim* and
'Heart of Darkness', Conrad has Marlow remark to the narrator
about his London interview with Flora, 'A confession of whatever
sort is always untimely. . . . You seek sympathy, and all you get is
the most evanescent sense of relief—if you get that much. For a confession, whatever it may be, stirs the secret depths of the hearer's character. Often depths that he himself is but dimly aware of' (p. 212).
But in *Chance*, although the narrator tries to build up Marlow's
stature (note his 'sympathetic impulses of mirth and pity'), he is an
opinionated, cranky, indifferent and rather dense speaker. At times,

Conrad does not know what to do with Marlow, even though he requires him to continue his narrative. What Palmer calls 'Marlow's analytic improvement of other characters' understanding' is often irrelevant to the characters' experience. [1] Whereas in *Lord Jim* Marlow uses parallels to Jim's experience (such as the French Lieutenant or Bob Stanton) to create contexts in which to evaluate Jim, in *Chance* he often uses abstractions which, because undefined by the dramatic action, fail to stir the reader's imagination. The following analyses of the conduct of Fyne's *dog* reveals, behind an unsuccessful effort at irony, a self-indulgent pleasure at using multisyllabic words for trivial events: 'The dog, a vivacious and amiable animal which for some inscrutable reason had bestowed his friendship on my unworthy self, rushed up the bank demonstratively and insinuated himself under my arm' (p. 43).

Not only Marlow's cynicism but also his verbosity undermines the fulfilment of the romance possibilities implied by the terms 'Knight' and 'Damsel'. When the narrator remarks that 'one never could be sure' whether Marlow meant what he said or not, he proposes the possibility that Marlow is playing with his audience. Conrad undoubtedly proposes this Catch-22 formulation to excuse whatever foolishness his narrator speaks; surely, there is no factual explanation or psychological reason for Marlow's speaking *other than what he meant*. But then, again, there are no dramatised reasons for much of Marlow's intermittent philosophising and occasional polemics; for example, the following epigrammatic passage *sounds* important, but does it derive from experience within the novel, or, indeed, does it really make much sense? 'I think that to understand everything is not good for the intellect. A well-stocked intelligence weakens the impulse to action; an overstocked one leads gently to idiocy' (p. 62). If, as Guerard claims, Captain Anthony 'initiates the line of immature, passive, irritable and unintelligent heroes', Marlow initiates that line of tellers. [2] What kind of psychological or moral analyses is the following remark to the nameless narrator? 'The idea of the son of the poet, the rescuer of the most forlorn damsel of modern times, the man of violence, gentleness and generosity, plunged up to his neck in ship's accounts amused me' (p. 238). Such a sentence conveys Marlow's complacency, self-indulgence, and generalising propensity. One can neither identify nor empathise with a speaker prone to such generalisations as the following: 'the incapacity to achieve anything distinctly good or evil is inherent in our earthly condition. Mediocrity is our mark' (p. 23).

Conrad replaces Marlow with Powell to report the psychodrama on board ship. Powell is supposed to be a sympathetic but conventional character with whose perspective the reader will feel comfortable. While he transmits to the narrator what he learns from Powell, Marlow lacks a substantial relationship with both of them. Either Marlow or the first-person narrator should be an active seeking mind in the process of coming to terms with experience or, alternatively, an imperceptive, myopic narrator whose telling is self-indicting. Marlow is really an *explanation of omniscience*; because he has had the opportunity—the 'chance', in an intended irony—to speak to and observe the major characters at crucial moments, he can tell the tale. The tale is undermined—'deadened' might be a better word—by the elaborate narrative technique whereby the anonymous narrator tells us what Marlow learned from Flora, Powell and Fyne; and, at times, what Fyne learned came from Mrs Fyne via Flora. The unintended effect of this process is to make the action remote and to reduce it to Lilliputian stature. As in *Clarissa*, the inefficiency of narrative technique becomes itself the focus of interest; the characters self-indulgently immerse themselves in a word world as an outlet for repressed libidinous energies. While the constant retelling of private dramas *seems* to transform them into semi-public events, the reader's interest is in the intricacies and idiosyncrasies of the characters' psyches.

At times Conrad tries to duplicate the dramatised crises that make Marlow function so effectively in 'Heart of Darkness' and *Lord Jim*. Such a moment occurs when Mrs Fyne's remark that Flora 'has chosen to disappear' overwhelms Marlow, and he experiences such disorientation that he thinks of himself as a trained dog: 'In an instant I found myself out of the dance and down on all-fours so to speak, with liberty to bark and bite' (p. 58). If one has any doubts that this bathetic image of dislocation transparently reveals Marlow's lack of seriousness and moral energy, one only has to compare it with Marlow's psychological agony when he loses his temper in the face of Jewel's challenge to Jim, or when he explains why he could not lie to the Intended in 'Heart of Darkness'. Indeed, Marlow now lives in a word world which is often an echo chamber of his past narrations; Conrad's frequent use of 'inscrutable' is a facile mnemonic device to recall the Marlow of 'Heart of Darkness'.

Rather than a dynamic, evolving personality, Marlow is a disguised version of the anonymous omniscient narrator that Conrad had previously avoided in his major works, even when he nominally used that convention. When Marlow's comments reinforce the dramatised action, they serve a functional choral role but they do not distinguish him as an individual moral identity in whom the reader is interested. Although hardly profound, his references to man's powerlessness and loneliness within the 'cruel', 'horrible', 'Infinite' universe—a universe that is indifferent to man's aspirations—are confirmed by the action. Like the omniscient narrator in *The Secret Agent*, he alludes to enduring traditions and thus proposes alternatives to the standards of the mediocre characters whose actions he describes; implicitly he emphasises the ironic discrepancy between his subject and the world evoked by such allusions. For example, Marlow describes de Barral in terms that suggest a religious visionary: 'His appearance was ecstatic, his motionless pale eyes seemed to be gazing down the vista of future ages . . .'; at his trial, he cries out 'in accents of passionate belief' (p. 83).

Since Conrad interrupted *Chance* to write *Under Western Eyes* and 'The Secret Sharer', it is not surprising that *Chance* also contains the double motif. *Chance* lacks the kind of doubling in which a character confronts another who is not himself, but because of crucial resemblances seems *of himself*. In *Chance*, 'doubling' is really no more than Conrad's insistence upon superficial resemblances. For example, at first Powell confuses the captain with de Barral: 'he received an absurd impression that his captain . . . was sitting on both sides of the aftermost skylight at once. He was too occupied to reflect on this curious delusion, this phenomenon of seeing double . . .' (p. 276). To be sure, each is a prisoner on board the ship; each is the jailer of the other. They are contesting for the love of the same woman; feeling that her father is a martyr, no doubt because she identifies with his suffering, which she had shared because of society's verdict, Flora acknowledges his claims. But, these similarities are either at the verbal level or they define parallels that an attentive reader already understands. Such putative character doubles in *Chance* provide a refuge for Conrad from intense psychological and epistemological analysis.

Chance has historical interest as an unintentional parody of the self-conscious narrator that was perfected by James, Ford and Conrad. Like most parodies, *Chance* teaches us something about the limitations and possibilities of the form that is caricatured. Henry James has made the most acute comment about the form of *Chance*:

It literally strikes us that [Conrad's] volume sets in motion

more than anything else a drama in which his own system and
his combined eccentricities of recital represent the protagonist
in face of powers leagued against it, and of which the
denouement gives us the system fighting in triumph, though
with its back desperately to the wall, and laying the powers
piled up at its feet.[3]

The almost geometric form threatens to snuff out content. The form,
like a series of Chinese boxes, imprisons the characters and mirrors
their repression; it is a form that dilutes and undermines passion by
setting it at a distance. The reader becomes anaesthetised to the
characters' passions and to dramatic situations because they are
remote from his experience. The seemingly baroque form of *Chance*
lacks a radial centre, a unifying core that informs the various episodes.
Hence, beneath the sophisticated scaffolding is really an inchoate
form reflecting Conrad's inability to master his narrative materials.
The reader finds himself discarding multiple explanations that eschew
the psychosexual complexities and, as a result, making little headway
into what is going on. Because of Marlow's evasion and verbiage, the
reader often must provide his own analyses of character and moral
implication. This is quite contrary to the reader's experience in *Lord
Jim* and *Nostromo*, where the novels' rhetoric shapes the reader's
responses. Unwittingly in *Chance*, at times Conrad puts the reader in
the position of the crewmen in *The Nigger of the 'Narcissus'* struggling
to rescue Jimmy Wait from beneath the wreckage and clutter.

II

If the shortcomings of *Chance* derive from the narrative technique
and the effect of that technique upon the form, its success rests on
Conrad's deft analysis of various kinds of physical, emotional and
moral imprisonment. Conrad subtly uses de Barral's physical
imprisonment as a trope for these more subtle kinds of imprisonment:
'One has a notion of a maiming, crippling process; of the individual
coming back damaged in some subtle way. . . . Did you notice that
there is something infernal about the aspect of every individual stone
or brick of them, something malicious as if the matter were enjoying
its revenge of the contemptuous spirit of man' (p. 352).[4] De Barral
becomes transformed into an imprisoned object, and cannot put that

identity behind him.[5] He refers to the captain as the 'Jailer' and, as if it were a prison or a brothel, regards the ship as 'a house of disgrace' (p. 371); he feels that he has simply exchanged one prison for another. His 'rigidity' suggests that he has become interchangeable with the bars that enclosed him. But every place in which he dwells is a prison; even the cab which takes him to the ship is called a 'confined space' and a 'rolling box' (pp. 365, 355). The prison has transformed him into an object that it encloses: 'There was something between [Flora and her father], something hard and impalpable, the ghost of these high walls' (p. 355). The curtains that divide the cabin between Anthony's quarters and those of Flora and her father were 'joined closely, and perhaps on purpose, made a little too long, moved no more than a solid wall' (p. 415). Anthony's section is called 'the most private part of the saloon' and 'that forbidden space' (p. 410). De Barral, of course, is imprisoned by his own obsessions: 'His fixed idea was to save his girl from the man who had possessed himself of her' (p. 377). His use of the term 'possessed' is indicative of how the quintessential materialist defines human relations. He tries to establish his dominance by his 'air of guardianship', and by his assuming the Pandarus role in relation to Powell, whom he encourages ('my daughter has taken quite a liking to you') and perhaps regards as a replacement for his hated rival Anthony (pp. 377, 409). De Barral was imprisoned before, during and after his release by the obsessions of his perverse personality; as Conrad perceives so often in his work, we are all imprisoned by our psychic needs.

On board, the prison is replicated. What Marlow says of de Barral's prison seems applicable to the situation on ship: 'You do indeed seem to feel along the very lines and angles of the unholy bulk, the fall of time, drop by drop, hour by hour, leaf by leaf, with a gentle and implacable slowness. And a voiceless melancholy comes over one, invading, overpowering like a dream, penetrating and mortal like poison' (p. 354). De Barral feels that in prison he has 'had his life stolen from him' (p. 294). Even though, as she tells him, 'I haven't been shut up like you', Flora has her own ghosts – a vivid past, including the governess and her suicide attempt – which imprison her (p. 360). When Flora and her father go to their room, 'Flora shuts [the door] carefully behind [them]', as if to suggest they are locked up together (p. 373).

Both Flora and Anthony are imprisoned by their own sense of inferiority; Anthony is sure she 'could not care for a man like me, a stranger' (p. 337). Imprisoned by her past no less than Lord Jim, she thinks she is insignificant and contemptible. In a sense the governess has psychologically imprisoned Flora by convincing her 'that she was in heart, mind, manner and appearance an utterly common and insipid creature' and that no one can love her except her father. 'She could not help believing what she had been told; that she was in some mysterious way odious and unlovable. It was cruelly true—*to her*. The oracle of so many years had spoken finally' (pp. 119, 263). Her father's imprisonment has, as the captain remarks, 'robbed you of your very name' (p. 226). Reacting to her disgrace, she has created the imprisoning illusion of her father's innocence and of the quiet happiness that they once shared. Taking him on board she thinks, 'If he bolts away . . . then I shall know that I am of no account indeed! That no one loves me, that words and actions and protestations and everything in the world is false—and I shall jump into the dock. *That* at least won't lie' (p. 370). She has misinterpreted Anthony's generosity and believes it indicates a lack of regard on his part. Yet she correctly realises that his proposal is a new kind of imprisonment. For when he refers to her putting herself in his 'keeping', inadvertently echoing the concept of human possession that de Barral holds, he is proposing an alternative to a dynamic, passionate relationship.

The asexual, self-absorbed de Barral's physical imprisonment is an apt metaphor for kinds of psychological confinement, including psychosexual imprisonment. The captain is imprisoned by his generous agreement with Flora; living in his own cabin he is physically separated from his wife: 'Intoxicated with the pity and tenderness of his part', he creates his own prison (p. 261). This generosity becomes a barrier that separates him from Flora, but the other side of his generosity is his sexual repression: 'She existed, unapproachable, behind the blank wall of his renunciation. "His" force, fit for action, experienced the impatience, the indignation, almost the despair of his vitality arrested, bound, stilled, progressively worn down, frittered away by Time' (p. 396). Deference to de Barral undermines Flora and Anthony's love, and puts both lovers in his power. De Barral's presence creates their epistemology. Captain Anthony speaks of her as if he had imprisoned her and she answers in kind. He tells her, 'I, who have said I could never let you go, I shall let you go'; and she responds, 'But I don't want to be let off' (pp. 429–30). They are both captives of their own sense of duty.

As Marlow notes, 'There is a Nemesis which overtakes generosity too, like all the other imprudences of men who dare to be lawless and proud' (p. 350). Conrad's attitude to the crew's sympathy for

Wait and Donkin in *The Nigger of the 'Narcissus'* and of the captain for Leggatt in 'The Secret Sharer' indicates that he would have regarded as sham sentiment the overgenerosity that separates Anthony from Flora. When Flora sadly tells her father, 'I mean to be honest', Conrad knows that she is unintentionally playing on the older meaning of 'honesty' as 'chastity' (p. 385). It is as if she were the prisoner on board: 'she felt herself being pushed back into that solitude, that moral loneliness, which had made all her life intolerable' (p. 428). Imprisonment is self-defined; while, as Marlow notes, we may be awed by institutional imprisonment, man is imprisoned by his past, his ideas, his loyalty and his routine. Conrad's implication is that all men are imprisoned by their own fixed ideas, which often are interchangeable with obsessions; as Marlow puts it, 'Each of us arranges the world according to his own notion of the fitness of things' (p. 289).

The shipboard arrangement imprisons the passions of the Anthonys. Reflecting Conrad's idealisation of heterosexual love, Marlow uses the language of crime and punishment to describe their arrangement:

> If two beings thrown together, mutually attracted, resist the
> necessity, fail in understanding and voluntarily stop short of
> the—the embrace, in the noblest meaning of the word, then
> they are committing a sin against life, the call of which is
> simple. Perhaps sacred. And the punishment of it is an invasion
> of complexity, a tormenting, forcibly tortuous involution of
> feelings, the deepest form of suffering from which indeed
> something significant may come at last, which may be criminal
> or heroic, may be madness or wisdom . . .   (pp. 426–7)

Until Anthony makes his renunciation, after Flora's visit, she is moving away from the primacy of her commitment to her father; indeed, if the strength of that commitment kept her from suicide, it just barely did. It is Anthony who has 'liberated' her 'from a condemned cell' (p. 330). Like Lord Jim, Anthony imprisons himself in his own self-image, and because of this he lets her lapse back into self-imprisonment: 'The inarticulate son had set up a standard for himself with that need for embodying in his conduct the dreams, the passion, the impulses the poet puts into arrangements of verses, which are dearer to him than his own self—and may make his own self appear sublime in the eyes of other people, and even in his own eyes' (p. 328). Yet perhaps Conrad is implying that, because all men are imprisoned by their 'mortal envelope' (like Franklin), they inevitably become the ironic victim of their illusions. When Anthony offers to let her go, Flora feels that she is being returned to prison, to a prison far more awful than the original one in which she had been living, because that one always contained the hope of sexual fulfilment and marital love.

The novel dramatises that each person is imprisoned by his own anxieties and obsessions. In a famous early letter to Mme Poradowska Conrad wrote,

> One must drag the ball and chain of one's selfhood to the end. It is the [price] one pays for the devilish and divine privilege of thought; so that in this life it is only the elect who are convicts—a glorious band which comprehends and groans but which treads the earth amidst a multitude of phantoms with maniacal gestures, with idiotic grimaces. Which would you rather be: idiot or convict?
>
> (20 July [?] 1894, *Mme Poradowska*, p. 72)

(It is interesting that Conrad speaks of Flora and her father as 'figures from Dickens', since *Little Dorrit* likewise concerns self-imprisonment and uses prison as a central metaphor for isolation and alienation.[6]) Initiation into love requires overcoming psychic imprisonment; Anthony and Flora relieve one another from self-imprisonment, only to allow her father, when he is released, to imprison them.

If allowed to become an obsession, a passion itself can imprison a man, as Marlow understands: 'A passion, dominating or tyrannical, invading the whole man and subjugating all his faculties to its own unique end, may conduct him whom it spurs and drives, into all sorts of adventures, to the brink of unfathomable dangers, to the limits of folly, and madness, and death' (p. 329). Such a ruling passion dominates all three major characters: Anthony's passionate love for Flora is matched by the passion of de Barral's resentment and jealousy and by Flora's passionate commitment to the one man whom she thinks has loved her, her father. That the term 'fixed idea', used to describe de Barral's self-conception, is also used to describe Powell when he sees himself in the role of rescuer is part of Conrad's effort to imply that one man's behaviour is never so different from another's potential behaviour as we might think or wish. Even Franklin, embittered by the change in his status and the disruption of what he recalls as an idyllic life on board the ship, is self-imprisoned. De Barral's interest in Flora is more than the paternal one he acknowledges; playing Pandarus to Powell is a partially sanctioned outlet. But, at one point after thinking of the marriage, 'his eyes [ran] over her with an attention which was surprisingly noticeable' and he proposes that they 'clear out before it is too late' (p. 386). Much older than Flora, who appeared to be only a girl to Powell, Anthony unwillingly assumes a paternal position to Flora. The incestuous overtones of her love for her father reflect her sense of unworthiness; because she is unable to believe that she is capable of evoking love and, in particular of deserving Anthony's love, her father becomes the outlet she requires for her libidinous energy. Yet, perhaps to sanction her feelings, Flora regards her father as 'more helpless than a child', for whom she must care (p. 336).

Chance continues Conrad's exploration of the family structure. Both Flora and Captain Anthony have been affected by self-indulgent fathers who offered little in the way of tenderness and gentleness. After his wife's death, de Barral assigned the child-rearing to a governess who despised her charge. Mrs Fyne and Captain Anthony had as father a poet who, while celebrating 'the domestic and social amenities of our age', in his own life 'showed traces of the primitive cave-dweller's temperament' (p. 38). In a sense his home became a prison for his children; subsequent to the son's running away, 'The daughter . . . remained in bondage to the poet for several years, till she too seized a chance of escape by throwing herself into the arms, the muscular arms, of the pedestrian Fyne' (p. 39). Although she can exchange her father for Fyne, she is still a prisoner of her past: 'Her father had kept her strictly cloistered. Marriage with Fyne was certainly a change, but only to another kind of claustration' (p. 66). The father completely dominated the daughter ('He was a savage sentimentalist who had his own decided views of his paternal prerogatives'), and when she escapes she devotes herself to defending the prerogatives of women (p. 38). Mrs Fyne seems to have played for Flora the role of a strong parental figure, a role she learned from her father.

Like Flora, Mrs Fyne is also victim of incestuous impulses. Indeed, there may be a hint in phrases such as 'paternal prerogative' or 'remained in bondage' that the poet had not repressed his impulses. Mrs Fyne's emotional and intellectual life is shaped and determined by her past. Despite his sympathetic description of her as the victim of her father, Marlow is hostile to Mrs Fyne, and his nasty sexual innuendoes about Mrs Fyne's female friends seem unjustified. Since Marlow admits to having some 'woman in [his] nature', can Mrs Fyne be considered a lesbian because of the 'masculine shape' of her cheeks?

For Marlow, and perhaps to an extent for Conrad, the stodgy, complacent, threatening Mrs Fyne crystallises his fear of women. Women, he believes, lack compunction: 'They are too passionate. Too pedantic. Too courageous with themselves' (p. 159). In a passage which reveals how sexually threatening women are to him, he speaks of Mrs Fyne's 'eminently feminine occupation of thrusting a stick in the spokes of another woman's wheel' (p. 151). Yet he acknowledges in himself a small portion of femininity in his 'composite temperament'. He contrasts himself to the *uxorious* Fyne's comic masculinity, highlighted by his 'extra-manly bass' (p. 147). To the extent that Marlow is androgynous, he most resembles Mrs Fyne. Marlow, the misogynist, has the same categorising sensibility as Mrs Fyne. Perhaps Conrad is uncomfortable with this androgynous identity that he perceives within himself. His surrogate's awareness of a feminine impulse challenges his own virile self-image and may explain his excoriating women and implicitly an aspect of himself he would very much like to deny.

It is unfair to indict an author of a past generation for holding views that by current standards are uncivilised. Yet Conrad's implication that the heterosexual woman whose desires are being fulfilled cannot be interested in woman's rights is surely myopic. Mrs Fyne is an easy target that Conrad has set up to mock the Women's Movement, which by 1912 had become quite militant.[7] Not only does she write 'a handbook for women with grievances . . . a sort of compendious theory and practice of feminine free morality', but, further, she is depicted as a lesbian (pp. 65–6). Whatever Conrad's intentions, she cannot be for us a representative figure of the feminist movement, any more than Flora and Captain Anthony can be raised to an allegorical level by entitling the two parts 'The Damsel' and 'The Knight'.

III

Chance, the first novel after the three major political novels, sustains and intensifies the stress on private life and passionate love as the only alternatives to a world threatened by materialism, political ideology and uncontrollable historical forces. In *Chance*, as in prior Conrad, each man is lonely, isolated and separate, and requires the recognition of another as friend, lover, parent, child or counsel to complete him. This kind of recognition in the form of empathy and understanding revitalises the recipient. Where there is substantial mutuality, as between Lingard and Mrs Travers in *The Rescue*, then both figures in the relationship become transformed. But there is something poignant when the other is perceived only as a detached and passive listener rather than a responsive soul.

If there is an alternative in *Chance* to repression, isolation and self-imprisonment, it is in the possibility of sympathy and understanding, and, most significantly, passionate love. The novel posits the alternative achieved by Flora and Anthony and endorsed by Marlow when he arranges the union between Powell and Flora. The ending should not betray us into believing that Conrad the optimist has triumphed over Conrad the sceptic or that Conrad's basic perception of man's place in the cosmos has fundamentally changed. Does marriage really ease the pain of living in a purposeless universe, in a world full of meanness and pettiness? Once one perceives the prominence of the prison metaphor within the texture of the novel, one realises that Conrad's indictment of English life has the harshness and bitterness of *The Secret Agent*. *Chance* discovers a heart of darkness beneath the civilised exteriors of Edwardian London, just as *The Secret Agent* discovers it in the political machinations not only of anarchists and reactionaries but also of those charged with upholding the status quo. In *Chance*, the London of *The Secret Agent* still exists in all its shabby, ugly decadence; mankind is separated by individual dreams and illusions. Marlow's contention that 'people, whether mature or not mature . . . are for the most part quite incapable of understanding what is happening to them' is dramatically illustrated (p. 117). Nothing is extrinsically changed by heterosexual love; can those who share it really exclude the sense 'of the hopeless obscure insignificance of our globe lost in the splendid revelation of a glittering soulless universe' (p. 50)? After all, within the novel Conrad stresses the inevitability of death and the near-certainty of disappointment.

Chance is, among other things, Conrad's burlesque of the novel of manners. The social conventions repeatedly constrain the behaviour of individuals whose conscious and unconscious efforts to circumvent these conventions produce idiosyncratic and often bizarre behaviour. The perception by Anthony and Flora that social forms are as unbending and inflexible as a wall is the central cause of their odd

courtship and their mutual imprisonment on the ship. In *Chance*
Conrad satirises bourgeoise smugness, self-righteousness and hypocrisy. The first part of the novel moves from the evocation of the
sea in the first chapter, in which Powell establishes the reductive
land – sea dichotomy, to the world of upper middle-class conventions
and proprieties (qualified by Mrs Fyne's advanced ideas and lesbianism), and finally to the financial parasitism of de Barral, the
epitome of civilisation's moral bankruptcy.

The relationship between Flora and Anthony takes place within
the context of a civilisation in decline. George Dangerfield has
written about the 'dangerous state of hysteria' in 1912–14 as
England's liberal democracy became increasingly paralysed by the
Women's Movement, worker unrest, and Tory intransigence that
bordered on rebellion:[8] 'For nearly a century men had discovered in
the cautious phrase, in the respectable gesture, in the considered
display of reasonable emotions, a haven against those irrational
storms which threatened to sweep through them. And gradually the
haven lost its charms; worse still, it lost its peace.'[9] Respect for the
opinions of others, self-restraint, and the willingness to compromise
political and social differences all reached a low ebb in the years
immediately preceding the First World War. Dangerfield speaks of
how 'people . . . saw their arrested, their static notions of respectability disintegrate before their eyes; and . . . scarcely understood what
they saw'.[10]

Those who claim that *Chance* is a romance disregard its concern
with the quality of English life. The first part begins with prowlers at
the doors and climaxes in a vision of London that recalls the urban
wasteland of *The Secret Agent*: 'The broad interminable perspective of
the East India Dock Road, the great perspective of drab brick walls,
of grey pavement, of muddy roadway rumbling dismally with
loaded carts and vans lost itself in the distance, imposing and shabby in
its spacious meanness of aspect, in its immeasurable poverty of forms,
of colouring, of life—under a harsh, unconcerned sky dried by the
wind to a clear blue' (p. 204). Marlow notices the 'brutal unrest of the
street' and 'the ugly street-noises' (pp. 215–16). The denizens' lives
seem even more drab than those of the people in Geneva in *Under
Western Eyes*, the preceding novel:

> Every moment people were passing close by us singly, in twos
> and threes; the inhabitants of that end of the town where life
> goes on unadorned by grace or splendour; they passed us in

their shabby garments, with sallow faces, haggard, anxious or weary, or simply without expression, in an unsmiling sombre stream not made up of lives but of mere unconsidered existences whose joys, struggles, thoughts, sorrows and their very hopes were miserable, glamourless, and of no account in the world.   (p. 208)

As Marlow and Flora speak, Marlow notices the crass commercialism of the city: 'It was as if the whole world existed only for selling and buying and those who had nothing to do with the movement of merchandise were of no account' (pp. 209–10). And Flora is the offspring of the man who is the epitome of this.

Juxtaposed to the ironic equation of thrift with 'the great moral evolution of our character' is a civilisation which, despite its façade of decorum epitomised by the tea-party and the Fynes' respectability, seems to be in devolution (p. 74). It is quite deliberate that the chapter in which the Fynes are exposed is called 'The Tea-Party', for that custom represents to Conrad the quintessence of the shallow civility practised by the Fynes. Marlow's obvious pun on 'pedestrian' is appropriate for the staid, unimaginative, and complaisant Fyne. Marlow sees that 'sincere conduct . . . at times resemble[s] brutality' (p. 158). When Marlow recalls how he was near a quarrel with Mrs Fyne for refusing to recognise the captain's role, he calls attention to 'the cold teapot, the emptied cups, emblems of hospitality' (p. 158). Guests who can be patronised or controlled are welcome, but passion is forbidden in the world of the Fynes (whose name is an ironic comment on their complacent view of themselves). The Fynes are the favourite target of his satire. Commenting on Mrs Fyne's telling Flora that she must be prepared for the worst, Marlow remarks, 'Compassion—judiciousness—something correctly measured. None of your dishevelled sentiment' (p. 141). He says of the Fynes, 'They were strangely consistent in their lack of imaginative sympathy' (p. 143). Although Marlow does not present any evidence for this view, he believes that Mrs Fyne is enraged at the elopement less out of sisterly concern than out of snobbish resentment that her children will have to play with her brother's children, the grandchildren of a convicted embezzler.

The revelation that the governess harbours resentment towards the class for whom she works is another aspect of Conrad's dissection of Edwardian assumptions. The governess, that traditional symbol of propriety, is motivated by sexual energy and class hostility. And that is what motivates Mrs Fyne, whose target is the masculine world; yet Marlow's views on women are often as reductive as Mrs Fyne's on men. He specifically compares the Machiavellian governess to Mrs Fyne:

> There is a certain amount of what I would politely call unscrupulousness in all of us. Think for instance of the excellent Mrs Fyne, who herself, and in the bosom of her family, resembled a governess of a conventional type. Only, her mental excesses were theoretical, hedged in by so much human feeling and conventional reserves, that they amounted to no more than mere libertinage of thought; whereas the other woman, the governess of Flora de Barral, was, as you may have noticed, severely practical—terribly practical.
>
> (p. 100)

While Mrs Fyne has her outlet for her passion in either fantasies or actual encounters with her young female visitors, the governess finds her outlet in fantasies with her fellow adventurer Charlie and, finally, hostility to the employing class. Marlow expresses Conrad's understanding that the human ties that bind all classes of mankind are stronger than class distinctions that separate them: 'Why shouldn't a governess have passions, all the passions, even that of libertinage, and even ungovernable passions; yet supressed by the very same means which kept the rest of us in order?' (p. 103).

IV

To the extent that Marlow's hostility to the Fynes is justified within the plot and does not reflect Conrad's impatience with English stolidity and complacence, it derives from his sympathy with his fellow seaman Captain Anthony. Conrad implies that Marlow is a kind of double of the captain. Marlow understands Captain Anthony's attraction for Flora. In the street while he is awaiting Fyne's return, 'a tentative, uncertain intimacy was springing up between [him and Flora]' (p. 207). Since they had 'dealt' with death, he felt 'a sort of bond between us' (p. 209). As a captain and as a bachelor very conscious of his unmarried state and ostentatiously intimidated by women, Marlow can sympathise with the difficulties of Captain Anthony, the thirty-five-year-old bachelor who finds himself lonely and bored at his sister's country home. He sympathises with Captain Anthony's attraction to Flora and to an extent shows through his own responses how she might have captivated Anthony. He perceives that her lips 'seemed warm with the rich blood of life and passion' (p. 205). That, despite his years on shore, Marlow still thinks he would return to sea reflects Conrad's own intermittent fantasy. The novel's reductive view of shore life confirms Anthony's oversimplications rather than undermines them; he is 'a confirmed enemy of life on shore—a perfect terror to a simple man, what with the fads and proprieties and the ceremonies and affections. He hated all that. He wasn't fit for it. There was no rest and peace and security but on the sea' (p. 221). After all, to Anthony, shore life represents his difficulties with his father and his current loneliness. Marlow's sympathy for Captain Anthony is accentuated by Mrs Fyne's undiplomatic rejection of maritime life: 'Then his choice of life—so extraordinary, so unfortunate, I may say. . . . I should have liked him to have been distinguished—or at any rate to remain in the social sphere where we could have had common interests, acquaintances, thoughts' (p. 185). More than he realises, that remark may be shaping his retrospective hostility to Mrs Fyne.

More frequently it is Captain Anthony's emotional life, not Marlow's, that most engages Conrad. At times the captain is a fictional character to whom the author consciously or unconsciously transfers his own mental and emotional crises. Anthony is the objectification of sexual and emotional problems Conrad feared having, in much the same way as Aschenbach is for Mann in *Death in Venice*. He also represents Conrad's earlier life as a man of action, and is an earlier inarticulate self to which Conrad feared he might revert. Because he discovered his identity as a writer late in life, Conrad associated inarticulateness not only with childhood and adolescence but also with young adulthood. Conrad understands how the *actions* of Captain Anthony ironically parallel the sentiments of his father, the writer, just as Conrad's own life had recapitulated his father's careers as a writer and a man of action: 'The father, fastidious, cerebral, morbidly shrinking from all contacts, could only sing in harmonious numbers what the son felt with a dumb and reckless sincerity' (p. 332).

Captain Anthony insists on living by the verbal behaviour of the land he despises. Yet he lacks the moral equipment to deal with the ambiguities of shore life. Indeed, he goes one better than the Fynes at creating conventions that interfere with the acknowledgement of feelings, although he 'was the last man to condemn conventionally any human being, to scorn and despise even deserved misfortune' (p. 334). For Captain Anthony, the totally sincere man, words have the actuality of facts. He believes in the sincerity of words and responds to Fyne's accusations—delivered pro forma at the behest of his wife, as if they were objective facts—that he was taking unfair advantage of Flora. 'Anthony, unaccustomed to the chatter of the firm earth, never stayed to ask himself what value these words could have in Fyne's mouth. And indeed the mere dark sound of them was utterly abhorrent to his native rectitude, sea-salted, hardened in the winds of wide horizons, open as the day' (p. 333). He becomes the prisoner of silence once he establishes the conditions that Flora must speak her consent to their living as man and wife. Yet, as Captain Anthony's passion, and the Fynes's talkativeness indicate, words are not essential to love.

Chance is not an allegorical romance, but a novel about delayed sexual maturity in a repressive culture. Captain Anthony responds to Flora because he has long repressed her passions; Flora agrees to elope as a desperate effort to define herself and allows Anthony to become the captive of his own generosity. Before the climactic scene they live within their own self-created conventions, which keep them sexually apart. But the form and content reveal the author's immaturity. Conrad's voyeurism is pervasive in this novel; he continually approaches sexual material as an onlooker—through Powell, Fyne, Marlow and the nameless narrator. Like Powell and Fyne, Marlow and the anonymous narrator seem to be either repressed or lacking passion. Marlow's efforts to raise the rhetorical ante are undermined by his obsessive though unacknowledged interest in the character's psychosexual lives: 'But those two are outside all conventions. They would be as untrammelled in a sense as the first man and the first woman' (p. 210). Conrad's effort to transform his characters into romance figures by entitling the parts 'The Knight' and 'The Damsel' is a thin disguise for his interest in the psychosexual dynamics of the attraction and subsequent marriage between Flora and Captain Anthony. Surely, whatever Conrad intended, both are ironic versions of the chivalric love tradition; the captain's attraction to her situation as victim has naturalistic explanations in her relationship with his father. Thus the fairy-tale about Flora's and Captain Anthony's idyllic life after de Barral's death is hardly plausible given the neurotic behaviour that preceded.

The problem with *Chance* is not Conrad's negative attitude toward love, but his clumsiness of presentation. It is as if Conrad required the oblique narrative technique as a necessary artifice to distance the psychosexual material. In any case, it seems likely that *Chance* reflects Conrad's self-regulating repression when addressing sexuality, and his realisation that the manners and conventions of pre-war England were artificial and obsolete. Indeed, it may be that novel's wooden quality derives as much from Conrad's desperate desire to believe that salvation lies in heterosexual love as from his inability to make Marlow's meditations a matter of serious concern to the reader.

NOTES

1. Palmer, *Joseph Conrad's Fiction* (Ithaca, NY: Cornell University Press, 1968), p. 208.
2. Guerard, *Conrad the Novelist* (Cambridge, Mass.: Harvard University Press, 1958), p. 262.
3. Henry James, *Notes on Novelists* (New York: Charles Scribner's Sons, 1914), p. 349.
4. See Thomas Moser, 'Conrad, Ford, and the Sources of *Chance*', *Conradiana*, vol. 7, no. 3 (1975), pp. 207—24; and Karl's brief discussion of sources for de Barral: *Conrad: The Three Lives* (New York: Farrar, Straus and Giroux, 1979), p. 741n.
5. In 'Autocracy and War' Conrad had written, 'A prisoner shut up in a noisome dungeon concentrates all his hope and desire on the moment of stepping out beyond the gates. It appears to him pregnant with an immense and final importance . . .' (*NLL*, p. 103).
6. Conrad indicates familiarity with Dickens in *A Personal Record*, pp. 71, 124, and in *NLL*, pp. 152—3.
7. See chs 3 and 4 of George Dangerfield's *The Strange Death of Liberal England* (1935) (the edition cited below is the Capricorn edition, New York, 1961). According to Dangerfield (pp. 148—9), from 1912 there was a considerable homosexual element in the Women's Movement.
8. Ibid., p. 95.
9. Ibid., p. 141.
10. Ibid., p. 427.

5 *Victory*: Conrad's indictment of detachment

I

Although London is not the setting, *Victory* (1915) is the last of Conrad's novels which analyses contemporary European culture. As we shall see, beginning with *The Shadow-Line* (1916), the subsequent novels beat a retreat from confronting the crisis of values which Conrad believed was undermining Western civilisation. For Conrad, this crisis was epitomised by imperialism, capitalism, the decline of family and national ties, and the replacement of human relationships based upon personal ties with relationships based on economic consideration. *Victory* depicts an 'age in which we are camped like bewildered travellers in a garish, unrestful hotel' (p. 3). Schomberg's hotel becomes a mnemonic device to recall that image, and Schomberg's malice, enervation, lust and greed are the quintessence of that age. In a world dominated by various forms of materialistic adventurism—from the coal-mine in the tropics, Zangiacomo's travelling band, and Schomberg's parody of a hotel—Heyst's courtesy and delicacy stand as a vestige of an older tradition. But his manners and formality also serve as a barrier not only to reaching a complete understanding with Lena, but also to contending with the forces of economic barbarism—Jones, Ricardo and Schomberg. 'Outward cordiality of manner' and 'consummate politeness' become Heyst's refuge. Recalling *The Secret Agent*, London is a shadowy and malevolent presence in *Victory*; its gloom and cold enfeeble Morrison's vitality. When Morrison dies there, almost in a grotesque parody of the Phoenix myth, the imperialistic Tropical Belt Company is born. Moreover, the setting for Lena's poverty-striken childhood is London, where 'houses . . . look like the tombs of an unvisited, unhonoured cemetery of hopes' (p. 174). *Victory* is about the decline in civility and morality not only in what Conrad had once called 'an outpost of progress', but in Western civilisation. Conrad perceived, as Mann had in *Death In Venice* (1912), that something had

60

gone wrong with the amenities and proprieties which are the glue that holds civilisation together.

In the 1912–14 period, when Conrad wrote *Victory*, the stable, secure England in which Conrad had found a home was in danger of disintegration. Beset by political turmoil in the form of labour unrest, the Women's Movement and the excesses and zeal of the Conservative opposition, which threatened to undermine parliamentary government, England must have seemed to him to be increasingly in danger of becoming like his native Poland. As Dangerfield writes, 'the public mind . . . [was] clouded with fearful dreams of anarchists and invasions'.[1] The ironically titled *Victory* is Conrad's response to an England which, torn by conflicting but powerful enclaves, suffered a loss of esteem in its own eyes as well as in those of other nations. According to Dangerfield,

> What could be expected of a liberal democracy whose parliament had practically ceased to function, whose Government was futile, and whose Opposition had said enough to put lesser men in the dock for treason? . . . For all her arrogance, her seeming perfidies, her perplexing moments of gayety, carelessness, and romance, she had enjoyed a preeminence among the nations which deserved—above all others—the epithet 'respectable.' . . . If the events of 1913 and 1914 could be followed to their logical conclusion, what would one find there but the weariness, the decadence of a great democracy?[2]

Discussions of *Victory* have not taken into sufficient account Conrad's reasons for creating Heyst, who, in many ways, is an embodiment of aspects of himself. *Victory* reflects Conrad's recurring fear that the thoughtful intellectual man would prove inadequate to the demands of action, especially if that man is also a romantic who colours all external facts and situations with the impressions of his imagination. Heyst is a prototype of the artist who observes life from a distance rather than participating in it; Conrad, the orphaned and exiled son of an activist and the observer in a foreign culture, feared becoming this figure from Axel's castle precisely because he found detachment so tempting. Heyst's stance of detachment characterises the artist who inevitably chooses to describe his vision of life rather than to participate in life. At first he exemplifies the aesthetic temperament that eschews moral engagement and regards the

problems of others as a spectacle to observe. As he wrote in the
Author's Note,

> Heyst in his fine detachment had lost the habit of asserting
> himself. I don't mean the courage of self-assertion, either moral
> or physical, but the mere way of it, the trick of the thing, the
> readiness of mind and the turn of the hand that come without
> reflection and lead the man to excellence in life, in art, in
> crime, in virtue and for the matter of that, even in love.
> Thinking is the great enemy of perfection. The habit of
> profound reflection, I am compelled to say, is the most
> pernicious of all the habits formed by the civilized man.
>
> (pp. x – xi)

That Conrad had propensities to detachment and over-fastidiousness
in personal relationships during his writing years is clear from his
letters. Heyst sounds like the voice of the Conrad of 1914 who
withdrew into himself after completing work on *Victory*: 'I have been
in a state of mental coma. This is the first day of approximate sanity or
consciousness' (22 July 1914, *LL*, ii, p. 155).

Heyst is a self-conscious reflective man who, like Dostoevsky's
underground man, is often immobilised by his own thoughts: 'The
young man learned to reflect, which is a destructive process, a
reckoning of the cost' (pp. 91 – 2). Heyst shows Conrad's realisation
that it is impossible to draw a magic circle around oneself that will
shut out the rest of the world. Heyst, like the underground man,
would like to believe his spirit sustained 'itself proudly on its own
contempt of the usual coarse aliments which life offers to the
common appetites of men' (p. 177). But his generous impulses take
him outside his self-consciousness when he intervenes to help
Morrison and finally to rescue Lena.

After his father's death, Heyst becomes a solitary existence; he
intentionally avoids personal ties as if this could remove him from
life's disappointments: 'He became a waif and stray, austerely, from
conviction' (p. 92). Heyst reflects Conrad's lifelong fascination with
the wanderer and the adventurer; indeed, in his later years he often
saw himself as a Ulysses figure. Himself an orphan deeply affected by
the memory of his father and of his surrogate father, Thaddeus
Brobowski, Conrad identified with the rootlessness of the exile.
Heyst's father is an embodiment of one aspect of Conrad, the bitter

cynical Conrad that recurs in the letters. Heyst's gradual growth away from his father's scepticism and negativism reflects a recurring movement of Conrad's from detachment and cynicism, attitudes to which he retreated at times of personal or professional disappointment and frustration.

Heyst's ennui and inertia objectify emotions that interfered with Conrad's creativity; his victory over detachment and non-involvement corresponds to Conrad's own victory over ill health, depression, and inability to write. In a typical letter, after complaining of the gout, he moans, 'The worst is that I haven't done any work for a month. No inspiration; a sort of languid feeling all over' (2 Aug 1913, *LL*, ii, p. 149). That 'Victory', the title, was the last word Conrad wrote in peace-time made it all the more difficult to change the title, even though war had broken out between his completing the novel in 1914 and publishing it in 1915. As he wrote in the note to the first edition, the word had profound personal meaning for him: 'What influenced my decision to [retain the title] most were the obscure prompting of the pagan residuum of awe and wonder which lurks still at the bottom of our old humanity' (p. vii). The 'awe and wonder' were associated with his own elation at completing the novel.

At a time when he was beset by illness and anxiety, Conrad's imaginative removal from London and Western Europe to remote islands might have been helpful to its completion. (While England is the focus of *Chance*, the movement back to settings of his active life— the sea and the East—began with the shipboard chapters of that novel.) Conrad draws also upon his past literary experience in *Victory* in a way that recalls how he had drawn upon his past seaman's experience to write *The Nigger of the 'Narcissus'*. Samburan, the tropical island nearly overgrown with vegetation, is a clear phonic echo of Sambir, the primitive setting of *Almayer's Folly* and *An Outcast of the Islands*. Heyst, the mature, temperamentally sympathetic man who responds empathetically to another person's difficulties, recalls Marlow. Heyst's introspective self-analysis suggests Marlow. Like Marlow, his values undergo profound change as a result of his experience. Like Marlow he sees himself as a detached 'independent spectator' even while he cannot resist involvement (p. 196). Heyst, like Jim after he is sent to Patusan (a three syllable word with most of the same letters and sounds as Samburan), seeks to live according to his dreams, but is prevented by the intrusion of a fatal double, Jones, whose role recalls Gentleman Brown. The idea of a group of Europeans in remote islands who are held together by national, maritime and racial pride and who impose their 'home' standards, is recalled by the anonymous narrator's echoing Marlow's original description of Jim when he describes Morrison as 'one of us'. That this resemblance proves superficial because no standards or values bind the men together indicates how Conrad has abandoned one tenet of his humanism. In the early sections the narrator speaks of Heyst as 'our man', the very term that had been applied to Nostromo, because Heyst seems to belong to everyone who confers an identity on him, although he actually belongs, like Nostromo, only to himself. Like Nostromo, he is perceived from the vantage point of public legend and gossip ('enchanted Heyst', 'hard facts', 'the enemy') by those who do not really understand him, but who are using their own words as a way of controlling their world. Like Sir Aethelred in *The Secret Agent*, the language-teacher in *Under Western Eyes* prior to his emergence as a moral creature, and both the speaker and the count of 'Il Conde', Heyst is unable to deal with the barbarians who threaten civilisation. While Heyst recalls Aethelred in his remote ineffectuality, Schomberg, Jones, Ricardo and Pedro suggest the anarchists and agents of totalitarianism, as well as their police adversaries in *The Secret Agent*.

Even as Heyst scrupulously subscribes to his father's hold upon him, he unconsciously seeks to overthrow that dominance and to play the role of the rebellious son who overthrows the autocratic father. 'Victory' describes the triumph not only of the instincts over the rational self, but also of the son over the father in a quest for his own selfhood. His father's truths do not sustain Heyst. Not only his response to Morrison and Lena but even his concern about Schomberg shows that he rebels against his father's shibboleth: 'Look on—make no sound' (p. 175). Conrad would not have subscribed to the father's dogmatism, excerpts of which are presented as confusing and vague generalisations; he would have considered the very attempt to reduce experience to abstractions as examples of folly and arrogance. Conrad, too, turned his back on his father's example when he chose exile and a seaman's career and, subsequently, a writer's career in a foreign culture instead of pursuing his father's revolutionary and political example by dedicating himself to Poland. That Conrad feared becoming 'a man of universal scorn and unbelief' is shown by Conrad's sympathetic identification with characters such as Decoud and Razumov, men who seek refuge in words and ideas and

who are Heyst's predecessors (p. 199).[3] Heyst's original resignation is
the antithesis of the kind that Conrad praised in *A Personal Record*.
Conrad had written, 'Resignation, not mystic, not detached, but
resignation open-eyed, conscious, and informed by love, is the only
one of our feelings for which it is impossible to become a sham'
(p. xxi). *Victory* is not only an exploration of emotional retreat, but
also, finally, a renunciation of it.

II

Heyst wishes to subtract himself from the conventions and manners
of society; he refuses to dissemble and to act diplomatically (which for
him means to act duplicitously): 'A diplomatic statement . . . is a
statement of which everything is true but the sentiment which seems
to prompt it' (p. 325). But Heyst's polish, fastidiousness and
refinement belong to the very world he has renounced.[4] Faced with
the hurly-burly of economic competition in modern life, Heyst seeks
refuge in detachment disguised as polish and courtesy. Conrad takes
pains to establish that Heyst's detachment is responsible for his
undoing. Heyst thinks that his 'finished courtesy of attitude,
movement, and voice' will provide him with a buffer and enable him
to take his father's advice (p. 8). But Heyst cannot withdraw from the
world, because like all of us he is part of the world. Heyst is lacking in
self-knowledge; his entire life is a delusion. As his response to
Schomberg indicates, he is concerned far more than Lena with the
opinions of others. The novel gradually reveals that Heyst is not the
man he appears to be: 'This observer of facts seemed to have no
connection with earthly affairs and passions. The very courtesy of his
manner, the flavour of playfulness in the voice set him apart' (p. 60).
But the façade of indifference belies Heyst's passion and sexuality.

The passionate attraction of Lena and Heyst takes place in the
context of a culture based upon the profit motive. Yet Conrad
understands the common instinctive denominator between Lena's
strong sex drive and Ricardo's atavistic acquisitiveness, just as he
understands that Jones and Heyst, except for occasional spasms of
passion, sublimate their passions in the rituals of behaviour that they
embrace. Those who subscribe to the predatory code of acquisitive-

ness at all cost assume that others follow the same motives. Thus,
speaking to Jones, Ricardo accuses Heyst

> When it comes to plunder drifting under one's nose, there's
> not one of them that would keep his hands off. And I don't
> blame them. It's the way they do it that sets my back up. Just
> look at the story of how he got rid of that pal of his! Send a
> man home to croak of a cold on the chest—that's one of your
> tame tricks. . . . What was all that coal business? Tame citizen
> dodge . . . (pp. 264—5)

The conduct of Schomberg, the Zangiacomos, and the Portugese
officials who would auction Morrison's brig testifies to the displace-
ment of human relations and amenities by economic considerations.

Heyst sees himself as a romance figure, but Conrad's novel
dramatises the impossibility of romance in the pedestrian modern
world. Although Heyst regards himself as too fastidious for his time,
Conrad regards him as a representative figure of an era lacking in
moral energy and conviction. If Heyst is 'a man of the last hour', or if
'he [dates] too late', it is because he represents an effete, ineffectual
mutation of man just as surely as Schomberg does. His Crusoeism is
mocked by impulses to involve himself. Whatever romance he tells
himself, he does involve himself in the coal business and he does elope
with Lena after she appears to him 'as if one waking suddenly should
see the figure of his dream turned into flesh and blood' (p. 92).
External events are the catalyst for bringing out his repressed
emotions; moreover, they bring into the open aspects of Heyst's
dream life. Heyst, like Jim, does not believe in his own moral energy:
'when the issue was joined, it would find him disarmed and shrinking
from the ugliness and degradation of it' (p. 357).

Heyst, a man of intelligence, sensibility and capacity, abnegates his
responsibility and retreats into a solipsistic world of his own creation.
A self-appointed modern-day Jeremiah, Heyst's father 'had spent his
life in blowing blasts upon a terrible trumpet which had filled heaven
and earth with ruins, while mankind went on its way unheeding' (p.
175); he was a 'destroyer of systems, of hopes, of beliefs' (ibid.). To
the prior passage one might add, 'and his own son', for his son is
unsuited to play either a personal or a social role. Originally Heyst
seeks to follow his father's example. In a magnificent passage Conrad
shows how Heyst, as a defence against involvement, perceives people
as objects in a mobile rather than as fellows with whom he shares

hopes and dreams. Thus the inhabitants of London seem immersed in life's stream 'like figures cut out of cork and weighted with lead just sufficiently to keep them in their proudly upright posture. . . . The fatuously jostling, nodding, spinning figures hurried irresistibly along, and [gave] no sign of being aware that the voice on the bank had been suddenly silenced' (ibid.).

The absolutist credo of Heyst's father does not prepare Heyst for the eventualities of life. Indeed, the problem with Heyst's withdrawal is that it is based on the unsound notion that one can shape one's life according to a paradigm. As surely as a Lawrence character, Heyst responds to the truth of his own instincts and passions. Since Conrad believed that man fulfils himself by responding to another, Heyst's notion that he might be a 'solitary achievement' is contrary to man's natural impulse for companionship, love and understanding. In the following passage, the words 'scheme' and 'system' are crucial because they imply the impossibility of organising life on rational grounds:

> Heyst was not conscious of either friends or of enemies. It was the very essence of his life to be a solitary achievement, accomplished not by hermit-like withdrawal with its silence and immobility, but by a system of restless wandering, by the detachment of an impermanent dweller amongst changing scenes. In this scheme he had perceived the means of passing through life without suffering and almost without a single care in the world—invulnerable because elusive. (p. 90)

While Conrad may have felt a certain attraction for this kind of minimalism, he knew that it isolated a person from the possibility of family and emotional life.

Heyst's response to Morrison in terms of 'that form of contempt which is called pity' is a step towards abandoning his father's advice—advice which he lacks the self-possession and arrogance to follow (p. 174). His humanity is not immune to pity and sympathy, and, despite his father's advice, he is moved to action, in part because 'He understood [Morrison's] feelings perfectly' (p. 18). Heyst cannot refuse Morrison because he does not know how to establish a footing on which he can lend Morrison money and not be his working partner. His involvement is truly a comedy of manners: 'No decent feeling was ever scorned by Heyst. But he was incapable of outward cordiality of manner, and he felt acutely his defect. Consummate politeness is not the right tonic for an emotional collapse' (p. 18). Heyst wishes to hide behind the façade of a tradition of elegant manners, but, to his credit, dismay and ruin, he cannot.

Because he knows that Morrison's offer of partnership in the coal venture derives from extreme gratitude (to the point of regarding him as a 'saviour'), Heyst's delicacy does not permit him to decline. He becomes entangled in the web of imperialism and venture capitalism that Conrad always despised after his 1890 Congo trip. Heyst is ashamed not of the nature of his past action, but of acting at all, and his fastidious moral conscience accuses himself of being responsible for Morrison's death. For a while Heyst had apparently deluded himself into believing that the company contributed to the '"stride forward" . . . in the general organization of the universe', and in particular 'for these regions' (p. 6). With his polished, complacent attitude to imperialism, and his disdain for personal health, he seems a cartoon of the Edwardian progressive. He develops his taste for isolation after the demise of the coal enterprise. Once the coal company fails, he intensifies his efforts to be detached and seeks to live on the island where the company had sought to build its empire.

Lena is Heyst's *Patna*; when he meets her, sublimated energies and passions emerge which inevitably lead him to make his jump—that is, to rescue and elope with her. If at first his response to Lena is based on more complicated grounds, gradually his repressed sexual drive combines with the need for companionship to break down his defences. Yet, although, as he realises, 'the very scorn is falling from me year by year', he thinks too little of himself and Lena to believe in Lena's fidelity. The cynicism inculcated from his father is finally enough to destroy him: 'I have refined everything away by this time—anger, indignation, scorn itself. Nothing's left but disgust' (pp. 329–30). That he is ready to think the worst of Lena when he sees Ricardo at her feet ironically shows how far Heyst has come from his original scepticism.

When Heyst perceives Lena with Ricardo, he is overcome by doubt of Lena which in part derives from self-doubt: 'Doubt entered into him—a doubt of a new kind, formless, hideous. It seemed to spread itself all over him, enter his limbs, and lodge in his entrails. He stopped suddenly with a thought that he who experienced such a feeling had no business to live—or perhaps was no longer living' (pp. 391–2). The fastidious Heyst himself feels guilty for this imagined betrayal. His self-doubt even extends to half-believing Schomberg's calumny that he lured Morrison to his death for money:

'The power of calumny grows with time. It's insidious and penetrating. It can even destroy one's faith in oneself—dry-rot the soul' (p. 362). Ironically the man who wished to be apart from man takes all man's evil upon his shoulders and becomes a kind of Christ-figure (his name even rhymes with 'Christ').[5] Accepting Schomberg's verdict may be a factor which prevents a violent response to Jones and Ricardo. Like Jim, he is undermined not only by the values he has inculcated from his father, but, like Jim on Patusan, also by the self-image he has acquired from experience.

Conrad is exposing the practical uselessness of the fastidious man; Heyst can dissemble to protect Lena, but he lacks the passion and instinct to use physical force. He adopts the ironic stance of the aesthetic and intellectual personality, but there is something precious and self-serving about his word world: 'Here I am on a Shadow inhabited by Shades. How helpless a man is against the Shades! How is one to intimidate, persuade, resist, assert oneself against them? I have lost all belief in realities' (p. 350). Heyst's problem is that he perceives himself and Lena as allegorical and romance figures when a different kind of response is required. He knows that he is confined by his own delicate sensibilities. He never learns to deal with his own passions. He lacks the will to attack Jones physically; he has the chance when the latter is distracted by his anger at Ricardo for failing to inform him of the presence of a woman. Unlike Heyst, Lena's 'heart found its solution in a blinding, hot glow of passionate purpose'—namely, saving Heyst (p. 367). On Samburan, she develops the energy and passion that Heyst still lacks. Even after Lena has saved him, his 'fastidious soul . . . kept the true cry of love from his lips' (p. 406). Conrad would have us note that 'the cry of true love' is itself from the simplified romance world that Heyst has created for himself. Like Decoud, Razumov, and Jim after the *Patna*, Heyst is another of Conrad's imaginative men who attempt to create a buffer against reality out of their dreams and fantasies; he wants to believe that 'Nothing can break in on us here' (p. 223). Yet, once she is out of his sight, his imagination fails him; his cynical intellect corrosively undermines his own dreams.

III

Not only is Heyst a double for part of Conrad's temperament, but

doubling of characters within the novel's imagined world is very
important to *Victory*. It is a central irony of the novel that virtually
every character parallels in some important way Heyst, the man who
would set himself apart from humanity and the man who thinks he is
different in kind from his fellows. Heyst duplicates the gentleness,
sympathy and kindness of Morrison, the 'true humanitarian', and
Davidson, 'The most delicate man' ever to sail in the islands (pp. 12,
52). Because he withdraws from the world and refuses to participate,
he is misperceived by his fellow men. Schomberg and Ricardo each
understand Heyst according to their own moral and psychological
needs. Heyst acts from the same motive of loneliness and the same
instinctive need as Schomberg or Ricardo. Heyst's lack of force and
conviction has a vague echo in Ricardo's assertive moral indifference:
'I just don't care' (p. 129). Lena's passionate intensity is the
counterpart to Heyst's own instinctive nature that, once awakened,
caused him to set aside his identity as 'a perfect gentleman' and elope.
But doubling, in the sense of empathetic understanding, is never fully
achieved. 'Understand' is as crucial a word and concept in *Victory* as it
is in 'The Secret Sharer'. Conrad proposes and discards the possibility
of understanding between Lena and Heyst. She thinks he is ashamed
of her and wants to hide her; he does not understand the depths of her
love, nor her lack of embarrassment.

In *Victory*, Conrad's use of character-doubling forces the reader to
consider the common humanity of seemingly disparate characters.
Lena and Ricardo recognise a kinship in their origins: 'Perhaps
because of the similarity of their miserable origin in the dregs of
humanity, she had understood Ricardo perfectly' (p. 308). He
perceives Lena as 'one of his own sort', 'an ally of his own kind' (pp.
336, 341). Both Ricardo and Lena have a sense of social inferiority to
the men they follow, and feel that they are being honoured by being
permitted to be a follower. As the two gentlemen watch Ricardo and
Lena, we realise that, rather than the woman who should be his secret
sharer, Jones, the grim homosexual, becomes Heyst's double. Just as
the volcano mocks Heyst's idleness, Jones's moral indifference is a
cartoon of Heyst's own. Jones becomes a mirror into which the reader
looks and sees a reflection of Heyst's repressed or unacknowledged
self. Jones and Heyst are exiles from England (the country in which
Heyst's Swedish aristocratic father had settled) and the upper class to
which they belong by manners if not by wealth. They have literally
become men of the world rather than men of a nation. Taken
together, Jones, the outlaw from the gentleman class, and Heyst, the

spectator of life, imply the incapacity of the upper class to meet its responsibilities. Jones is not only Heyst's but also Schomberg's double, the darker atavistic other beneath the civilised exterior of the commercial spirit.

Those who argue that *Victory* is an affirmative novel ignore the narrator's cynical, melancholy tone. The narrator is nominally a first-person character who has heard the tale from Davidson, but he actually functions for the most part as a traditional omniscient presence. Reflecting Conrad's temperament in 1914, the narrator is a sceptical, gloomy presence hovering over the tale. By the time he tells the story, he knows the tragic outcome, which almost seems to justify the stance Heyst adopted before entering the world of action and personal involvement. At times, the narrator's commentary is as cynical as the views of Heyst's father. The narrator calls life the 'plot of plots', as if he regarded man's life as a trick played by fortune upon him. He generalises Heyst's 'sense of incompleteness' as 'the fatal imperfection of all the gifts of life, which makes of them a delusion and a snare' (p. 212).

The action confirms the narrator's gloom. Like Heyst, he sceptically questions the sense of *any* action. The narrator's stance is the one Heyst abandons. It is he who sustains the crucial image of the age as an 'unrestful hotel', as when he describes those who come to gamble with Jones and Ricardo at Schomberg's hotel: '[They] looked like collected samples of intensely artless, helpless humanity—pathetic in their innocent watch for the small turns of luck which indeed might have been serious enough for them' (p. 118). For the narrator, 'one of us' expands in meaning to imply not merely those who inhabit the tropics, but all men who are tempted to shape the world according to their visions by denying some part of their humanity. Heyst, the man of facts, adopts a philosophy that does not take account of impulses and passions. Throughout *Victory*, it is with sympathetic irony that Conrad's narrator watches Heyst, the man who would control the world, as circumstances intervene between himself and his aspirations. Heyst is one of us because, in a world lacking coherence and clarity, he is undergoing a trial of values and a quest for certainty that most of us must undergo.

The narrator's interest in Heyst's psychology and his melancholy probing into the significance of Heyst's life undermine the possibility of allegory because allegory depends upon the dramatisation of an *a priori* value system; allegory makes only limited use of particular facts about character and detailed descriptions that are not part of its dialectic of values. But, consistent with Conrad's prior voices, the narrator is arguing not only for the relativity of truth, but also the impossibility of objective values. 'For every age is fed on illusions, lest men should renounce life early and the human race come to an end' (p. 94). As the narrator says of Mr Jones, 'He was pursuing truth in the manner of men of sounder morality and purer intentions than his own; that is he pursued it in the light of his own experiences and prejudices. For facts, whatever their origin (and God only knows where they come from), can only be tested by our own particular suspicions' (p. 157). Such views, recalling the early Marlow, who insisted that we 'live, as we dream—alone' argue for the continuity of Conrad's fiction.

To an extent one can justify the much-criticised narrator's view of women. The narrator's generalisations about women are in the context of his indictment of men whose conduct lacks stability and purpose. The narrator is generalising from the world within the novel when he speaks of 'a woman's innate mistrust of masculinity, of that seductive strength allied to an absurd, delicate shrinking from the recognition of the naked necessity of facts, which never yet frightened a woman worthy of the name' (p. 308). The narrator is proposing that the salvation of the race lies in women because contemporary life shows that men have forfeited the right to moral leadership and because it is women more than men who have retained the necessary passion and energy. None the less, because his view of women is so different from ours, his interpretation of character is often at odds with our reading of a scene. Because of the incongruity between his view and ours, he becomes finally a spokesman for an obsolete cultural perspective. Although Conrad hardly intended it, when speaking of women his narrator is a figure of historical interest rather than an omniscient voice on whom we can rely.

IV

Yet on the whole the narrator is a reliable critic of a decadent civilisation. *Victory* resumes the social satire of *The Secret Agent* and *Chance*, but its targets are more specifically the Edwardian world in which Conrad had lived. Samuel Hynes has written in *The Edwardian Turn of Mind*,

The *forms* of values had become the values; institutions had become more important than the ideas they embodied. If propriety expresses the forms of morality without the convictions, then the Edwardian period was an Age of Propriety, of propriety carried to absurd extremes. Conventional standards of behavior which had developed from the evangelical ethics of a century earlier had become rigid and empty gestures of decorum, important not because they implied moral rightness, but because they seemed to protect social stability, public morals, religion, and the British Empire against the threat of change.[6]

Heyst's addressing Morrison 'in the manner of a prince addressing another prince' represents an obsolete tradition based on courtesy and form (p. 12). Yet Heyst's 'consummate good-society manner' also enables him to avoid personal commitment and makes him a representative figure of the Edwardian aristocracy (p. 13).

Victory is a novel that represents the ennui, anxiety, and moral and intellectual confusion of pre-war England.[7] On every page it bears witness to human ineffectiveness. In virtually all of Conrad's other works, one man, if only the narrator, embodies or dramatises the possibility of effective moral action. Not so in *Victory*. Perhaps the ennui and drift of the historical and intellectual milieu deprived Conrad of the usual humanistic modulation to his pessimism. Conrad reflected what Hynes has defined as 'the vague, anxious mood of the time—a mood of nostalgia for the past, regret for the present, and apprehension for the future'.[8] Ricardo, Jones and Pedro represent the worst fears of the Social Darwinists about the physical decline of the species and about the kind of creatures who would survive. Rather than offering pastoral retreat and renewal, Dorset (the setting, Conrad knew, of Hardy's pastoral world) is a place to which Morrison succumbs to the 'native climate'. Lena is a 'child of [London's] streets' in 'the hopeless grip of poverty' (p. 78). With his emaciated, debilitated appearance, his decadent pencilled eyebrows and his 'tired way of speaking', Jones is a gruesome prognostication of the direction in which the English gentleman is moving. Jones retains the forms but not the morality or energy of his class. Ricardo recalls C. F. G. Masterman's gloomy description of a new type of Englishman to be found in the cities: 'easily wearied: yet voluble, excitable, with little ballast, stamina, or endurance—seeking stimulus in drink, in betting, in any unaccustomed conflicts at home or abroad'.[9] Lena understands that Ricardo is the quintessence of what she has been trying to escape all of her life: 'It seemed to her that the man sitting there before her was an unavoidable presence which had attended all her life. He was the embodied evil of the world' (p. 298). Without personal or national ties, without any values but survival, he embodies creeping mediocrity. Allied with a decadent upper class personified by Jones and a barbarous lower class epitomised by Pedro, Ricardo represents a threat to the stability of Western civilisation. Despite his name, Martin Ricardo is an English sailor who has completely renounced the maritime ethic that Conrad embraced. Ricardo scorns the work ethic: 'If you sell your work—what is it but selling your own self?' (p. 145). (Ricardo's disdain for exchanging labour for wages, as an excuse for outlawry, may be like Michaelis in *The Secret Agent*, a contemptuous cartoon of Marxism.[10]) As Schomberg realises, Ricardo and Jones are 'identical souls in different disguises' (p. 130). Apelike Pedro is both a vestige of man's primordial antecedents and a prolepsis of man's devolution; that he intrudes into European outposts implies the imminent threat of barbarism to Europe. Ricardo best summarises the trio's common lack of humanity when he says, 'I have no feelings' (p. 133). In *Victory* all men lack community and national ties; none of the white men belongs to the British merchant marine or has any commitment other than to himself.

In *Victory*, language itself seems deprived of its subtlety, polish and meaning. Crude clichés, heavily stressed monosyllabic diction and abruptly truncated, aggressive syntax not only underline Ricardo's crudity but also show the devaluation of language. Despite superficial polish, Jones's words have no relation to his intent. Heyst is the introspective self-distrusting ironist who has replaced the Victorian man of action; the latter, despite some doubts, believed in his values and principles and knew that life was worth living. In depicting the effective invasion of the remote island Samburan by the villainous trio, Conrad may have been ironically alluding to the persistent fear of invasion in England during the first decade of the twentieth century as well as to the decline of the upper class as standard-bearers of civilisation.[11] When Heyst says, 'You don't seem to have quite enough pluck for your business', Jones does not quite deny the charge: 'Strange as it may seem to you, it is because of my origin, my breeding, my traditions, my early associations, and such-like trifles' (p. 383). Jones simultaneously scorns common humanity and admires its instinctive potential. In his most poignant remark Jones says, 'I tell you, a gentleman is no match for the common herd' (p. 388). Among other things, *Victory* is about the decline of the class on which Conrad believed European civilisation had depended for its moral leadership.

Heyst may represent Conrad's perception that a certain kind of man—polished, tolerant, polite, considerate of others, and of impeccable integrity and the highest personal standards—was becoming obsolete in England. For all his quirks, Heyst adheres to Edwardian propriety and decorum with the single exception of his elopement. As Dangerfield writes, 'the long season of bourgeois respectability was drawing to its close'.[12] The invasion of Samburan by Jones, the man who both belongs to and is alienated from the very class on which England had depended for moral and political leadership, may reflect Conrad's perception that England had more to fear from inner decay than from outside invasion.[13] If we recall the pre-war hysteria over the German invasion, highlighted by the apocryphal sighting of German airships, the impact of Jones's invasion—whose expeditionary force is launched by the German Schomberg—will not be lost upon us.[14] The alliance between Ricardo and Jones spoke to the secret fear in pre-war England that an alliance between the disaffected element of the wealthy and the anarchical element in the working class would destroy England's parliamentary democracy.

The negativism of Heyst's father may represent the anonymous 1905 pamphlet *The Decline and Fall of the British Empire*; in any case, it is an extreme rejection of the more optimistic of the Social Darwinists. It may also be a criticism of *A Commentary* by Conrad's friend John Galsworthy. Reading through that volume, composed of satirical sketches originally written for *The Nation*, confirms Hynes's observation: 'The whole treatment is heavy, humorless, and grotesquely over-simplified, and this is in part a function of the mode of observation; the observer is a consistent, though uninvolved character who sees everything from an upper-class, sympathetic, but detached point of view. He sees feelingly, but never enters the human situations. . . .'[15] Before he became involved, Heyst's own attitudes resembled those of Galsworthy.

Victory is a novel which attacks imperialistic pretensions, decadent aristocracy and business morality, only to give those forces the laurels of victory. The title 'Victory' finally implies the triumph of materialism and greed over feeling and personal relationships. By using 'business' interchangeably with 'game', Conrad emphasises the Edwardian effort to disguise in understatement its competitive and aggressive impulses. With his recurrent talk about sport, form and breeding, while carrying on his criminal enterprises, Jones is a satire of amoral capitalism. He is travelling for 'sort of sport' (p. 100). Jones and Ricardo are card sharks who, at one point, plan on taking Heyst's supposed fortune in a card game; Jones remarks, 'A game is as good a way as any to let him understand that the time has come to disgorge. . . . It's not a bad form to give to the business—which in itself is crude . . .' (p. 336). Jones is a confidence man not only for monetary reasons, but also because he needs an outlet for his sadistic form of play. 'Game' is also associated with 'scheme' (as when Ricardo remarks, 'No use giving the game away' [p. 339]), and with problem' when Jones remarks, 'Why not go over there and see if we can't get to the bottom of this game?' (p. 340). They are ironically echoing a metaphor Heyst uses for life itself when he explains to Lena why he remained loyal to Morrison: 'Truth, work, ambition, love itself, may be only counters in the lamentable or despicable game of life, but when one takes a hand one must play the game' (p. 203). He joined Morrison's coal project 'as one joins a child's game in a nursery' (p. 213). Finally, the multiple uses of 'game' reduce all activities to the level of play and undermine the possibility of serious purpose. If man's activity is a form of play in a world he cannot control, then necessarily his life is bathetic.

The persistent references to money and business have a similar reductive effect. Conrad is concerned with the kind of men that capitalism has produced; Schomberg, Jones, Ricardo, the Zangiacomo band and the Tropical Belt Coal Company are symptomatic of the rampant commercialism of an age Conrad despises. Schomberg is the archetypal capitalist, whose credo is ironically summarised by the narrator: 'business is business, and its forms and formulas must be observed'; for him, people are 'accounts' (p. 98). In such a *Zeitgeist*, Heyst and his father, men who seek to live life by values, have no place. That Heyst ironically describes his father's rejection, a rejection which he adopts but does not adhere to, in materialistic terms shows that he cannot really inhabit a discrete moral sphere: 'Suppose the world were a factory and all mankind workmen in it. Well, he discovered that the wages were not good enough. That they were paid in counterfeit money' (pp. 195–6).

Preying upon the hopes and dreams of others, Jones's gambling becomes a trope for the commercial impulse. His gambling table collects 'samples of intensely artless, helpless humanity—pathetic in their innocent watch for the small turns of luck which indeed might have been serious enough for them' (p. 118). Jones is depicted as death-like because he preys upon men, stifling their hopes and dreams; symbolically and actually, he is at war with time, the ingredient of man's hopes for a better future, whether it be economic or personal; he argues 'that one must do something to kill time. Killing time was not forbidden' (p. 113). That he is ostentatiously opposed to heterosexual relations, which Conrad regarded as one salvation from human loneliness, is another of his life-denying qualities. Obviously, with his pathological fear of woman, a caricature of a homosexual, Jones has sublimated his vestiges of passionate energies into the desire for gain and the need for violence; he even finds speaking of violence, as when he killed Pedro's brother, an outlet. Throughout the novel commercial dealings provide an outlet for whatever remains of instinctive, passionate energy; when Ricardo expresses his love of cards the narrator remarks, 'The effect of this outburst was augmented by the quiet lowering of the eyelids, by a reserved pause as though this had been a confession of another kind of love' (p. 124).

Ricardo worships Jones's manner and uses words such as 'proper' and 'correct' as his own norms to define behaviour. Ricardo is a cartoon of British class worship; he assumes that Jones's supercilious and condescending attitude is part of the mysterious rites of a gentleman. The object of Ricardo's esteem is a psychotic whose fixation is hatred of women. When Jones says, 'I am the world itself', we realise he epitomises the cynicism, commercialism, exploitation of the modern world. He is an inversion not only of Heyst, but also of the values civilisation has stood for: '[Jones] depended on himself, as if the world were still one great, wild jungle without law. Martin was something like that, too—for reasons of his own' (p. 113). The jungle image suggests that the gentleman class, for all its polish, has not necessarily progressed from its primordial origins.

The relationship between Jones, Ricardo and Pedro parodies the obsolete social hierarchy of the past. The intellectual man of the world governs the libidinous Ricardo, whose savagery is barely controlled by his underdeveloped social self. Ricardo, in turn, treats his immediate inferior Pedro as an animal. Conrad is again rejecting the idea that civilisation has progressed. The atavistic trio Ricardo, Pedro, and Jones illustrates the folly of the idea that man has improved. Jones has adopted what he believes to be the morality of the 'common herd' and yet has sought to separate himself from what he calls 'the unceremonious classes' on the basis of manners and dress (p. 390). Until Ricardo surrenders to his passion, Jones's analysis of

Ricardo is accurate—and as applicable to Lena as to his servant: 'Ricardo is of the faithful retainer class—absolutely identified with all my ideas, wishes, and even whims' (p. 379). His political subservience to Jones depends upon his rejecting the system of wages. Conrad uses the word 'repressed' to describe Ricardo because he wishes to show how close to the surface violent impulses can be. He lacks minimal self-control. Once Ricardo experiences sexual desire, his ties to the governor dissolve.

V

Victory is an ironic title for what may well be Conrad's most pessi-mistic novel. Malice, not love, has triumphed. Heyst's 'infernal mis-trust of all life' keeps 'the true cry of love from his lips' even after Lena saves him (p. 406). Given Conrad's lack of belief in the hereafter, there is nothing purifying about Heyst's funeral pyre for Lena and his self-immolation. Isn't his suicide a continuation of his search to separate the strand of his life from a cosmos he despises? Davidson's final world, 'Nothing!', spoken to give emphasis to his previous comment, 'There was nothing to be done there', is a suitable epigraph that not only summarises what Heyst and Lena have accomplished in their desperate quest for love and happiness, but also stands as Conrad's comment on what man can achieve in this world. With its plethora of murders and suicides, the melodramatic climax—an acceleration of an inevitable movement that begins with the villain's arrival on Samburan—explodes the possibility of a meaningful conclusion. In a sense, the ending undermines the viability of an allegorical interpretation by discarding a dialectic of values in favour of a sea of blood. What survives is an 'indolent' volcano whose 'dull red glow, expanding and collapsing spasmodically like the end of a gigantic cigar' surrealistically mocks the former inhabitant's own habits and temperament, and Schomberg's hotel, that grim image of *our* age (p. 4).

Victory is often quite fine, but it is not among Conrad's major achievements. It does not justify the extent of its growth from the short story Conrad originally planned. Despite its length, it does not fully develop Heyst's psychology nor show how he is modified by experience. Nor does Conrad provide sufficient parallels to create the kind of complex moral vision of his best fiction, such as 'Heart of Darkness', *Lord Jim, Nostromo* and 'The Secret Sharer'. The important characters other than Heyst never develop beyond cartoons; for example, despite their prolonged appearance in the novel, the outlaw gentleman Jones and his feral follower Ricardo are repetitious variations of a few humour qualities. Once the villainous trio arrives, the novel dissolves into operatic melodrama with a strong 'cops and robbers' component but little sustaining mystery. And this takes up about half a novel of over 400 pages. Were *Victory* narrated by a meditative central consciousness probing into the meaning of Heyst's impressions, perhaps the novel, and in particular the first half, would have been successful. Despite some tentative but soon abandoned efforts to establish Davidson in this role, Conrad turns to a leisurely omniscient narrator whose chatty, often flaccid, style does not have sufficient intensity, density or discrimination to engage the reader's attention at the level of the 1898–1900 Marlow tales and the major political novels.

NOTES

1. Dangerfield, *The Strange Death of Liberal England* (New York: Capricorn, 1961 [original ed. London, 1933]), p. 123.
2. Ibid., pp. 366–7.
3. See Meyer's discussion of Conrad's ignoring his screaming baby on a train (*Joseph Conrad: A Psychoanalytic Biography* [Princeton, NJ: Princeton University Press, 1967], p. 129).
4. Two excellent discussions of Heyst are contained in Robert Secor, *The Rhetoric of Shifting Perspectives: Conrad's 'Victory'* (University Park, PA: Pennsylvania State University, 1971), and Donald Dike, 'The Tempest of Axel Heyst', *Nineteenth-Century Fiction*, vol. 17 (Sep 1962), pp. 95–113.
5. See Karl's discussion (*Conrad: The Three Lives*, pp. 765–70) of the manuscript and revisions for publication, including the change of the major figure's name from Berg to Heyst. According to Karl, 'in revising the manuscript for the book text, Conrad altered not only wordiness but also our view of Berg, transforming him from a retiring idealist interested in human welfare to the ironic Heyst' (ibid., p. 766).
6. Samuel Hynes, *The Edwardian Turn of Mind* (Princeton, NJ: Princeton University Press, 1968), p. 5.
7. See ibid., ch. 2, 'The Decline and Fall of Tory England'.
8. Ibid., p. 69.
9. C. F. G. Masterman, *The Heart of the Empire* (London: Fisher Unwin, 1901), quoted ibid., pp. 61–2.
10. Conrad may be satirising the labour unrest of 1910–14, which was threatening to undermine the social and political fabric of pre-war England. Dangerfield writes of 'the sudden class hatred, the unexpected violence, the irrational moods' which characterised what he calls 'The Worker's Rebellion' (p. 217). Workers were no longer content with the shibboleths that preached that each man should soberly accept his station in life and that an honest day's work was the noblest

work of god. As Dangerfield puts it, 'The workers did not want to be safe any more; they wanted to live, to take chances, to throw caution to the winds: they had been repressed too long' (*The Strange Death of Liberal England*, p. 235). Ricardo, of course rejects the work ethic of Victorian England. Ricardo represents, perhaps, what Dangerfield calls the 'increasing horde of the casually employed, the unemployed, and the unemployable [who] drifted through the country' (ibid., p. 233).

11. See Hynes, *The Edwardian Turn of Mind*, p. 43.

12. Dangerfield, *The Strange Death of Liberal England*, p. 333.

13. Interestingly, prior to giving the novel its final title, he thought of it as the *Island Story* (see Karl, *Conrad: The Three Lives*, p. 747).

14. Dangerfield remarks, 'The public was only aware of an inner tension, a need for stimulants; and what could be more exciting than to gather all the political rages, all the class hatreds, all the fevers for spending and excitement and speed, which then seemed to hang like a haunted fog over England—to gather them and condense them into one huge shape and call it *Germany*' (*The Strange Death of Liberal England*, p. 119).

15. Hynes, *The Edwardian Turn of Mind*, p. 76.

6 Wartime fiction

I

The First World War had a profound effect on Conrad. It particularly troubled him that his beloved sea had become a battleground on which man fought with deadly weapons:

> Mines: Submarines. The last word in sea-warfare: Progress— impressively disclosed by this war. . . . Mankind has been demoralised since by its own mastery of mechanical appliances. Its spirit is apparently so weak now, and its flesh has grown so strong, that it will face any deadly horror of destruction and cannot resist the temptation to use any stealthy, murderous contrivance. It has become the intoxicated slave of its own detestable ingenuity. (*NLL*, pp. 162–3)

During the war Conrad often felt enervated and bored and complained at times of his inability to concentrate (*LL*, ii, p. 172, 180). But, when he did write, he dramatised serious moral crises and focused on the act of telling as an experience of self-definition. His intense concern for the welfare of both Poland and England as well as for his son Borys, who became a second lieutenant in 1915 and was from early 1916 to the end of the war at the French front, recalled him to his characteristic themes of loyalty and betrayal. That once again he should produce excellent work when most self-conscious about the difficulties of writing is characteristic of his entire career. In 1915 he wrote the magnificent short novel *The Shadow-Line*, which, while returning to the concern of 'The Secret Sharer' with the excruciating loneliness of a first command, is distinctly different in its emphasis on the captain's fulfilling a clearly defined ethical ideal.[1]

Written in 1915 and based on his command of the *Otago* in 1888, *The Shadow-Line* explores the difference between merely practising skills and providing leadership to a community.[2] In contrast, the seemingly similar 'The Secret Sharer' emphasised the captain—

narrator's personal psychological development rather than his ability
to occupy a position in terms of standards established by maritime
tradition. By fulfilling the moral requirements of a clearly defined
position, the captain—narrator fulfils himself; he overcomes ennui,
anxiety and anomie and merges his psychological life with the demands of the external world. To oversimplify: *The Shadow-Line*
affirms that hyperconsciousness is a moral, rather than, as in 'The
Secret Sharer', a psychological, problem. The later work demonstrates
how hyperconsciousness and its symptoms can be overcome by
discovering the authentic self that exists beneath self-doubt and
anxiety. *The Shadow-Line* illustrates the important difference between internal doubts and external behaviour; the captain, like the
French Lieutenant in *Lord Jim*, may be as fearful as the next man,
but his conduct is shaped and ordered by belief in a system of
values.

In 1916 Conrad wrote his final short stories, 'The Warrior's Soul'
and 'The Tale'. Both surpass in quality the short romances of *Within
the Tides*. Each depicts the ambiguity and complexity of excruciat-
ingly difficult moral decisions. In both stories, Conrad briefly uses an
introductory omniscient narrator to posit the dramatic context for a
self-justifying monologue. Yet the two tales are quite different. In
'The Warrior's Soul', the narrator becomes an sympathetic apolo-
gist for a companion whose commitment to personal values took
precedence over political distinctions. The last short story that
Conrad was to write, 'The Tale', is in the pattern of his retrospective
reminiscences where the speaker rather imperceptively evaluates his
own past conduct. While 'The Warrior's Soul' shows the obsolescence of aristocratic ideals, 'The Tale' shows the failure of an
undisciplined individual to fulfil the ideals of the British marine. In
the latter, a seemingly mature sea captain, despite his good intentions,
lacks the essential self-control, tolerance and judgement to make the
requisite moral distinctions between neutrals and enemies.

II. *THE SHADOW-LINE* (1916)

The Shadow-Line: A Confession is the last of a series of tales—others
include 'Youth' (1898), 'Heart of Darkness' (1899), 'Falk: A
Reminiscence' (1903) and 'The Secret Sharer' (1910)—in which
Conrad created a mature captain reminiscing upon a journey which,
to the captain—narrator, represents the successful progress from

innocence to experience and from youth to maturity. In each of these tales, the narrator nostalgically recalls how the journey had tested and refined his character and prepared him for future challenges. At the same time, he selects and arranges the past events to create a self-image with which he feels comfortable. For this reason, the present verbal behaviour of the speaker is as much a focus as the past action he describes. Yet, despite its resemblance to preceding tales in which the self-dramatising narrator testifies to the completion of a successful personal quest, I believe that *The Shadow-Line* needs to be discussed in terms of quite different intellectual and aesthetic assumptions.

The interest of the dramatic monologue and the Victorian novel in the consciousness of individual characters demonstrates the continuation and development of the Romantics' stress on dramatising the thoughts and feelings of the individual. But in the 1890s several writers took this emphasis on subjectivity one step further. For Wilde in *The Picture of Dorian Gray* (1891) and elsewhere, Hardy in *Judy the Obscure* (1895) and Conrad in his Marlow tales, experience itself is value, and self-knowledge becomes the ultimate goal of life. Joyce's epiphanies, Lawrence's psycho-autobiographical *Sons and Lovers* (1913), which deliberately focuses on his personal obsessions, and Conrad's belief that 'another man's truth is only a dismal lie to me', emphasise how these writers began their careers by asserting the value of subjective experience as a means to self-knowledge and by assuming that individual experience has a representative value. But during the second decade of the twentieth century one can perceive a reaction to subjectivity and a search for extrinsic standards. Robert Langbaum has written how modern writers—he includes Joyce, Yeats, Eliot, Lawrence and Mann in his generalisation—'reaffirm the authenticity of the self by finding that individual identity emerges, like smaller Chinese boxes out of larger, from an archetypal identity.'[3] Within a period of ten years, Conrad, Joyce, Yeats and Eliot increasingly stressed objective, conservative values as a means to separate themselves from, and give moral shape to, the intellectual turmoil they felt. For Yeats, these values are associated with the eighteenth-century aristocratic world of Burke and Swift; for Eliot, the values are derived from the Anglo-Catholic religious tradition; and for Joyce and Mann classical humanism gives intellectual, if not moral, order to contemporary life. Major tenets of Eliot's early critical theory assert the value of objectivity in art: the separation between the man that suffers and the mind that creates, and the quest for 'an objective correlative' to express characters' thoughts and feelings. (It may be worth noting that this is the decade in which 'objective' Cubism and Futurism developed in response to the supposed 'subjectivity' of Impressionism in painting.)

As Eliot and Joyce use allusions to classical and Christian traditions to imply alternative values to the modern disintegration, within *The Shadow-Line* Conrad explicitly juxtaposes a vision of maritime ideals to the experience of a specific community on board a ship. He uses as supporting figures Giles and Ransome, who exist for their representative, if not allegorical, significance. In 'A Prayer for my Daughter' (1919), Yeats recognises the value of established traditions:

> How but in custom and ceremony
> Are innocence and beauty born?
> Ceremony's a name for the rich horn,
> And custom for the spreading laurel tree.

After indicting Prufrock for the failure to understand that internal order depends upon religious truths and showing how Gerontion, despite his intellectual awareness, lacks religious passion, Eliot predicates spiritual and moral health on commitment to the specific beliefs of the Anglo-Catholic tradition. Even a seeming exception such as Lawrence seeks to reinterpret rather than eschew traditional religious myths. That the hortatory and prophetic voice in *The Rainbow* (1915) speaks in religious language and evokes biblical personae as he urges passion and instinct, demonstrates the fundamentally conservative Evangelical influence on Lawrence. By placing modern Ireland in biblical and epic contexts in *Ulysses* (1922), Joyce objectifies the subjective fantasy of his character, Stephen Dedalus, to forge within himself the uncreated conscience of his race. What these writers share, then, is an emphasis upon the need to revive and redefine cultural paradigms and archetypes.

Much as Shakespeare demonstrated how kingship brought out inherent qualities of leadership for both Henry IV and Henry V, Conrad demonstrates in *The Shadow-Line* how the narrator's belief in the captaincy as a moral abstraction shapes his character. In *The Mirror of the Sea* (1906), Conrad explicitly defines qualities essential for maritime leadership: industry, enthusiasm, faithfulness; good sense; an 'eternally watchful demeanour'; service for its own sake rather than for gain; affection for the ship and its crew; and the ability to respond to the individual needs of each man on board. While the maritime hierarchy has provided the narrator with the necessary experience as first mate and the requisite skills, he has not been tested by the moral and social demands of command. Approaching sixty and finally having received substantial public recognition as a writer, Conrad could confidently resolve the struggle between the inner and outer man by positing a clear solution: adherence to a system of values that tradition has established as a viable means of ordering and controlling personal doubts. For Conrad, the sea was not merely a subject-matter to which he continually returned as a writer, but the canvas on which—*before* he became a writer—he had created an image of himself as a man of ability and responsibility. As Morton Dauwen Zabel has written,

> It was in the sea and its ships that he found the sense of community, dedication, and responsibility that had failed him in Poland and France, and though his relations with it were eventually to show all the complexity of emotion and conflict of intelligence that could be expected in a man of Conrad's nature, his feeling of identification with its life and 'passion' remained with him to the end.[4]

Before going to sea on board the British freighter *Mavis* in 1878, Conrad had disappointed his surrogate father, his uncle Thaddeus Bobrowski; and had shown himself in his French years, to quote Baines, as 'irresponsible, undisciplined, inconsiderate, sensitive, highly-strung, passionate, apparently rather susceptible to female attraction, and apparently prone to morbid depression'.[5] But the British maritime code had provided him with a clear and precise system of values and a meritocracy by which he could measure his success in an alien culture.

The narrator's vocabulary emphasises the ethical dimensions of his tale concerning the 'maturing and tempering' of his character (p. 129). In search of 'truth', the narrator leaves the ship on which he has been serving as first mate. Because resigning his position is alien to his own standards and he does not understand his motives, the retrospective narrator hyperbolically proposes radically immoral roles for himself. He compares himself to 'some poor devil going out to be hanged' and an 'impenitent criminal' (p. 8). That he compares himself to a criminal twice more (for berating Burns and for neglecting to check on the quinine supply) shows how he now adopts roles for himself that acknowledge a sense of guilt. Such oft-repeated maritime values as 'duty', 'service' and 'responsibility' emphasise the tale's ethical dimension. As they are redefined through the dramatic action, 'humane' and 'sympathetic' come to mean responding individually to the personality of each man without compromising one's commitment to the rest of the community. 'Duty' evolves to include not merely performing one's assigned function—like the captain of the harbour launch—but also devotion to ship and its community. 'Responsibility' for the captain means not only to act courageously and to oversee every aspect of the ship; it also means to accept blame personally for his shortcomings and to acknowledge to himself the inevitable discrepancy between human fallibility and the awesome demands of his position.

In *The Shadow-Line*, the captain does not permanently overcome anxiety, guilt and despair, but learns to cope with them. At the very moment when he is acting most heroically, he feels that his own inadequacy is being revealed by events. He understands the need to go on deck when the weather changes; he takes the lead in hauling the sail; he knows every inch of his ship, and without a crew he steers the ship into port. Yet, he is simultaneously beset by inner turmoil and by an apocalyptic vision of the end of his world.[6] Even while he writes the diary because of 'a personal need for intimate relief', the 'abstract sentiment of . . . command' to which he is committed shapes his conduct (pp. 50, 106). It has been noted that the state described in Baudelaire's sonnet 'La Musique', from which the epigraph, 'D'autres fois, calme plat, grand miroir de mon désespoir', is taken, describes both his condition at the *outset* of the tale and the period of intolerable calm during his first command.[7] But the novel rejects as self-indulgent Baudelaire's correspondence between the inner and outer man and the romantic sensibility it implies. As the narrator learns the full dimension of 'faithful service', the solipsistic perspective of section 1 is left behind; duties and standards, rather than immediate emotional gratification, shape his conduct. The ensuing chapters gradually reveal that the ennui of the young captain is *not* the result of 'immobilizing neurotic depression',[8] but boredom experienced by the exceptional man who *requires* the ethical imperatives of responsibility.

The novel discovers that position and character are in a symbiotic relationship. In other words, the viability of an ethical tradition depends upon its being continually reinvigorated by individuals who believe in it and live by its demands. Originally the captain found sustenance in the belief that the position itself confers value upon him. His previous seaman's experience has taught him to trust in the ability and judgement of those who (like Kent, the previous captain) hold that role. But he learns that the position confers no automatic dignity and morality. Not only has his predecessor's malfeasance constituted a virtual abdication of the position, which he naïvely believed automatically conferred a conception of service and responsibility on the men chosen for it; but the resentful first mate, Burns, who hoped to be the successor and who had taken the ship to port, debases the position that the narrator had previously held. Each captain must discover within himself the resources to measure up to his idealised concept of command. At first the captain had felt that he was in a state of preparedness, until he met a series of circumstances that challenged his self-confidence.

When the young narrator receives his command, he thinks of it as a *personal fulfilment* rather than in terms of his ethical responsibility to the shipboard community, to the owners, and to a maritime code. In a solipsistic moment upon first boarding the ship, he looks in the mirror and self-indulgently congratulates himself on ascending to the command:

> I stared back at myself with the perfect detachment of distance, rather with curiosity than with any other feeling, except of some sympathy for this latest representative of what for all intents and purposes was a dynasty; continuous not in blood, indeed, but in its experience, in its training, in its conception of duty, and in the blessed simplicity of its traditional point of view on life.   (p. 53)

But the captain's self-confidence is challenged; the crew is overcome by illness, with Burns as one of the victims; continuing calm makes it impossible to take the ship out to sea; and soon the young captain discovers that his and the doctor's failure to check on the quinine supply have left him with a dearth of medicine. Ian Watt perceptively describes the captain's plight: 'The narrator gradually comes to realize that his new role as captain, which he had first envisaged as the final, total, and indeed magical solution of all his life-problems, actually involves an intricate network of moral imperatives, psychological discoveries, and social responsibilities.'[9] The captain imagines that once he finally takes his ship out to sea, his problems will dissolve, that the 'mortal coil of shore affairs' (p. 73) will give give way to the simplified existence of the sea.[10] But, as he confronts the 'dead calm', he feels his 'sense of balance' threatened by the pressure of 'lonely responsibilities' (pp. 74, 75).

The mature captain's younger self needed to entertain imaginative and primitive interpretations that he now knows are factually false. He emphasises the similarity between Burns's notion that the ship is bewitched and the belief of his younger self in the quinine as a 'magic powder working against mysterious malefices that [would secure] the first passage of my first command against the evil powers of calms and pestilence' (p. 88). When he discovers the absence of quinine, he has his own paranoid delusions, believing momentarily that he is a victim of 'a sort of plot, a sinister attempt to deceive, a thing resembling sly vengeance—but for what?—or else a fiendish joke' (p. 93). And he goes further towards Burns's epistemology when he speaks of 'the fever-devil who has got on board this ship' (p. 103). The captain anthropomorphises the malaria, imagining that it has 'stretched its claw after us over the sea' (p. 79), and the winds, which, he recalls, 'raised hopes only to dash them into the bitterest disappointment' (p. 84); in times of stress and anxiety, his mind reverts to irrational explanations. The young captain groped for an appropriate epistemology and semiology with which to explain the plight in which he found himself as captain of a diseased crew during a period of inexplicable calm. He desperately strove to understand why the cosmos seems to have especially directed its fury at him. Conrad understood man's atavistic need to apostrophise the unknown forces that he confronts. Writing in the section of *Mirror of the Sea* entitled 'The Character of the Foe', Conrad remarked:

> Looking back after much love and much trouble, the instinct of primitive man, who seeks to personify the forces of Nature for his affection and for his fear, is awakened again in the breast of one civilized beyond that stage even in his infancy. One seems to have known gales as enemies, and even as enemies one embraces them in that affectionate regret which clings to the past. . . . For after all, a gale of wind, the thing of mighty sound, is inarticulate. It is a man who, in chance phrase, interprets the elemental passion of his enemy. . . . It is, after all, the human voice that stamps the mark of human consciousness upon the character of a gale.   (pp. 71, 78, 79)

As 'Heart of Darkness', *Lord Jim* and 'Karain' illustrate, Conrad felt that most of the accepted distinctions between civilised and primitive

men were apocryphal. Whether in oral expression at sea or the
formalised verbal behaviour of written prose, all men, Conrad
believed, create fictions by which they bring the incomprehensible
universe into the ken of human understanding.

The diary device provides Conrad with a solution that he had not
previously tried to the major technical problem of the retrospective
reminiscence: how to differentiate clearly between the responses and
attitudes of an experiencing former self and the reminiscing speaker,
whose identity is quite different from his younger self. For Conrad,
the problem of how to dramatise two separate selves, the younger self
and a mature speaker who has successfully completed his rites of
passage, is crucial. If the reader experiences the speaker's mature
personality in the present, there is a danger that the former self will
exist only as a remote image of past events; conversely, if the reader,
despite the preterite, feels that he is experiencing the former self rather
than the mature narrator, he may feel that the author has become a
ventriloquist for a character that no longer exists and may be unclear
about the narrator's present identity. By juxtaposing crucial passages
from a diary with the narrator's present verbal behaviour, Conrad
isolates the captain's former self from the refractions of memory and
thus convincingly shows that the crisis is not an event completely
distorted by a distance of years. The diary testifies to the propensity of
the captain to fantasise disasters: 'I have nothing to do to keep my
imagination from running wild amongst the disastrous images of the
worst that may befall us' (p. 106). (The possibility that the
imaginative seaman might be more vulnerable to immobilisation
recurs in Conrad from Jim and Jukes to the captains of 'The Secret
Sharer' and The Shadow-Line.) The tenuous connection between the
captain's rapidly changing impressions, the abrupt transitions and the
alternation from objective facts to inner responses creates a verbal
correlative to his sense of isolation and anxiety:

I suppose the trouble is that the ship is still lying motionless,
not under command. . . . What's going to happen? Probably
nothing. Or anything. It may be a furious squall
coming. . . . And what appals me most of all is that I shrink
from going on deck to face it. It's due to the ship, it's due to
the men who are there on deck—some of them, ready to put
out the last remnant of their strength at a word from me. And
I am shrinking from it. From the mere vision. My first
command. Now I understand that strange sense of insecurity in

my past. I always suspected that I might be no good. And here
is proof positive, I am shirking it, I am no good.   (pp. 106–7)

His reductive and hyperbolic language illustrates his anxiety and
insecurity, but, despite feelings of guilt and self-doubt, he takes the
initiative during each crisis, and is never derelict in facing his
problems.

Because *The Shadow-Line* is concerned with the decisions the
narrator must make if he is to fulfil the ethical demands of the
captaincy, it is structured (rather like a morality play) to illustrate
alternative possibilities of conduct for the captain. The narrator is a
pilgrim in quest of truth and faith, but these values must come from
within. The action does not trace the narrator–protagonist's gradual
evolution, but brings out qualities already present in a man who,
despite his 'feeling of unworthiness', is properly trained and prepared
for the burdens of command (p. 117). Because he wishes to stress the
viability of objective values, Conrad creates characters primarily as
significant examples for the narrator, not as independent personalities
who affect his conduct and values. (Compare the one-dimensional
roles of Giles, Ransome and Burns with the complex, psychological
relationship that Marlow has with Kurtz, and that the captain in 'The
Secret Sharer' has with Leggatt.) Virtually every character has a
didactic dimension. Although he is 'choleric', 'inquisitorial' and
'peremptory', Ellis represents the effectuality and morality of the
hierarchical principle (p. 30). By contrast, the superciliousness and
condescension of Hamilton show that the quality of self-confidence
has an egoistic dimension which is not worthy of the regard of the
maritime community. The doctor, whom the captain finds friendly
and kind, was derelict in his duty. Indeed, because the doctor and
captain allow a personal relationship to displace their sense of duty,
neither properly inspects the medicine cabinet. On the other hand,
despite his jealousy and nastiness, the captain of the launch—who is
the 'first really unsympathetic man' the narrator has ever known—
performs his function and does him no harm (p. 47).

Ransome, the cook, provides an important example for the
captain. Quality does not depend on rank. Despite his 'defective
heart', Ransome had complete control of himself; his 'soul [is] as firm
as the muscles of his body' (p. 112), for 'he had schooled himself into a
systematic control of feelings and movements' (p. 68). His existential
moral commitment to a standard of conduct that places community
before self demonstrates the officer's credo that the captain must

attain. Because his every action endangers his physical health, his courage and service are all the more admirable. Ransome knows and understands that man lives within a dimension of time, subject to the vicissitudes of circumstances he cannot control. But for his part the young narrator must learn that life is not an 'enchanted garden' and that command is not invested 'as if by enchantment' (pp. 3, 39). (Crossing the shadow-line to adult responsibility involves some repression of adolescent fantasy.) Always giving voice to the impulse of the captain's conscience, Ransome becomes his alter ego. By the appropriate comment and apt glance, he urges the captain to his duty. When the captain begins 'talking somewhat in Mr. Burns' manner' and voicing superstitious notions about 'the fever devil', Ransome gives him 'one of his attractive, intelligent, quick glances' (pp. 103–4). Ransome behaves heroically and puts the interest of the community ahead of self ('[He] puts out his strength . . . for some distinct ideal. . . . Every effort, every movement was an act of consistent heroism' [p. 126]); but, once the voyage is completed, he insists upon leaving the ship and preserving his life. As both 'The Secret Sharer' and *The Nigger of the 'Narcissus'* demonstrate, Conrad stresses a balance between self-abnegation and self-interest. Ransome's assertion of his will to live, at first resisted by the captain, is tacitly understood by the captain as an essential act of self-preservation. For Ransome's 'savage determination' to preserve his own life is really part of the same moral intensity which enabled him to behave heroically.

If Ransome represents the desired superego, the sense of community responsibility that the captain must achieve, the superstitious and paranoid Burns represents the irrational and neurotic impulse that he must overcome within himself. I believe Conrad would have us regard the captain's decision to take Burns on board as an instance of 'sham sentiment', as rather analogous both to the moment when the captain in 'The Secret Sharer' volunteers to keep Leggatt on board when the latter offers to leave, and to the intermittent tendency of the crew aboard the *Narcissus* to place Wait's comfort ahead of their responsibility to their ship. (This, I think, is what he has in mind when he writes, in the Author's Note to *A Personal Record*, of 'that humanitarianism that seems to be merely a matter of crazy nerves or a morbid conscience' [p. ix].) Partly because Burns occupies the narrator's former position of first mate, the captain had identified with Burns despite his ambivalent feelings; 'In the face of that man, several years, I judged, older than myself, I became aware of what I had left already behind me—my youth' (p. 55). That Burns is not capable of performing his responsibilities means that the captain (ignoring the doctor's advice to get another chief officer) has put emotional and psychological needs ahead of the welfare of the ship. Just as Gentleman Brown insinuates himself upon Jim, and Leggatt appears as a potential ally to an insecure, paranoid young captain, Burns plays upon a vulnerable captain who already feels uneasy about coming between Burns and his expectations:

> He pleaded for the promise that I would not leave him behind.
> I had the firmness of mind not to give it to him. Afterwards
> this sternness seemed criminal; for my mind was made up.
> That prostrated man, with hardly strength enough to breathe
> and ravaged by a passion of fear, was irresistible. And, besides,
> he had happened to hit on the right words. He and I were
> sailors. That was a claim, for I had no other family.   (p. 70)

During the worst of the crisis, he mistakes Burns stumbling on all fours for 'an added and fantastic horror', but again he demonstrates his ability to cope with vicissitudes no matter how frightened he feels (p. 115).

Originally the narrator patronises Giles, the man who demonstrates qualities necessary for successful command: mature judgement, tolerance, leadership, self-possession, and selfless service to the maritime community. He regards Giles, as Jukes did MacWhirr, as 'the most dull, unimaginative man'. Despite the narrator's insistence that he wants to go home, Giles understands that the captain is one of those select few fit for command. By his humane conduct to the pathetic steward, Giles *shows* him how command depends upon tolerance and partial sympathy for all human beings. The young narrator does have the character not to blame the steward for his late arrival at Captain Ellis's office. But, whereas he inconsiderately (and slightly sadistically) allows the steward to wonder whether he had informed Ellis about the former's plot, Giles immediately reassures the steward. While the captain condescendingly observes, 'I would scorn to harm such an object' (p. 38), Giles recognises the man's few virtues and refuses to accept the verdict that the steward 'doesn't seem very fit to live' (p. 39). The 'self-conscious complacency' that he ascribes to Giles aptly applies to himself (retrospectively, the narrator realises that Giles was indeed a man of quality: 'It never occurred to me that I didn't know in what soundness of mind exactly consisted and what a delicate and, upon the whole, unimportant matter it was' [p. 21]). The captain, who regards Giles as something of an eccentric, has learned that moral quality is different from and far more important than artificial standards about normality and sanity. By his own admission, he is not 'sane' when he gives crucial orders to meet the change in the weather: 'I was like a mad carpenter making a box. Were he ever so convinced that he was king of Jerusalem, the box he would make would be a sane box' (p. 101).

Giles knows what the narrator must learn: 'Both men and ships live in an unstable element, are subject to subtle and powerful influences, and want to have their merits understood rather than their faults found out' (*The Mirror of the Sea*, p. 27). The final meeting with Giles which concludes his reminiscence is really something of an atonement to the formally maligned father figure. In a profession where death and misfortune are necessary parts of everyday life, 'a man', Giles tells him, 'should stand up to his bad luck, to his mistakes, to his conscience, and all that sort of thing. Why—what else would you have to fight against? (*The Shadow-Line*, pp. 131−2). The narrator now knows that a ship's captain cannot be concerned with himself, that 'You owe [a ship] the fullest share of your thought, of your skill, of your self-love' (*The Mirror of the Sea*, p. 56). As Watt has noted, that he repeats the verb 'steer' several times emphasises the significance to him of his having taken complete command, for the wheel of a ship is to him 'a symbol of mankind's claim to the direction of its own fate' (*The Shadow-Line*, p. 76).[11] Because he shows the leadership and self-command demanded by the tradition, the men respond to the present occupant of the hierarchical position. The journey has been a test in which his own egocentricism and immaturity are replaced by an earned knowledge of his capacity for command.

But achieving self-command is a continuous process rather than a goal one reaches. Giles tells the narrator, 'You will learn soon not to be faint-hearted. A man has got to learn everything—and that's what so many of those youngsters don't understand' (p. 132). The captain's imminent departure on his next journey indicates his own tacit acknowledgment of this; in a sense the shadow-line has to be continually met. That Conrad does not have Giles speak in nautical terms is deliberate. As the dedication implies ('To/Borys and all others/who like himself have crossed/in early youth the shadow-line/of their generation/with love'), Conrad wishes to expand the title image to include his son Borys and his generation, whose shadow-line

was created by the European war, and who had to face challenges for
which one can be professionally and technically prepared, but for
which ethical preparation is impossible. His emphasis on the maritime
autocracy and its concomitant hierarchy is part of his deep conservative streak, which made him impatient with the moral and social
anarchy that results from democracy. (One thinks of his disappointment with both contemporary London in *The Secret Agent* and even
Geneva in *Under Western Eyes*.) It may be that the World War was
a factor in making Joyce, Lawrence and Conrad aware that the
subjective epistemological journey and the discovery of one's own
truth are not enough in a world where each man's fate is tied to that
of his fellows' by political circumstances. Some of Conrad's younger
contemporaries, such as Yeats, Pound and Lawrence, carried the
search for objectivity into authoritarian political doctrines which
advocated clearly outlined community responsibilities for each man.
But Conrad knew of the arbitrariness of political autocracy from his
Polish background and was never tempted to suggest that what he
called the 'autocratic realm of the ship' be adopted as a model for
countries (*The Mirror of the Sea*, p. 17). Within the hermetic world of
the sea, Conrad could embrace an alternative to the utilitarian spirit
without flirting with repugnant ideology. *The Shadow-Line* implies
that only by rediscovering the traditional values of courage, duty and
responsibility can men individually face the turbulence of events—
whether political or meteorological—beyond their control. Finally,
the young narrator has found within himself the ethical ideal by
which Giles lives and by which Conrad wished to measure his work:
'There is something beyond [the attainment of proficiency]—a higher
point, a subtle and unmistakable touch of love and pride beyond
mere skill; almost an inspiration which gives to all work that finish
which is almost art—which *is* art' (*The Mirror of the Sea*, p. 24,
Conrad's emphasis).

III. UNCOLLECTED STORIES: 'PRINCE ROMAN' (1910) AND 'THE BLACK MATE' (1908)

Before discussing 'The Warrior's Soul' and 'The Tale', I should like to
discuss briefly the other uncollected tales that Richard Curle
published with them in the posthumous volume entitled *Tales of
Hearsay*. 'The Black Mate' is a trifle; a version was apparently written
for a short-story contest in 1886, but the tale was not published until
1908.[1,2] But 'Prince Roman' deserves attention because it expresses
Conrad's conservative political strain in its most transparent form.

'Prince Roman' is in the form of a reminiscence and was probably originally supposed to be part of the 1908–9 autobiographical essays that became *A Personal Record* (1912).[13] While Conrad may have been saving it for another volume of memoirs, it stands on its own as an effective story. The tale is a nostalgic recollection by a Polish nationalist of a man whose conduct and attitudes represent to him the patriotism and dignity of the aristocracy.[14] Written immediately after *Under Western Eyes*, it shows the value of self-respect and dignity, even while implying the obsolescence of such values. To the narrator, Roman is a mythic figure standing for patriotism and consummate integrity.

The Pole juxtaposes his original boyhood disappointment at Roman's appearance with his present admiration of the legendary aristocrat who had acted 'from conviction'. Conrad's narrative technique emphasises the remoteness of the era when the aristocracy played a significant role. Rather than have a contemporary of Roman's narrate the tale of his heroism or even have the nostalgic speaker give his impressions of his boyhood encounters with the old prince in 1868, Conrad has an unidentified speaker tell the story that he heard from the Polish nationalist several years ago. This frame narrator concurs with the Polish nationalist that the present aristocracy has deteriorated: 'No longer born to command . . . it becomes difficult for them to do aught else but hold aloof from the great movements of popular passion' (p. 30).

When he was a young child, the Polish speaker had been shocked to discover that a Prince could be 'deaf, bald, meagre, and so prodigiously old' (p. 35); he had noticed the 'harmonious simplicity' of Roman's face and realised that the face must have been beautiful in its day. Later, after learning Roman's story, he sees that once, before hardship, disease, and disappointment took their toll, the prince almost did fit his romantic, fairy-tale conception of a prince. After Roman's idyllic marriage had ended with his wife's premature death, he heroically and anonymously participated in the defence of his nation; after joining the popular movement against the Cossack invaders, he discovered such traditional values as 'sense of duty' and 'love of country'. But the narrator's interest is in the parable of aristocratic commitment, not in the psychology of Roman's patriotic awakening. Usually Conrad is sceptical of political zeal, but not in this story of loyalty and patriotism.

Until his imprisonment and subsequent impressment into the Russian forces, Roman is a figure from romance: 'Young, charming,

[and] heroic' if not 'fortunate' (p. 33). The Polish speaker is always sympathetic to Roman's patriotism and magnifies Roman into a folk hero. He imagines the line of Cossacks as a gigantic dragon-like creature devouring the land and its people: 'It was like an immense reptile creeping over the fields; its head dipped out of sight in a slight hollow and its tail went on writhing and growing shorter as though the monster were eating its way slowly into the very heart of the land' (p. 38). And within the Pole's parable the prince is depicted almost as a kind of St George – Perseus figure ready to take arms against the ghoulish monster. He refuses to surrender even when the uprising is doomed. His 'undying hope', according to the Pole, is different from the vain 'mad cult of despair' (p. 48). The tale's climax and the supreme moment of Roman's life are when he refuses to accept the opportunity, offered by the presiding officer's leading questions, to escape the wrath of the Russian victor.

As the following passage makes clear, the Polish speaker is a thinly disguised version of Conrad:

> How much remained in that sense of duty, revealed to him in sorrow? How much of his awakened love for his native country? That country which demands to be loved as no other country has ever been loved, with the mournful affection one bears to the unforgotten dead and with the unextinguishable fire of a hopeless passion which only a living, breathing, warm ideal can kindle in our breasts for our pride, for our weariness, for our exultation, for our undoing.   (p. 51)

Even after Prince Roman has been reduced physically and suffered twenty-eight years of humiliation, he returns to take his part in the community. To Conrad, Roman represents the full flowering of the aristocratic patriotic consciousness with which he proudly identified his father's commitment to the revolt of 1863. The Polish speaker views the Poland of the 1830s as a nation which despite oppression is united in love of country and tradition. The Jew, Yankel, is a respected partisan of the uprising, and the minor noble offers his son as a companion to Roman in a gesture of respect for the prince's position. To the intense regret of the Polish narrator *and to Conrad*, the organic community, uniting aristocrat, small landowner and peasant in love of country, is no longer possible in an age that regards patriotism as 'a relic of barbarism'. Prince Roman's idealism recalls what Conrad said of his father in the Author's Note to *A Personal*

Record: 'He was simply a patriot in the sense of a man who believing in the spirituality of a national existence could not bear to see that spirit enslaved' (p. x). In contrast, Prince John's excessive distrust of 'popular and democratic tendencies', and his willingness to collaborate with the St Petersburg regime, place him at odds with Polish nationalism. And Roman's daughter and her husband are content to emulate those artificial and insincere aristocrats who 'move in the cosmopolitan sphere'; they are the forerunners of the aristocrats whom the narrator indicts at the outset for their inability to command.

'The Black Mate', originally conceived for a penny magazine and later revised, is little more than a trifle and thoroughly belies Cunninghame Graham's verdict, expressed in his Preface to *Tales of Hearsay*, that 'there is no evidence of immaturity' in it. Conrad wrote 'The Black Mate' in 1886 as an unsuccessful entry in a prize competition for sailors conducted by *Tit-Bits*, but only the 1908 version that appeared in *London Magazine* seems to have survived. His wife disputed Conrad's contention that this was his first story and claimed to have been the source of the tale's subject. She believed the myth, created in *A Personal Record*, that until he began *Almayer's Folly* in 1889, he had 'never made note of a fact, or an impression, or of an anecdote' except for his letters. Internal evidence suggests that the story was originally composed well before *Almayer's Folly* and was only retouched for *London Magazine*; this was hardly the calibre of fiction Conrad was writing in 1908.

The story is of some historical interest because it is a clumsy experiment with a partially involved narrator whose perspective is influenced by his relationship to circumstances in the narrative. Since the speaker provides the hair dye to make the forlorn Bunter look younger and helps shape Bunter's attitude towards Johns, he is a minor actor in the story. In an attempt to create an impression of psychological and moral depth, Conrad has his speaker postpone the disclosure of Bunter's secret. But this is a clumsy contrivance that fails to create suspense and to engage the reader's curiosity. For the mystery consists merely of Bunter's dyeing his hair.

Rather than criticising Bunter's malingering or rebelliousness, the speaker excuses his irresponsible view of his duty by constantly alluding to his present poverty. Referring to Johns as a 'wretched insect' and to Mrs Bunter's uncle, who disapproved of her marriage, as an 'old cannibal', the narrator anticipates the recurring oral aggressiveness of Conrad's narrators and characters to those they dislike. The first-person narrator is an empathetic advocate of Bunter's perspective and selects and arranges the data to show his reader that under the circumstances Bunter acted honourably. He quotes Bunter's soap-operatic explanation for his deceit: 'You know that since I've been squeezed out of the Western ocean packets by younger men, just on account of my grizzled muzzle—you know how much chance I had to ever get a ship. And not a soul to turn to. We have been a lonely couple, we two—she threw away everything for me—and to see her want a piece of dry bread—' (p. 117). Although the narrator plays down Bunter's dereliction of duty—he feigned illness 'a good many days'—and extenuates his murderous impulses towards his captain, Bunter's fidelity is to himself and his wife, not to his ship. And he is rather casual about Bunter's homicidal urge towards the captain which he merely considers 'a dangerous form of self-indulgence' and attributes to a 'disordered imagination' (p. 101).

In a brief 1910 review entitled 'The Life Beyond', Conrad expresses disdain for the widespread Edwardian interest in the scientific proofs of life after death. 'What humanity needs', he writes, 'is not the promise of scientific immortality, but compassionate pity in this life and infinite mercy on the Day of Judgement' (NLL, p.69). Johns is not only a caricature of a spiritualist, but also a tentative psychological sketch of a man whose aggressiveness compensates for the abuse received from a dominating sister. Yet the speaker's serious tone belies the silly comedy of the central situation: to explain the change in his hair colour to a man who believes in ghosts, a man pretends that he has seen a ghost. When the anticipated revelation comes, the mystery is so trifling that the joke is almost unintentionally on the teller and protagonist, both of whom take themselves too seriously. Yet Conrad does use the final vision of the grotesque Johns, now senile, compulsively repeating his ghost story, to imply the equation of spiritualism with pathological behaviour.

IV. 'THE WARRIOR'S SOUL' (1917) AND 'THE TALE' (1917)

'The Warrior's Soul' and 'The Tale' show how the war renewed Conrad's interest in dramatising how a sensitive idealist could be placed in a morally and psychologically untenable situation where he cannot avoid excruciating decisions. If 'The Warrior's Soul' begins as if it were going to be a patriotic companion piece to 'Prince

Roman', it soon becomes clear that the carnage and dehumanisation produced by war are the focal points. The title, 'The Warrior's Soul', refers to three men: the narrator; the young soldier, Tomassov, who must make the decision to perform a mercy killing; and the despairing Frenchman, who requests that he be killed.

After a young man's apparent glib remark (which we do not hear) to the effect that the Russian army ought to have slaughtered the entire French army, an old Russian officer recalls his experience in the Napoleonic wars. (A nominal narrator contributes a few sentences to establish the scene before yielding to the officer's monologue.) Speaking to young listeners, the officer confidently defends the performance of the Russian army against Napoleon with a parable about the complexities of honour in wartime. At first, the old soldier takes umbrage at the insinuation that the army was anything less than complete in its victory or sense of purpose. But, as he recalls the horrible actualities and moral ambiguities of war, he drops his rather chauvinistic attitude and reveals his humanity. He remembers the retreating French army as 'a crawling, stumbling, starved, half-demented mob' (p. 3). He could not slaughter 'galvanized corpses that didn't care'. This prologue prepares us to sympathise with Tomassov and to appreciate his moral dilemma when the French officer insists that Tomassov has a duty to kill him. The narrator's perception of the amorality of *all* war sets the stage for Tomassov's attempt to fulfil a moral commitment. He remembers the 'funeral' setting and his thoughts that day of the Frenchmen dying 'in the midst of a nature without life'; Tomassov's attempt to make a delicate moral decision—and a macabre one at that—in a world which is shouting an everlasting no to morality, has frozen the event and his concomitant daydream forever in his memory (p. 20).

The tale belies the narrator's original effort to impose a Christian framework of values (the Russian army were 'simple servants of God', who helped 'God' deal with the invaders [p. 6, 4]), and verifies his thought, upon awakening from his dream, 'that the earth was a pagan planet and not a fit abode for Christian virtues' (p. 20). Indeed, in the story's second phase, religious images are mockingly applied to Tomassov's worship of the Frenchwoman. She is Tomassov's one 'divinity', and the drawing-room is the shrine (p. 10). Like the chivalric code of honour and the Christian concept of a benevolent universe, the romantic worship of an unattainable woman is an anachronistic conception. Finally, the carnage of war gradually makes all three value-systems irrelevant to the narrative. But,

interestingly, the narrator finds no alternative standards with which
to understand or evaluate Tomassov's act. He seems to draw back
deliberately from imposing a judgement on the rectitude of
Tomassov's decision to obey the French officer.

Tomassov reluctantly becomes a murderer because of his commitment to a chivalric code of honour which the actualities of war have
rendered obsolete. The romantic Tomassov *needs* to believe in
humane values and a standard of conduct. He is so overcome with
gratitude that he fails to see that the French officer's informing him of
the coming outbreak of hostility is not an act of 'friendship' to him,
but merely a gesture to titillate a cloyed mistress: 'For [Tomassov]
love and friendship were but two aspects of exalted perfection. He
had found these fine examples of it and he vowed them indeed a sort
of cult' (p. 16). He is as oblivious to the Frenchman's condescension as
he is unaware of his motives. His own act of honour whereby he fulfils
his commitment to de Castel is an act of generosity. Like the captain
in 'The Secret Sharer', Tomassov must choose between duty and self-
preservation. He sacrifices everything for his conception of duty. De
Castel's horror becomes Tomassov's horror, and Tomassov becomes
as much a victim of war as de Castel. The grotesque irony is that, to
fulfil his role as an Abel figure and thus be his brother's keeper,
Tomassov must be a Cain figure and murder his brother.

Conrad uses the officer to express his own despair over the World
War. The officer's elegiac tone combines with his perceptions of the
futility of war to reveal his present ethical dilemma. Tomassov's
macabre act of chivalry has been responsible for crystallising the
grotesqueness of war. De Castel's loss of faith is more intelligible
because the officer has a perception of the depravity of war and how it
divests life of its meaning. He refuses to commit himself to any pat
explanations, but recalls the devoted meditation of Tomassov, as the
latter stands over the man he has killed. That Tomassov's career is
ruined by his idealistic convictions confirms the world's lack of
morality. He now knows that only 'a horrible peace' can be achieved
on a foundation of corpses. But, more importantly, the intensity and
vividness of his own nightmare that day clearly dominate his
conscience and shape his response to his jingoistic audience:

> I had the intimate sensation of the earth in all its enormous
> expanse wrapped in snow, with nothing showing on it but
> trees with their straight stalk-like trunks and their funeral
> verdure; and in this aspect of general mourning I seemed to

hear the sighs of mankind falling to die in the midst of a
nature without life. They were Frenchmen. We didn't hate
them; they did not hate us; we had existed far apart—and
suddenly they had come rolling in with arms in their hands,
without fear of God, carrying with them other nations, and all
to perish together in a long, long trail of frozen corpses. I had
an actual vision of that trail; a pathetic multitude of small dark
mounds stretching away under the moonlight in a clear, still,
and pitiless atmosphere—a sort of horrible peace.   (p. 20)

The undeservedly neglected 'The Tale' reflects Conrad's anxiety
for Borys's safety at the front, his concern about the potential
corrupting effects of war upon maritime life, and his perception that
war reduces life to grotesque moral choices.[15] The anxiety of
wartime patrol caused the captain to behave irrationally and cruelly,
even though his motives were well-intentioned. He likes to think of
himself as a man whose simple morality is no longer relevant in an age
where engines rather than finesse move ships. But the captain has
made a decision that resulted in the death of an entire crew.

The captain—narrator genuinely wanted to discover whether the
boat he encountered was a neutral. But fear and anxiety prevented this
man who hates lies from being able to distinguish the truth in a
situation requiring mature judgement. Ironically, he misinterpreted
the facts he discovered. Even in the retelling, he never admits that his
paranoia *created* the reality he perceived. He is like Jukes in
'Typhoon', whose capacity for imagining disaster threatens his sanity.
During the fatal night, he was obsessed with invisible threats. Isn't his
preference for darkness irrational in a situation where the ability to
sight potential menace is the best safeguard? Finding a suspect object,
probably some sort of tank for refuelling submarines, reinforced his
anxiety. After his officer speculated that it had been left by some
unforeseen necessity, such as the need to leave quickly, the captain
proceeded along a series of surmises to his fatal decision. He
hypothesised that the object left by the neutral had refuelled the
submarine which was now ready to attack British ships. In a significant reversal of roles which reveals Conrad's opinion of the speaker,
the man who should be the voice of maturity took the initiative in
positing suspicions, while the younger second officer was the
moderating influence. The speaker self-righteously revolted 'against
the murderous stealthiness of methods and the atrocious callousness of
complicities that seemed to taint the very source of men's deep

emotions and noblest activities' (p. 67). And yet he used the very morality he despises to destroy the Northman.

Because of his contempt for the Northman's opportunistic philosophy that a neutral should serve its own self-interest, the captain's inclination was to believe the worst. The Northman apparently lacked the sense of self-survival necessary to realise the sort of threat the captain represented. Unable to take a chance, self-pitying, believing that he had an 'internal disease', and desperately needing a sympathetic ear, which he thought he had found in the captain, the Northman was a pathetic figure. While the Northman told his tale, the captain listened to an 'inward voice, a grave murmur in the depth of his very own self, telling another tale, as if on purpose to keep alive in him his indignation and his anger' (p. 73). It was this other tale, this alternative to what happened, that was responsible for plummeting the captain into his private hell, haunted by agonising guilt; yet even now he is still trying to make himself believe he might have been justified. He acted upon the fiction that he was confronted by an 'enormous lie' and imputed pernicious motives to the Northman. Remembering his fantasy that the whole ship was 'a picked lot' promised a 'fistful of money', he recalls that 'He felt alarmed at catching himself thinking as if his vaguest suspicions were turning into a certitude. *For indeed, there was no shadow of reason for his inferences*' (p. 76, emphasis added).

The captain is a final tortured victim of his own macabre trick, even though he refuses to abandon the pretence that he does not know whether or not the neutral was a conspirator. What makes his decision to give the boat an incorrect course so insane is that *only if* the Northman *had been lying* and had been refuelling the enemy's submarines would the crewman have lived; presumably, then, the captain would have apprehended them. If the Northman were telling the truth, how could he have known how to avoid the deadly rock? Because he could not cope with the ambiguity of the Northman's appearance and sort out subtle evidence, the captain deceitfully sent a crew to its death. The woman can sympathise with him, and he can self-indulgently worry about the correctness of his behaviour, but what about the tragic loss of life? Both of them seem to have little concern about his hubristic attempt to play God. Yet the omniscient narrator is not necessarily ironic when he speaks of how the woman 'knew [the captain's] passion for truth, his horror of deceit, his humanity', qualities that he may well have displayed on every other occasion (p. 81). Neither of them realises the extent of the self-indictment provided by his narrative. The captain returns to the woman, who sustains his own estimation of his moral worth; she allows him to inhabit temporarily a world where illicit sexuality for a moment placates the demands of his conscience and pushes aside the agony of sailing on a sea 'sown thickly with the seeds of hate' (*NLL*, p. 162).

The narration reveals the extent that the captain is haunted by his behaviour toward the neutral. His sense of guilt shapes his rhetorical strategy. He pretends, when his mistress requests a tale, to tell of 'another world' where the capitals had no names and where a commanding officer and a Northman lived. It is transparently clear that the woman realises, as we do, that the speaker is the officer, because he drops the pretence early, if only for a moment, when he says, 'And since I could find in the universe only what was deeply rooted in the *fibres of my being* there was love in it, too' (p. 62, emphasis added). The fiction of another world is a poignant effort to escape the moral complexities which overwhelm him. The speaker distances the events emotionally and makes it possible for him to discuss them. He retells the events from the point of view of grim humour, itself a kind of defence mechanism, while he uses the convenient fantasy that these events belong to another world so that he can engage himself in the painful, guilt-burdened retelling. As he renders his recollections half-ironically and half-defensively, we feel both his and Conrad's intense nostalgia for the simplified maritime world that once existed: 'Everything should be open in love and war. Open as the day, since both are the call of an ideal which it is so easy, so terribly easy, to degrade in the name of victory' (p. 67). Yet, ironically, the woman's allusions to her neglected responsibilities imply that their relationship involves duplicity, and we are learning that the captain has, whatever his intentions, degraded his ideal of war.

NOTES

1. For an extensive discussion of the relationship between 'The Secret Sharer' and *The Shadow-Line*, see Carl Benson's excellent article 'Conrad's Two Stories of Initiation', *PMLA*, vol. 69 (Mar 1954), pp. 46–56; repr. in Harkness, *Conrad's 'Secret Sharer'* (Belmont, Calif.: Wadsworth, 1962), pp. 83–93. Benson considers *The Shadow-Line* to be 'the communal counterpart' to 'The Secret Sharer'. He argues that *The Shadow-Line* has 'as its moral core the redemption of the captain through his realization that no man . . . is truly *self*-sustaining, that

the lot of the one is ineluctably involved with that of the many' (ibid., pp. 83, 84; emphasis Benson's). Jerome Zuckerman, 'Architecture of *The Shadow-Line*', *Conradiana*, vol. 3 (1971–2), pp. 87–92, argues that the 'treatment of command' in *The Shadow-Line* lacks the depth that it has in 'The Secret Sharer', because in *The Shadow-Line*, Conrad 'excessively [idealises] the crew and [minimises] the captain's difficulties with them' (p. 90).

2. Conrad had written in Richard Curle's copy of the novel, 'This story had been in my mind for some years. Originally I used to think of it under the name of *First Command*. When I managed in the second year of war to concentrate my mind sufficiently to begin working I turned to this subject as the easiest. But in consequence of my changed mental attitude to it, it became *The Shadow-Line*' (Richard Curle, *The Last Twelve Years of Joseph Conrad* [London: Sampson, Low, Marston, 1928]; quoted in Karl, *Conrad: The Three Lives* [New York: Farrar, Straus and Giroux, 1979], p. 770.)

    According to Karl, Conrad 'was trying nothing less than to regain an existence which was passing forever from him' (ibid., p. 779).

3. Robert Langbaum, *The Modern Spirit: Essays on the Continuity of Nineteenth and Twentieth Century Literature* (New York: Oxford University Press, 1970), p. 171. I am especially indebted to the essay entitled 'The Mysteries of Identity: A Theme in Modern Literature' (pp. 164–84).

4. Morton Dauwen Zabel, Introduction to Conrad's *'The Shadow-Line'*, *'Typhoon', and 'The Secret Sharer'* (Garden City, NY: Doubleday, 1959), p. 6.

5. Baines, *Conrad: A Critical Biography* (New York: McGraw-Hill, 1960), p. 58.

6. After the air turns black at the conclusion of the seemingly interminable calm, the narrator imagines that 'the blackness would overwhelm silently the bit of starlight falling upon the ship, and the end of all things would come without a sigh, stir, or murmur of any kind, and all our hearts would cease to beat like run-down clocks' (p. 108).

7. See Ian Watt, 'Story and Idea in Conrad's *The Shadow-Line*', *Critical Quarterly*, vol. 2 (Summer 1960), p. 141. The entire article, pp. 133–48, is an invaluable study.

8. See Guerard, *Conrad the Novelist* (Cambridge, Mass.: Harvard University Press, 1958), p. 30.

9. Watt, in *Critical Quarterly*, vol. 2, 138–9.

10. Watt notes (ibid., p. 141) that this and a number of other phrases are taken from *Hamlet*.

11. Ibid., p. 145.

12. For a discussion of the circumstances of composition and publication, see Lawrence Graver's 'Conrad's First Story', *Studies in Short Fiction*, vol. 2 (Winter 1965), pp. 164–9.

13. The book's original English title was *Some Reminiscences*. See Karl, *Conrad: The Three Lives*, p. 771n.

14. The story is based upon Conrad's childhood encounter with an uncle, Prince Roman Sanguszko (see ibid., p. 69).

15. Karl writes, 'the war meant for the historically oriented Conrad the kind of anarchic action in which everything he believed was disrupted, stained, or destroyed. . . . Europe had become the arena of savages, in which one hoped that one's own savages would prevail' (ibid., pp. 763–4). 'The Tale', I think, demonstrates the validity of this observation.

7 'An air of expectant life': The significance and continuity of *The Rescue*

I

Writing *The Rescue* (1920) was Conrad's most difficult task as an author. Between 1896 and 1899, he worked on *The Rescue* intermittently before abandoning it in the middle of what is now part IV, after Edith Travers arrives on Lingard's brig. At one point he went eight days and produced one page:

> To be able to think and unable to express is a fine torture. I am undergoing it—without patience. . . . Other writers have some starting point. Something to catch hold of. . . . They lean on dialect—or on tradition—or on history—or on the prejudice or fad of the hour; they trade upon some tie or some conviction of their time—or upon the absence of these things. . . . I have had some impressions, some sensations—in my time;—impressions and sensations of common things.
>
> (19 June 1896, *LL*, i, p. 192)

Conrad's complaint that his past does not provide a resource as it does for other writers shows his self-consciousness about writing in a foreign language for an audience whose history and culture he does not understand. In a prior letter to Garnett he had written, 'I had some hazy idea that in the first part I would present to the reader the impression of the sea—the ship—the seamen. But I doubt having conveyed anything but the picture of my own folly' (10 June 1896, *Garnett*, p. 58). His wish to write a sea novel is finally fulfilled when he turns from Lingard to the *Narcissus* for his subject.

The letters to Garnett are most revealing. By 1898 he equates *The*

Rescue with despondency and failure: 'This is a free evening before I go into harness again to pull out of the mire, out of the slough of despond that damned and muddy romance' (2 Feb 1898, *Garnett*, p. 130). That Conrad speaks of a romance in 1898 hardly supports the idea of a radical generic shift from novel to romance in his later fiction. In fact, *The Rescue*, which was completed in 1918–19, argues for the continuity of Conrad's imagination.[1] Notwithstanding the inevitable need to complement something already written, we should expect to see more fundamental differences between the two parts if Conrad's conception of his fiction had changed. In those letters mentioning *The Rescue* he is likely to be at his most morbid and gloomy:

> I see how ill, mentally, I have been these last four months. The fear of this horror coming back to me makes me shiver. As it is it has destroyed already the little belief in myself I used to have. I am appalled at the absurdity of my situation—at the folly of my hopes, at the blindness that had kept me up in my gropings. Most appalled to feel that all the doors behind me are shut and that I must remain where I have come blundering in the dark. (Aug 1898, *Garnett*, p. 142).

The last sentence refers perhaps to his having committed himself to a writing career and to a book he cannot write. In another letter to Garnett during the same month he had written, 'I am writing hopelessly. . . . I feel suicidal' (3 Aug 1898, *Garnett*, p. 141).

His letters show that the revival of his friendship with Garnett accompanied the completion of *The Rescue* in 1918–19: 'It was a great and comforting experience to have your ever trusted and uncompromising soul come forward again from the unforgotten past and look closely at my work with the old, old, wonderful insight, with unimpaired wisdom and in unalterable friendship' (22 Dec 1918, *Garnett*, pp. 259–60). Completing *The Rescue* is a testimony to the ties with Garnett, ties which may well have been the catalyst for finishing the novel: 'Such friendship gives to one's life a sense of continuity, keeps off that dreadful suspicion of futility which dogs our footsteps and as we grow older treads on our very heels. It was a most unexpected experience and it—nothing else—makes *The Rescue* memorable to me' (16 Nov 1919, *Garnett*, p. 266). In a real sense, *The Rescue* was the rescue of their friendship, because discussion of his work once again provided a situation which required Garnett's

advice, approval and emotional support. Even more than with his
other alter egos—Ford, Pinker, Sanderson and Cunninghame-
Graham, such situations were the basis of Conrad's correspondance
and friendship with Garnett.

Although the 1894–1904 period was among the most remarkable
decades any writer ever had, Conrad regarded himself as a failure
because he was unable to complete *The Rescue*, which was begun as
The Rescuer in 1896 and changed to its present title in 1897. Yet his
sense of inadequacy owing to not succeeding on *The Rescue* created
the necessity of writing, and he sought relief from his frustrations by
turning to other works. His remarkable production during the
1896–1904 period derived from his obsession with productivity in
the face of the self-accusation of sloth. Paradoxically, not being able
to complete *The Rescue* was pivotal in his career and intensified his
motivation to write. After his uncle Thaddeus Bobrowski died in
early 1894, he seems to have internalised his uncle's work ethic; in the
letters, Conrad judges his writing career by the standards of diligence,
order, self-discipline and efficiency that his uncle had preached.
Writing in the 1920 Author's Note, he reveals not only the
persistence of the work ethic in his psyche, but also the catalytic
function that the inability to work on *The Rescue* played in his career:

> I dropped the 'Rescue', not to give myself up to idleness,
> regrets, or dreaming, but to begin 'The Nigger of the "Narcissus" '
> and to go on with it without hesitation and without a pause. A
> comparison of any page of 'The Rescue' with any page of the
> 'The Nigger' will furnish an ocular demonstration of the
> nature and the inward meaning of this first crisis of my writing
> life. For it was a crisis undoubtedly. The laying aside of a work
> so far advanced was a very awful decision to take. It was
> wrung from me by a sudden conviction that *there* only was the
> road to salvation, the clear way out for an uneasy conscience.
> The finishing of 'The Nigger' brought to my troubled mind
> the comforting sense of an accomplished task, and the first
> consciousness of a certain sort of mastery which could
> accomplish something with the aid of propitious stars,   (p. ix)

I have argued that Conrad wrote to define himself, because as an exile,
an orphan and an ambitious seaman he felt unfulfilled.[2] It is not
surprising, if we understand that writing was an act of defining his
identity in a foreign country, that frustration and disappointment

intensified both his desire and his need to write. Conrad's frustrations with *The Rescue* are reflected in his preoccupation with the efficacy of language and the problem of communication in 'Heart of Darkness', which he wrote during one of his respites from *The Rescue*. In the month prior to beginning that work he had written to Ford, another of the secret sharers upon whom he depended,

> I get on dreamily with *The Rescue*, dreamily dreaming how fine it could be if the thought did not escape—if the expression did not hide underground, if the idea had a substance and words a magic power, if the invisible could be snared into a shape. And it is sad to think that even if all this time came to pass—even then it could never be so fine to anybody as it is fine to me now, lurking in the blank pages in an intensity of existence without voice, without form—but without blemish.   (Nov 1898)[3]

According to this letter he had two related but distinct problems: (1) the elusiveness of ideas and concepts to the organising power of the mind; (2) the difficulty of finding the exact expression, a process far more difficult in a language other than the one in which he learned to think and perceive. The original title, 'The Rescuer' has its narcissistic implications, because on one level Conrad, exile, orphan, unemployed seaman, rescues his own identity, and on the other, by the act of writing, he is the rescuer of an English version of the evanescent impressions within his mind at a time when he had committed himself to settling in England. With bitter irony he spoke of the need to rescue himself from the novel he was writing; he spoke of the novel as a 'monster' stalking its prey—its creator.[4] The relationships between language and impressions, between perceptions and ideas, are quite different in an adopted language from those in a language one has known since infancy. Conrad knew that his writing was inevitably different in style and tonality from what it would have been in Polish. It is this knowledge that gives depth to what seems at first a glib remark about why he wrote in English: 'It was I who was adopted by the genius of the language, which directly I came out of the stammering stage made me its own so completely that its very idioms I truly believe had a direct action on my temperament and fashioned my still plastic character' (*A Personal Record*, p. vii).

His self-conscious preoccupation with finding the right word, his quest for precise tonality, resembles a composer's search for the right note. He does not use his adopted language instinctively. He is fascinated with finding the right combinations of words as if words were colours and he were a Fauvist painter. His quest for precision and control takes the form of his thinking of words as if they were objects that must be controlled, mastered and, yes, rescued:

> Words blow away like mist, and like mist they serve only to obscure, to make vague the real shape of one's feelings. . . . Were I to write and talk till Doomsday you would never really know what it all means to me. You would not know because you never had just the same experience. . . . Enough words. The postman will carry away this letter, the mist shall blow away and in the morning I shall discern clearly what tonight I am trying to interpret into writing—which remains. Let it remain, to show with what thundering kick the gods of life shut the door between our feeling and its expression. It is the old tale, the eternal grievance. If it were not for the illusion of the open door—sometimes—we would all be dumb, and it wouldn't matter, for no one would care to listen.   (18 Oct 1898)[5]

The notion of a door separating feeling and expression reflects the ratiocinative process by which Conrad converts perception into meaning, a process which is characteristic of one struggling with an adopted language. (According to Baines, Conrad undoubtedly spoke with a 'strong foreign accent throughout his life'.[6]) In the Author's Note to *The Rescue*, he spoke as if his failure to discover the apt word, to open the door between feeling and expression, was his reason for not completing the novel: 'The contents and the course of the story I had clearly in mind. . . . What I had lost for the moment was the sense of a proper formula of expression, the only formula that would suit. . . . I suspect that all the trouble was, in reality, the doubt of my prose, the doubt of its adequacy, of its power to master both the colours and the shades' (pp. viii–ix).

When he describes how he finally completed the novel, about which he had been worrying intermittently since 1899, it was as if he were seeing an adventure through to its completion. 'I am settling my affairs in this world and I should not have liked to leave behind me this evidence of having bitten off more than I could chew. A very vulgar vanity' (7 July 1919, *Garnett*, p. 263). In the Author's Note, which deliberately forges a link between himself and his subject, Conrad refers twice to the completion of *The Rescue* as an adventure and once to the author as an adventurer. He regarded *The Rescue* in terms of a ship that had never sailed, or, alternatively, as if it were an abandoned ship to which he finally returned in fulfilment of an ethical obligation. He in a sense rescues his novel by completing it; thus the title refers not only to Lingard's rescue of the white people and of Hassim and his sister, as well as their prior rescue of him, but of Conrad's rescue of a text that had drifted from his control. He defines his return to the long-abandoned novel in terms that could apply to Lingard's approach to the yacht within the narrative. In describing how as author he carried out his responsibilities, Conrad deliberately contrasts his behaviour with Jim's when the *Patna* collided with the derelict and he abandoned ship. He describes how he dutifully returned to the novel and reinvigorated its life: 'As I moved slowly towards the abandoned body of the tale it loomed up big amongst the glittering shallows of the coast, lonely but not forbidding. There was nothing about it of a grim derelict. It had an air of expectant life. . . . At once without wasting words, we went to work together on our renewed life' (p. x).[7] Describing the act of writing in terms of a rescue is both particularly appropriate to this novel and characteristic of Conrad's perceiving his writing in terms of his sea experience. Conrad is substituting two figures for Jim as the prototype of the imaginative man: Lingard, the morally responsible man of action who lives in a romance world of his own creation, and himself, the author who fulfils his commitments. Jim represented to Conrad his concern in 1899 about the vulnerability of the imaginative man. But, in the 1920 Author's Note, Conrad qualifies that view; he uses his finishing *The Rescue* as a striking example of the moral and the artistic integrity of the imaginative man.

II

The real question is whether the despair that Conrad experienced when writing *The Rescue* is related to something within the subject. Is there something in the nature of the plot or characterisation which impeded his progress and caused him to abandon the novel in 1899? I suspect that it is the character of Lingard. In his letters on the novel, the character of Lingard recurs, often in association with exclamations of despair: 'As to the "lyrism" in connection with Lingard's heart. That's necessary! The man must be episodically foolish to explain his action. . . . And every day *The Rescuer* crawls a page forward. . . . I have long fits of depression, that in a lunatic asylum would be called madness, I do not know what it is' (2 June 1896, *Garnett*, pp. 55 – 6).

The Rescue was to be the story of Tom Lingard, the heroic figure that lurked in the background of the earlier Malay novels, *Almayer's Folly* and *An Outcast of the Islands*. *The Rescue* takes place before *Almayer's Folly* and *An Outcast* and focuses on a younger Lingard. Yet he never is able to bring into really sharp focus that shadowy character, whose ethics and personality are irrelevant to the world in which Conrad writes and who would be judged immoral by his readers. Conrad himself is baffled by Lingard as a dramatic character and cannot get hold of him. Moser has shown how in the original manuscript Lingard is more of a romantic egoist than in the final text: 'Through certain crucial cuts from the original manuscript, the later Conrad obscures the most interesting facts of Lingard's psychology; the subtle difference between himself and other seamen; his egoistic longings for power; his lack of self-knowledge; his moral isolation.'[8] But, while those weaknesses fascinate Conrad throughout his career, he required in this novel an idealised character. Two Lingards, the flawed one and the idealised one, compete for his attention. It may be that his inability to resolve these competing versions of Lingard stalled him.[9] Certainly, a vestige of the Lingard that Moser described reappears in the final version; an analogy would be the phenomenon of pentimento in painting, where remnants of earlier, painted-over versions reappear.

Because as the consummate man of action Lingard embodies a heroic fantasy self that seemed an actual alternative to the agonies of his writing career, Conrad had difficulty achieving the necessary distance and control when writing about him. Lingard's obsession with his brig reflects Conrad's nostalgia for the life he has put behind him: 'If I lost her I would have no standing room on the earth for my feet' (p. 229). That Lingard must choose between loyalty to the Malay world (Hassim and Immada and their goals) and to the home world (Mrs Travers) reflects Conrad's divided allegiance between the world of adventure he has left behind and the English world in which he found himself writing of his past. When Lingard, the man in total communion with his ship, rescues the yacht, the ironic emblem of the leisured class, which Conrad had turned his back upon when he had left Poland and which he resented in his adopted country, he mimes Conrád's fantasy that he will rescue Polish civilisation, which he has deserted. As we shall see, this fantasy of rescuing a nation is essential to *The Rover* (1923).

Changing the title from *The Rescuer* to *The Rescue* in 1897 may have been an effort to free himself from bondage to his subject. He might have seen that the emphasis on the protagonist as the title figure made it all the more difficult to achieve the objectivity he required. Years later, he writes about *The Rescue* in tones of anxiety and ennui: 'I only wish I could absorb myself utterly, forget myself in it—but this is impossible. I have neither the power of detachment nor yet that intensity of belief in my work which perhaps would have made it possible' (8 June 1916, *LL*, ii, p. 172). One problem with the published novel is the uncontrolled fluctuations of distance between the narrator and Lingard. Lingard is at times a naïve romantic hero unaware of the complexities of life. Yet at other times he is Conrad's double. Conrad is torn between identifying with the heroic *Übermensch* of the pastoral maritime world and undermining his romantic ego with his ironic omniscient narrator.

In spite of himself, Conrad identified with Lingard because Lingard is the past self who represents a simple, comprehensible mode of existence. In 1896–9, the more that he feels the stress of writing and the more his present life frustrates him, the more Lingard becomes a figure with whom he identifies and *the more difficult the task of writing becomes*. Because he had received advances, the task became more excruciating to his fastidious conscience. While writing *The Rescue* he speaks not simply of escaping to sea but of commanding a ship, although there is no evidence he had the opportunity to do the latter: 'Half the book is not written and I have only to 1st Nov. to finish it. I could not take a command till December because I am in honour bound to furnish the story to time. Yet to go to sea would be salvation. I am really in a deplorable state, mentally. I feel utterly wretched. I haven't the courage to tackle my work' (26 Aug 1898, *LL*, i, p. 246). By contrast, Lingard, Conrad's imaginary self, has complete autonomy on board the brig and complete freedom from mundane responsibilities. The issues Lingard must face are not the pedestrian day-to-day activities of earning a living, worrying about family health, or getting along with a wife, the concerns that occupied Conrad; Lingard confronts issues that require courage, passion and boldness.

The Rescue has two coterminous imagined worlds: one is a conventional world dominated by the petty political machinations of the natives and including Travers and d'Alcacer; the other is a romance world, dominated by Lingard, into which only Edith Travers and at times Immada and Hassim enter. Ironically, this great adventurer is concerned with measuring himself by standards and conventions that are irrelevant to the kind of life he has chosen. Lingard's faith in himself and his self-concept are in the process of being undermined. Lingard, for all his renunciation of the home world, can no more divorce himself from it than Jim. In Edith's presence, he judges himself according to standards that are valid in Edith Travers's social world, standards that he has ostensibly rejected: 'And I know what a gentleman would do. Come! Wouldn't he treat a stranger fairly? Wouldn't he remember that no man is a liar till you prove him so?' (p. 164). Unlike Kurtz, Lingard cannot free himself from the home values; even though his only memories of that world are 'poverty, hard work—and death', he reminds Hassim that he is racially sympathetic to whites whom he considers 'my people, forever' (p. 218). Lingard's commitment to the world he has left behind reflects Conrad's own refusal to acknowledge that he had permanently put behind him Poland and the sea.

Whatever the original intent, the novel shows Lingard's transformation from naïve romantic to Conradian sceptic, and this transformation begins in the 1896–9 version. Lingard is defined at the outset as a man lacking in self-consciousness: 'Like most of his class, [Lingard] was dead to the subtle voices, and blind to the mysterious aspects of the world—the man ready for the obvious, no matter how startling, how terrible or menacing, yet defenceless as a child before the shadowy impulses of his own heart; what could have been the thoughts of such a man, when once surrendered to a dreamy mood, it is difficult to say' (p. 11). But soon the man described as 'unconscious of everything and everybody' is torn between his ties to Hassim, the native who has rescued him, and the opposing ties to Edith Travers, who has captivated him (p. 127). For the first time, he feels a conflict within himself: 'He had to face unsuspected powers, foes that he could not go out and meet at the gate. They were within, as though he had been betrayed by somebody, by some secret enemy. He was ready to look round for the subtle traitor. A sort of blankness fell on his mind and he suddenly thought: "Why! It's myself"' (p. 329). He realises that he has internalised the crucial personae of his life and turned them into a function of his own dreams: 'O, yes [Hassim and Immada

existed]—within his breast!' (p. 329). The demands of two or more
moral commitments pulling one's consciousness in separate directions
are central to Conrad's fiction. If one thinks of the three Malay novels
as a trilogy, then Lingard's *moral energy* stands in stark contrast to that
of Almayer and Willems. The potential Kurtz or Jim virtually
disappears in the later half which was written in 1918 – 19.

In fact, *The Rescue* continues the emphasis both of the earlier Malay
novels and much later work on personal and family relationships.
(Scepticism about political activities, we recall, was crucial to the
political novels.) Unlike Jim and Kurtz, Lingard is defined by human
ties. Lingard regards Immada and Hassim 'like his children'; he loves
Immada 'like my own daughter' (pp. 330, 158). But Lingard is
constantly seeking family ties that he lacks. In *Almayer's Folly* and *An
Outcast of the Islands*, Conrad had shown that an older Lingard adopts
Almayer's wife as a surrogate daughter and Willems as a surrogate
son. In *The Rescue* Lingard, like Heyst and Captain Anthony, is
another of Conrad's humanists, men who in the guise of adventurers
respond to traditional values and commitments. Touched that his life
had been spared by Hassim, he commits himself to Hassim's political
fantasies.

The novel traces a reduction in Lingard's stature and a necessary
adjustment in his self-image. What enabled Conrad to complete the
novel is that he no longer needed to identify with Lingard and could
move to the objectivity that he required. Earlier, Lingard was so
inextricably bound to Conrad's psyche that he was invulnerable to
either irony or criticism. Lingard, no less than Nostromo, is born into
a morally complex world, represented at the outset by the narrator's
worldly scepticism, irony and regret: 'A new power had come into
the world, had possessed itself of human speech, had imparted to it a
sinister irony of allusion' (p. 210). That power is not simply Edith,
nor even the moral confusion engendered by his conflicting responsibilities; it is also the awareness within himself that he has
relative rather than absolute power over himself and his world. In
fact, when he learns of Carter's aggression against the natives, which
breaks his compact with Daman, he thinks that 'the world [was]
coming down about his ears' (p. 328). Still something of a romantic
egoist, Lingard regards his world as a metonymy for the world
'which had lost its consistency, its shape and its promises in a moment'
(ibid.). But Lingard also knows that the disaster 'was in himself, too,
somewhere in the unexplained depths of its nature, something fatal
and unavoidable' (p. 329). Lingard ceases to be King Tom when his

passions respond to Edith Travers. In the stockade her intimate presence provides a necessary relaxation from the stance of invulnerability and omniscience on which his reputation depends. His response belies the myth of invulnerability in which he comes to believe. The rest of the novel is a working out of his changed perspective. In the later pages, Conrad emphasises Lingard's fall from innocence by comparing him with Adam: 'He was in the state of a man who, having cast his eyes through the open gates of Paradise, is rendered insensible by that moment's vision to all the forms and matters of the earth; and in the extremity of his emotion ceases even to look upon himself but as the subject of a sublime experience which exalts or unfits, sanctifies or damns—he didn't know which' (p. 415).

Conrad uses an aesthetic perspective, which includes the references to *Genesis* quoted in the previous paragraph, to distance and control Lingard. This perspective also emphasises the distance between the worlds of Lingard and Mrs Travers. She perceives him in aesthetic terms befitting her education: 'This was no stage play; and yet she had caught herself looking at him with bated breath as a great actor on a darkened stage in some simple and tremendous drama' (p. 282). Later, as Lingard and Daman exchange parting words, she 'had the sensation of acting in a gorgeously got up play on the brilliantly lighted stage of an exotic opera whose accompaniment was not music but the varied strains of the all-pervading silence' (p. 295). She regards her prior life as a sham, and in native costume thinks of her European past as a disguise and her life as part of a show. Civilised life is implicitly shown to be less real than the artifices of stage and opera: 'Civilization . . . offered to one a certain refinement of form, a comeliness of proceedings and definite safeguards against deadly surprises' (p. 408). The references to theatre and opera may also be an effort to place the love between Lingard and Edith Travers in a romance setting. But, these references arrest the linear movement of the narrative and contribute to an 1890s atmosphere of overripe mannerism and precious aestheticism. These images, which recall those of *The Arrow of Gold*, far more frequently occur in the sections written to complete the novel.

Within *The Rescue* man can neither shape his destiny nor break out of the social roles in which he is cast. The various kinds of captivity become images for self-captivity; each man and woman acts idiosyncratically and compulsively because of his or her own hopes and fears, his or her anxieties and doubts. What temporarily sets Edith

Travers and Tom Lingard apart is the strength of their characters,
which enables them to act on impulses and passions and to respond to
new phenomena. Like Captain Anthony and Heyst, Lingard becomes
a captive of his passions. The natives' suspicions that he is a 'willing
captive in Belarab's stockage' and the 'slave of these strange white
people' are not inappropriate (p. 445). The stockade which encloses
him and Mrs Travers suggests a parallel to the 'cage' which encloses
the other European prisoners; 'like captives of an enchanted cobweb,
[Travers and d'Alcacer] moved about, sat, gesticulated, conversed
publicly during the day' (p. 278). Do not the stockade and cage
suggest traditions and conventions that inhibit passion and spon-
taneity? Yet, because to her the world is a prison, Mrs Travers wishes
to escape it and be 'shut off from the world alone with Lingard as if
within the four walls of a romantic palace and in an exotic
atmosphere' (p. 283). Travers, like every other character, including
Lingard, is the captive of his personality and past. Like the
imprisonment of Jim after he has arrived in Patusan, the imprisonment of Travers and d'Alcacer demonstrates the limiting nature of
man's control over his life. In a sense, Conrad himself was the prisoner
of the novel he could not complete. We might recall Conrad's
preoccupation with expressions suggesting the imprisonment of
language in his letters about *The Rescue*.

Because the novel revolves around his dominant personality, in a
sense every character is a function of Lingard. While parallels
between differing men suggest man's common humanity, some of
the doubling depends on superficial resemblances and lacks psychological subtlety. At times, virtually every character is presented as
an externalisation of an aspect of Lingard. Although the parallel
between Lingard and Jörgenson is suggested in Part I, the parallel is
more prominent in the half written later. Jörgenson is an obvious
double. He is the man Lingard might become; 'I was like you—once',
he tells Lingard (p. 100). Jörgenson knows that the natives 'had a hold
and a claim on King Tom just as many years ago people of that race
had had a hold and a claim on him' (p. 388). At some level, he regards
Lingard as a surrogate son. He wants Tom to reiterate and thus
authenticate his fate by being 'absorbed, captured, made [the native's]
own either in failure or in success' (p. 388). Yet Jörgenson,
compulsively locked in his past, is a grim wraith that Lingard must
reject if he is to grow (just as Conrad knew he must reject the example
of his father, Apollo). But there are other potential doubles. When
Lingard thinks of Jaffir's body, he had 'a distant conviction . . . an

almost physical certitude, that under the cotton sheet shrouding the dead man something, too, had left the ship' (p. 454). Lingard understands that Carter is a younger version of himself. And even Travers's lassitude parallels Lingard's, once the latter is under the influence of passion. The narrator proposes other putative doubles, but, because these relationships are not developed by either action or analysis, they remain merely surface parallels. D'Alcacer and Jörgenson, both spectators in the worlds they inhabit, are 'much of the same build' and can wear the same clothes (p. 279). In a sense, d'Alcacer is as detached from the life of men as Jörgenson.

Despite these superficial resemblances to others, Lingard, like his creator, has been an outsider. Of the people on the yacht he says, 'Home's the place for them. Not for me' (p. 178). He has rescued himself from poverty and anonymity by courage and boldness: 'I *am* an adventurer . . . and if I hadn't been an adventurer, I would have had to starve or work at home for such people as you' (p. 134, Conrad's emphasis). Lingard's class antagonism may derive from Conrad's uncertain status in England as an exile. The gulf that divides Lingard from the yacht people is a social one. He believes he has been insulted because he 'didn't look enough like a gentleman' (p. 164).

The only plausible secret sharers are Edith and Lingard, and even here Conrad does not give breadth and subtlety to their psychological dependence on one another. Despite their class differences, Edith and Lingard feel an immediate rapport; in Lingard's presence Edith says to Carter, 'I do know him. . . . There is not, I verily believe, a single thought or act of his life that I don't know' (p. 236). As in 'The Secret Sharer' each seeks 'understanding' from the other, and both believe that the other provides the responsive consciousness that each desperately seeks. While it is doubtful that Edith perceives the actual situation when he wins her husband's release, he says, 'You understand everything'; Mrs Travers and Lingard look 'as if they had been made for each other' (p. 310). Their relationship fulfils each other's needs. When she encourages him to give back the prisoner, he idealises her conduct: 'Where was there another woman in the world who would have taken it like this?' (p. 340). Yet one could argue that they are bound together by a common misunderstanding derived from their irrational needs to compensate for what their lives lack. Both are adrift from their emotional and psychic moorings: 'In a few hours of life she had been torn away from all her certitudes, flung into a world of improbabilities' (p. 244). They both live in the illusion that a friendship and mutual concern for others binds them, even while an intense sexual attraction is developing. Both provide the other with a passage to kinds of experience from which they were cut off.

Quite accurately, Travers accuses Edith of having the same kind of scorn for her social sphere that Lingard has, and even accuses her of having the impulses of an 'adventurer and a primitive'. Edith wants to strip herself of the layers of acculturation which she believes inhibits her real self. In Lingard she sees a man who is not polluted by these layers. *The Rescue* discredits the life epitomised by Travers. *The Rescue* continues the satire of European civilisation and sustains the point made in both prior Malay novels that primitive and so-called civilised men are not fundamentally different. Despite European pretensions, motives do not differ much, as Mrs Travers understands when she responds to Travers's request for an explanation of his capture: 'Matters of high policy and of local politics. Conflict of personal interests, mistrust between the parties, intrigues of individuals' (p. 273).

In Lingard's presence, Mrs Travers discovers a self that had almost been obliterated by the conventions of so-called civilised society, and her personality expands 'to its full significance'. Mrs Travers feels a kinship with Immada, whom she thinks of as her 'humble and obscure sister': 'She glowed with a sudden persuasion that she also could be equal to such an existence; and her heart was dilated with a momentary longing to know the naked truth of things. The naked truth of life and passion buried under the growth of centuries' (p. 153). That she wears Immada's clothes and feels comfortable in them underlines Conrad's contention that only customs and ceremonies separate the two apparently different women. Mrs Travers is Conrad's objectification of a person who turns her back on what the world considers success and opts for passion, instinct and real feeling. But, finally, she lacks the courage to pursue her own psychological needs—as in fact Conrad may have felt about himself when he concluded *The Rescue* on a conventional note and eschewed the Ibsen ending of a lasting adulterous relationship between two adults of different social classes.

III

The Rescue is preoccupied with the effects of words. Given Conrad's difficulty in writing the novel, it is not surprising that it became the grounds for a dialectical struggle between his doubts about the efficacy of language and his hope that he could impose a verbal shape on his imaginings. In 1896–9 he used the text to rescue his own writing and personality from chaos. In the published novel, historical and political turmoil becomes a metaphor for his own chaotic relationship with the text, as well as for the unacknowledged and dimly understood areas of human consciousness represented by the passion between Lingard and Mrs Travers and by Lingard's and Hassim's mutually self-destructive commitment. *The Rescue's* recurrent discussions about language derive from Conrad's identification with Lingard as an expatriate trying to make a new life in a remote setting. His efforts to order the native world parallel Conrad's efforts to control his text and Conrad's preoccupation with the written word. Thus, the primitive, seemingly chaotic setting on which Conrad is struggling to impose his vision resists language: 'The night effaced even words, and its mystery had captured everything and every sound—had left nothing free but the unexpected that seemed to hover about one, ready to stretch out its stealthy hand in a touch sudden, familiar and appalling' (p. 42). That, within the final text, words struggle for independence reflects Conrad's self-doubt and mimes the conflict within his mind. Had he not spoken of words as mist that obscures experience? Yet Lingard within the novel does speak effectively, does open the door that divides feelings from expression. Lingard dramatises that meaning can be rescued from underground.

Lingard is not only Conrad's prototypical seaman, but also, like his creator, a man who, after overcoming difficulty in expressing himself, uses his words as powerful instruments to affect others and ultimately as the means of defining his identity: 'Of necessity he was not one of those men who have the mastery of expression. To liberate his soul was for him a gigantic undertaking, a matter of desperate effort, of doubtful success' (p. 211). For a time Lingard is a kind of Prospero figure, a magician—artist who can control the world in which he lives. Jaffir regards him as a 'providential man' sent by heaven.

Lingard—albeit temporarily, for finally he too fails—is able to write his significance on this world, and it is in this sense that he is Conrad's surrogate and that completing *The Rescue* is a triumph. Lingard's appeal to Mrs Travers in part derives from her fascination with his 'simplicity of images and expressions', in contrast to 'the fragments of official verbiage' with which Travers speaks (pp. 147, 157). When he tells her his tale, he 'liberate[s] the visions of two years into the night

where Mrs. Travers could follow them as if outlined in words of fire'
(p. 161). As a teller he makes her *see*. His experience becomes hers; he
is the 'narrator' whose tale affects Mrs Travers:

> The story appealed to the audacity of her thoughts, and she
> became so charmed with what she heard that she forgot where
> she was. She forgot that she was personally close to that tale
> which she saw detached, far away from her, truth or fiction,
> presented in picturesque speech, real only by the response of
> her emotion. . . . She heard him pronounce several names;
> Belarab, Daman, Tengga, Ningrat. These belonged now to her
> life and she was appalled to find she was unable to connect
> these names with any human appearance. They stood out
> alone, as if written on the night; they took on a symbolic
> shape; they imposed themselves upon her senses.   (p. 163)

That Lingard wears the masque of an artist in the 1896–9 section
shows that, if he is the man of action that Conrad had left behind, he
was also the man of language that he sought to become.

When Conrad returned to the novel in his later years, he became
even more fascinated by Lingard's powers with words.
Rediscovering Lingard as a prototype of the artist—indeed, of the
artist as an heroic figure—enabled him to complete the novel. He has
sympathy with the powerful seaman who was also a master of
language. When Lingard does speak to Edith Travers, he communicates effectively to the point of captivating her: 'The power of
his speech' gets the release of Travers and d'Alcacer (p. 296). Like
Kurtz, Lingard's gift is his voice, which is 'his very own self: He
persuaded, he moved, he disturbed, he soothed by his inherent truth'
(p. 417).

It is striking that even the section completed in 1918–19 reflects
the pessimistic tone of the early letters that Conrad wrote concerning
it and the frustration he had writing it. Returning to the novel
apparently revived those feelings. Reflecting Conrad's mood while
writing *The Rescue*, the narrator presents the imagined world in a
shroud of gloom. For example, as the natives stand on deck while
Carter and Shaw quarrel, the narrator notes, 'There was not a star in
the sky and no gleam on the water; there was no horizon, no outline,
no shape for the eye to rest upon, nothing for the hand to grasp. An
obscurity that seemed without limit in space and time had submerged
the universe like a destroying flood' (p. 241). Similes imply the

threatening nature of a cosmos that embodies a nightmare of violent destruction. The intense reds and purples alternating with black punctuate the texture of the novel: 'A trail of purple, like a smear of blood on a blue shield, lay over the sea' (p. 146); or, 'a vestige of the sun remained, far off, like a red spark floating on the water. It lingered, and all at once—without warning—went out as if extinguished by a treacherous hand' (p. 14). Darkness and shadows dominate Mrs Travers's apocalyptic hallucination:

> She saw herself standing alone, at the end of time, on the brink of days. All was unmoving as if the dawn would never come, the stars would never fade, the sun would never rise any more; all was mute, still, dead—as if the shadow of the outer darkness, the shadow of the uninterrupted, of the everlasting night that fills the universe, the shadow of the night so profound and so vast that the blazing suns lost in it are only like sparks, like pin-points of fire, the restless shadow that like a suspicion of an evil truth darkens everything upon the earth on its passage, had enveloped her, had stood arrested as if to remain with her forever. . . . When she murmured into the darkness a faint 'so be it' she seemed to have spoken one of those sentences that resume and close a life.   (p. 151)

The obscurity reflects Conrad's blurred sense of direction and paralysed sense of purpose; recall the 1898 letter I quoted earlier, in which he spoke of 'blundering in the dark'. Mrs Travers's fear of infinite physical and moral darkness reflects, as does her stoic acceptance of it, Conrad's own attitudes. Because Lingard's mind is resistant to such thoughts until he gradually awakens to the complexity of his situation, Mrs Travers's sensibility, along with the narrator's, becomes the outlet for the melancholy and gloom expressed in Conrad's letters.

The Rescue is pervaded by such intrusions of darkness, which are not only physical facts but also moral and metaphysical ones in the world of *The Rescue*. Frequently, as in the above passage, darkness seems to enclose, reduce and subsume speech into its vast nothingness. The darkness is progressive and dynamic and becomes a metaphor for Lingard's moral confusion as well as for the political chaos on the islands. Even as darkness represents Lingard's doubt and anxiety, it reflects Conrad's own. Once Lingard departs from the brig, Hassim and Immada 'entered the same darkness which had received, enveloped and hidden the troubled souls of Lingard and Edith' (p. 240).

The reader expects that the possibilities of love, political stability and communication will not be fulfilled. As they leave the brig, Edith and Lingard hear a dog's prophetic bark, which 'rent the black stillness, as though the instinct of the brute inspired by the soul of night had voiced in a lamentable plaint the fear of the future, the anguish of lurking death, the terror of shadows' (p. 241). Cumulatively these images penetrate the reader's consciousness and make the outcome of the plot almost a superfluity. Darkness becomes an ironic comment upon the possibility of meaning and a kind of ultimate argument for silence. In no other work, including 'Heart of Darkness', does Conrad depend so much upon the texture rather than plot and characterisation to carry the meaning, but the iteration of the darkness and language motifs becomes tedious in a novel of *The Rescue*'s length. The above passage is one of many in which characters are revealed alone stripped of their illusions and aware that the universe is hostile to their aspirations.

But there is another, more positive, aspect of darkness. In the crucial scene with Lingard in the small boat, Edith lapses from her conscious daytime self:

> And all this—the wan burst of light, the faint shock as of something remote and immense falling into ruins, was taking place outside the limits of her life which remained encircled by an impenetrable darkness and by an impenetrable silence. . . . The darkness enfolded her like the enervating caress of a sombre universe. It was gentle and destructive. Its languor seduced her soul into surrender. Nothing existed and even all her memories vanished into space. She was content that nothing should exist.   (p. 244)

As if she were a Lawrence character, Edith Travers welcomes the darkness that releases her from her conscious self and insulates her from awareness of her plight. Her acceptance of darkness parallels the awakening of her instinctive, non-verbal self. The novel contains a dialectic between, on the one hand, darkness as nothingness, moral confusion and obscurity, and, on the other, darkness as a subconscious, passionate potency and atavistic energy with which civilised man has lost touch. Ultimately the former triumphs, but Lingard achieves a kind of stature through his commitment to the latter. For a time, Edith discovers her buried libidinous self, but finally it, too, like Lingard's energy, courage and passion, is irrelevant in a cosmos where distinctions between appearance and reality, and between good and bad, seem blurred by an immense darkness. But darkness as sexual mystery and atavistic energy is displaced by the apocalyptic explosion of *Emma*, the fortress ship: 'All the world was darkened round [Lingard] as if the life of the sun had been blown out of it in a crash'; his mind is 'crowded by the mute images of universal destruction' (pp. 447–8).

That in the final scene Lingard's stature shrinks to human size in Edith's eyes confirms the movement of the plot, which has undermined his pretensions to be an *Übermensch*:

> The world resembled a limitless flat shadow which was motionless and elusive. Then against the southern stars [Edith] saw a human form that isolated and lone appeared to her immense: the shape of a giant outlined amongst the constellations. As it approached her it shrank to common proportions, got clear of the stars, lost its awesomeness, and became menacing in its ominous and silent advance.   (p. 463)

At the end he realises that, despite his despair, he does have his memory of her: 'I see now that as long as I live you will never die' (p. 465). His refusal to blame her vindicates him in Conrad's eyes; Conrad admires his generous and tender response to another's feelings, the stoical control when a lesser man would give vent to resentment. Her last view of him, in a foetal position next to Jaffir's grave (also a symbolic grave for the primitive self that Lingard must leave forever behind), underlines his innocence and defencelessness. (One thinks of Bloom in *Ulysses* at rest after he has returned home in 'Ithaca'.) By facing the consequences of his actions, and by judging himself, Lingard has a moral stature that he previously lacked and that none of Conrad's prior heroes achieves. It is the kind of muted victory that Conrad achieved when he finished writing the flawed novel—a victory of perseverance, an existential triumph in the face of trying circumstances and recognition of personal fallibility.

NOTES

1. Dismissing Conrad's claim, in a letter dated 2 October 1918, that the novel

showed 'modifications of my judgment, of my taste, and also of my style during the 20 years covering almost the whole writing period of my life', Karl writes, 'On the contrary, he returned to his early style, and his work on *The Rescue* is homogeneous' (*Conrad: The Three Lines* [New York: Farrar, Straus and Giroux, 1979], p. 816; Karl quotes Conrad's letter).

2. See Daniel R. Schwarz, *Conrad: 'Almayer's Folly' to 'Under Western Eyes'* (London: Macmillan; Ithaca, NY: Cornell University Press, 1980).

3. Quoted in Baines, *Conrad: A Critical Biography* (New York: McGraw-Hill, 1960), p. 223.

4. See letter of Good Friday 1899, in *Garnett*, p. 153.

5. Pierpont Morgan Library, quoted in Baines, *Conrad: A Critical Biography*, p. 219.

6. Ibid., p.445.

7. Indeed, he describes his reason for not returning sooner in terms that recalls Stein's advice in *Lord Jim*, 'to the destructive element submit yourself': 'Thus every stroke of the pen was taking me further away from the abandoned "Rescue", not without some compunction on my part but with a gradually diminishing resistance; till at last I let myself go, as if recognizing a superior influence against which it was useless to contend' (p. x).

8. Moser, *Conrad: Achievement and Decline* (Cambridge, Mass.: Harvard University Press, 1957), p. 146.

9. In '"The Rescuer" Manuscript: A Key to Conrad's Development—and Decline', *Harvard Library Bulletin*, vol. 10 (1956), pp. 325–55, Moser has argued that 'the yacht people were the rock upon which "The Rescuer" foundered'.

8 *The Arrow of Gold*: The collapse of form

In considering *The Arrow of Gold* (1919), we need to ask why Conrad wrote it and why he failed. One reason he wrote it was that he believed the subject-matter would appeal to a larger audience. As Conrad aged, it became important to him to expand his audience: 'As a matter of feeling—not as a matter of business—I want to be read by many eyes and by all kinds of them, at that' (21 Dec 1918, *LL*, ii, p. 214). But his essential motives for writing *The Arrow of Gold* were to recapture the intense emotions of his youth and to affirm his belief in passionate love.

While writing *The Arrow of Gold*, he had little respect for what I believe is his least successful novel: 'No colour, no relief, no tonality; the thinnest possible squeaky bubble' (31 Dec 1917, *LL*, ii, p. 198). Anticipating poor reviews he wrote to Galsworthy, 'Never before was the act of publication so distasteful to me as on this occasion' (8 Aug 1919, *LL*, ii, p. 226). He knew that writing from dictation made it very difficult to achieve the subtle relationship between reader and text on which he prided himself. Yet on some occasions, he took the novel seriously, because it was something of a romantic idyll for the ageing author. Conrad spoke of the novel as a 'portraiture of vanished years, of feelings, that had once their actuating power' (21 Dec 1918, *LL*, ii, p. 214). In a sense the novel is a sequel not only to *A Shadow-Line*, as Palmer has suggested, but also to *A Personal Record* and *The Mirror of the Sea* (Conrad's recollections of his initiation into the sea).[1] In the Author's Note, he defines his subject as 'the quality of initiation (through an ordeal which required some resolution to face) into the life of passion' (p. ix). At times George recalls Conrad's voice in *A Personal Record*: 'My adventurous pursuit kept me in contact with the sea where I found occupation, protection, consolation, the mental relief of grappling with concrete problems, the sanity one acquires

from close contact with simple mankind, a little self-confidence born
from the dealings with the elemental powers of nature' (p. 242).

The Arrow of Gold cannot be separated from Conrad's life. It is the
only novel in which for his principal subject Conrad journeyed back
beyond his career as a British sailor, and it is the one novel that uses as a
major source the period prior to his suicide attempt. Conrad identifies
with George and chooses for the novel's setting Marseilles as he knew
it in the 1870s, when he was George's age. He was called 'Monsieur
Georges' and had contact with both Carlist and Bohemian circles in
Marseilles.[2] Like his narrator, he ran guns for the Carlists and took a
trip to the West Indies. Not only does Conrad write in Richard Curle's
copy of the novel, 'All the persons are authentic, and the facts are as
stated',[3] but he claims that 'Rita . . . is true fundamentally to the
shore connections of that time' (Aug 1919, *LL*, ii, p. 224). George is
not only a younger version of himself, but also a fantasy that enables
him to recapture the energy, passion, irrationality and intemperance
of a time over forty years previous. He says that he could not read
the proofs, because they recalled past memories: 'My dear (as D. Rita
would have said) there are some of these 42-year old episodes of
which I cannot think without a slight tightness of the chest—*un petit
serrement de coeur*' (1919, *LL*, ii, p. 229).[4] In another letter he
reminisces, 'The "Divine Madness" was so strong that I could have
walked into a precipice, deliberately, with my eyes open, for its sake.
And now it seems incredible; and yet it is the same old heart—for
even at that distance of time I can't smile at it' (3 Nov 1919, *LL*, ii,
p. 232). These letters indicate that Conrad's intention was to recol-
lect passionate love rather than accurately to render the details of his
Marseilles period.[5]

A younger self and adventurer baffled by sexuality, George is
Heyst's opposite in age, temperament and behaviour. Both characters
are embodiments of strikingly different aspects of the mature
Conrad, and neither aspect can be understood in isolation from the
other. George is the man of impulse and passion, the man who lives
by his wits and takes part in the political activities of the world. He has
friends, position and seems to function within both the sea and
cosmopolitan worlds. Yet, like Heyst and Captain Anthony, he too is
basically a lonely man who has no religious, political, or philosophic
values to sustain him as he seeks a heterosexual other to complete
himself. Conrad in the mid 1870s was often a man far different from
George. Although at the outset George is inexperienced in love, he is
bold, confident and in full command of himself in other activities. As

a man who inspires confidence in others and on whom others can rely, he is hardly the Conrad that emerges from other evidence, including the Bobrowski letters and 'Document' and the suicide attempt.[6]

Conrad's presentation of George was undermined by his inability to deal with a period that climaxed shortly after with attempted suicide in 1878 and the humiliation of his uncle's subsequent appearance and reassertion of his position as surrogate father to an unruly, irresponsible and incompetent child. One reason why George does not show character development is that Conrad's psyche will not allow his memory to take a character based on his younger self up to his suicide attempt in late February or early March 1878.[7] In fact, as Karl notes, Conrad 'moved his own 1877-78 activities back to 1875–76'.[8] Conrad transforms the self-inflicted gunshot wound into a wound incurred in a chivalric duel in which George defends his honour. George remains unrelated to the major aspects of Conrad's mature identity as he saw himself in 1918: the outsider who had become a successful British captain and the writer who overcame numerous handicaps, including illness, self-doubt, debts, and a language that was not his by birth. One suspects that he chose to isolate his Marseilles days prior to his attempted suicide because at age sixty he wished to escape the inevitable strain of exploring his psyche and retreat into a memory of adolescent passions. Yet he wanted to write about what he considered part of his maturation. Written in 1917–18, *The Arrow of Gold* reaches for leisure and romance in what Conrad called in his Author's Note 'days of stress and dread' that are perhaps private as well as public (p. vii).

By not giving George a personal history or family background, Conrad insulates himself from his own past. In no Conrad novel do we learn so little about the characters' pasts. It is as if Conrad needed to disguise his complex psyche to preserve the fiction that he was a *tabula rasa* prior to meeting Rita: 'Except for a little habit of responsibility which I had acquired [my adventures] had not matured me. I was as young as before. Inconceivably young—still beautifully unthinking—infinitely receptive' (p. 8). But Conrad does not provide the essential ingredients for a complex characterisation. In his fiction he usually seeks to explain behaviour in terms of past experiences, so that the crucial test is an inevitable result of a concatenation of situations, circumstances, and facts. Obvious examples are Jim in *Lord Jim* and Razumov in *Under Western Eyes*, but the pattern informs virtually every major characterisation. In the prior novels with a psychosexual theme, such as *Chance* and *Victory*,

relationships are explored in terms of the experience characters bring
to them. But the period framed by the two carnivals does not lend
itself to a pattern of growth, because of Conrad's dramatisation of his
younger self in the person of George. He cannot impose the kind of
upward movement that would support the premise that the novel is
about initiation into adult emotions.

II

The older retrospective speaker, like Marlow, tries to recapture by
means of memory a period of excitement and achievement. But the
oscillation of tone between self-irony and lyricism which gives
'Youth' its subtle texture is absent. Like 'Youth', *The Arrow of Gold* is
a voyage of initiation; within the year that comprises the action of the
body of the novel, George journeys from innocence to experience.
Or, rather, he supposedly matures; in actuality, we do not really see a
change in his behaviour; nor do we hear a mature voice or feel the
Conradian conflict between a reminiscing speaker and the younger,
more impulsive self. The speaker's tale passes through the hands of the
editor who writes the notes. The editor might have played a role
similar to that of the language teacher in *Under Western Eyes* who
presents Razumov's diary, but in *The Arrow of Gold* the editor's
temperament is absent from the selection and arrangement of
material. He simply informs us that he has filtered out both direct
addresses to, and personal memories shared with, the 'childhood
friend' who is the nominal audience for George's reminiscence.
Whatever Conrad's intention, the editor – narrator's introductory
and concluding frame notes do not provide sufficient ironic control.
That George, in order 'to keep a better hold of the actuality', relies on
notebooks written while the events took place, does lend credibility
to past events; but he acknowledges that his notes provide 'an
irregular, fragmentary record' (p. 88).
     Conrad's nostalgic identification with George's passion seems to
cause a breakdown in narrative control. He not only cannot separate
himself from George and Rita, but also is unable to grasp fully how
his characters are behaving. In part, *The Arrow of Gold* fails because, in
reaching for intensity, Conrad inadvertently presents bathos. In
evoking passionate love, he renders infatuation and puppy love. If he
is in fact recalling an idealised love in the person of Rita; he presents a
woman without fundamental character. Conrad cannot move from

immersion in the past to reflection upon it. George never emerges from the inchoate adolescence of the early pages. At several points Conrad's narrative distance dissolves, and he emotionally participates in George's sexual initiation, his disdain for formality, his class resentment, and his use of the sea as a refuge from the turmoil on land. While George is meant to be a passionate soul who is poised and detached except when overwhelmed by his passion for Rita, he reveals himself as self-absorbed, idiosyncratic and at times manic. As the novel progresses and the process of reading unfolds, George's increasing hyperbole and hysteria undermine the novel's structure. Put another way, the process of reading discovers the flawed, disunified architectonics of the novel. The intended structure of the novel is subsumed by the raging torrent of George's rhetoric, a rhetoric which is supposed to mime passion but which stands as an unintentional parody of the emotions it is supposed to represent. This is all the more striking because the telling is retrospective and supposed to contain the Conradian tension between past and present perspectives. One could cite countless examples of rhetoric that are disproportionate to the occasion or inappropriate for the scene. Indeed, the entire narrative is placed within the context of an ersatz intensity which interferes with the possibility of making the kind of subtle moral distinctions that are characteristic of even Conrad's less distinguished fiction. At times George speaks with the frenzy of a man possessed.

Let us examine a few passages where George seeks refuge in a word world. Even before he recounts Mrs Blunt's veiled threat he writes of the meeting with her; 'There must have been an amazed incredulity in my eyes, to which her own responded by an unflinching black brilliance which suddenly seemed to develop a scorching quality even to the point of making me feel extremely thirsty all of a sudden. For a time my tongue literally clove to the roof of my mouth' (p. 184). Now surely the brilliance of a person's eyes does not induce drought and the concomitant feelings of extreme thirst. Since the recollections of the supposedly intense scenes between the lovers are the passages on which the book must stand or fall, we should recall the climactic scene when they meet accidentally at the house where he stays and which Therese runs. In her surprise she says, 'you are a cold illusion'; he responds with what is supposed to pass for wit: 'Well, I don't know that you are so much mist. I re-member once hanging on to you like a drowning man' (pp. 297–8). Recalling the scene years later he remarks, 'I must say, though, that I was swimmy in my head and now and then had a noise as of the sea in my ears' (p. 298). Unfortunately, Conrad is not trying to be grimly ironic concerning the hyperbole of his younger self. While George has just returned from a disastrous sea voyage, it is still difficult to believe that his sea experience is informing his perceptions, particularly at a time when he knows that Rita's life is threatened by a maniac. Conrad's clumsy groping for terms to describe experiences that elude his imagination undermines the novel's intended stress on heterosexual love between an inexperienced man and an experienced woman. His desperate quest for the appropriate language continues when George proceeds to tell her how he felt after they last parted: 'It was then that you took body in my imagination and that my mind seized on a definite form of you for all its adorations—for its profanations, too. Do not imagine me grovelling in spiritual abasement before a mere image' (p. 299). To our dismay, Conrad has George describe how he worshipped Rita as if she were the Virgin Mary.

As if he realised that his narrative failed to achieve the significance he sought and lapsed into meandering memories of a remote past, Conrad deliberately tries to imply a mythic structure as a means of transforming these particular, quirky, idiosyncratic characters into significant figures. In *The Arrow of Gold*, George conceives himself as a romance hero. Rather than, as in *Victory*, ironically viewing the protagonist's vision of himself as a romance hero, in this novel Conrad endorses George's perspective. George is nicknamed 'Young Ulysses' because he is an adventurer who lives by his wits; Rita alternately plays the role of Calypso, Circe and Penelope. Conrad in *The Mirror of the Sea* conceived of himself as a modern counterpart to Ulysses; as we shall see, he perceived Peyrol, the hero of the last novel he completed and a character that embodied his fantasy of a bold and significant death, as Ulysses. As he approached death, Conrad enjoyed creating heroic versions of himself. Writing *The Arrow of Gold* and *The Shadow-Line*—novels about his achieving personal and professional maturity—was an essential prelude to *The Rover*, the novel in which, as we shall see, he expresses his fantasy of a heroic death.

Conrad tentatively proposes George (St George) as a knight in shining armour, an heir to the Redcrosse Knight who sets out to rescue the imprisoned princess and restore her to her appropriate position. By rescuing the symbolic vessel of truth and beauty he will restore the European wasteland, epitomised by the bankrupt, self-serving Carlist movement, the cynical narcissistic aestheticism of Allègre and his circle, the mocking bohemianism of his friends, and the Dionysian Carnival.

The Carnival, prelude to Lent and occasion of masks and disguises, is the central image of the novel. A crystallising image of the *Zeitgeist*, it stands for artificial and disguised emotions, ersatz political causes, bohemian life-styles and precious aesthetic principles. George's response to the second carnival within a year is supposed to show a maturation that is never dramatised:

> My lucid thinking was, as it were, enveloped by the wide shouting of the consecrated Carnival gaiety. I have heard many noises since, but nothing that gave me such an intimate impression of the savage instincts hidden in the breast of mankind; these yells of festivity suggested agonising fear, rage of murder, ferocity of lust, and the irremediable joylessness of human condition: Yet they were emitted by people who were convinced that they were amusing themselves supremely, traditionally, with the sanction of ages, with the approval of their conscience—and no mistake about it whatever! (p. 272)

Although clumsily handled in *The Arrow of Gold*, savagery and instinct underneath the trappings of civilisation are as much the focus of this later work as of 'Heart of Darkness'. Once again we see the continuity of Conrad's fiction. The violent cold, dry mistral becomes an ironic metaphor for the sterile world in which Rita and George live: 'The same masks, the same yells, the same mad rushes, the same bedlam of disguised humanity blowing about the streets in the great gusts of mistral that seemed to make them dance like dead leaves on an earth where all joy is watched by death' (p. 263). Not only in George's mind, but also in the mythic structure that Conrad proposes, George will rescue Rita and revitalise the moral and physical wasteland.

Conrad also proposes George as Pygmalion, who will awake Galatea by means of his love; but, like Allègre, his predecessor in that role, who had sought to recreate the archetypal female in aesthetic terms, he does not succeed. George's perception of Rita as an archetypal woman, representing beauty, sexuality and passion, is part of Conrad's effort to magnify the stature of the action. That George does not fully arouse Rita's passions is indicated by the serendipitious nature of the beginning of their affair and by her leaving him after the duel. Such is Conrad's nostalgic sympathy with

George's passions that George's failure undermines the novel's form. Just as George cannot fully control Rita, who is conceived in terms of an aesthetic object, Conrad cannot achieve sufficient aesthetic control in the novel that contains her.

With its unexplored and undeveloped mythic pretensions, its confused characterisations, its discontinuous narrative, its strained imagery and its shrill tone, *The Arrow of Gold* presents an inchoate form, an *ur*-novel, from which the reader must extract the novel that Conrad did not write. Clearly, Conrad meant the structure to depend upon defining two kinds of artificial worlds—the political and the aesthetic—and then juxtaposing both to passionate heterosexual love. But, since he fails to present clearly the psyches of Rita and George, the novel does not unfold into coherent patterns of significance. Mill, the other roomers (the father and his two daughters who have pretensions to be actresses) and the journalist that tries to intimidate Rita either appear in vignettes that barely relate to one another or disappear entirely for long periods of time. The basic narrative itself is really a series of set scenes that do not quite cohere. While this could be attributed to the narrator's retrospective memory, it is actually the result of Conrad's unsuccessful effort to come to terms with his experience. Moser's complaint is not without validity: '[*The Arrow of Gold*] had virtually no center of interest, no basic conflict to be resolved, no climax toward which to move'.[9]

The major structural principle of the novel Conrad has written is Rita's eccentric and unstable personality. Around her shifting and often unclear identity revolves the entire cast of characters. She motivates action, triggers every crisis, and defines by her presence or absence every scene. At times she seems to enjoy her own unhappiness; at other times she has sadistic impulses. No reason for her leaving George after the duel is given. Nor can we assume from prior behaviour that she is loyal to him during his ten-month recuperation. After the attempted suicide of her cousin Ortega, her nemesis since childhood, she was about to depart. It was not George's rebuke or his throwing the phallic arrow at her that detained her, but the intimidating presence of Therese. She shuts the door and remains as George's lover for no other apparent reason than her need to defy Therese's bourgeois version of Roman Catholic values. She is obsessed with flouting her sister's morality, because Therese represents a kind of maternal figure to her. (An apostate Roman Catholic, Conrad during his Marseilles days would have found Rita's attitude to her sister's piety particularly daring and naughty.) In a sense, this woman of supposed passionate intensity becomes his lover by default. If even so shrewd a critic as Guerard is taken in when he calls her 'one of Conrad's very few charming and mature women',[10] it may be because George's misleading analysis of Rita claims charm and maturity for her. The problem is that her behaviour within the novel's dramatic scenes does not support such a claim. That Conrad misread his own creation also may have led some critics astray:

> A thing like that cannot go on for ever; and Rita with her greater maturity, greater experience of the world and in her perfect sincerity in the face of the situation sees it clearly.
>
> A connection of that kind would have spelt ruin for a young fellow of 19 without fortune or position or any young fellow for the matter of that. Had R. been merely sensual and selfish she could have kept George chained to her by his passion. Rita is what she is; but whatever she is, she is honest as the day. By going away beyond his reach she gives him the supreme proof of her love, stronger than mere passion, stronger than the fear of her own and of his suffering.   (9 May 1922, *LL*, ii, p. 270)

One of the novel's major problems is that Rita is supposed to stand for women's eternal sexuality and instinctive (as opposed to ratiocinative) wisdom. But the narrator who is supposed to transform her from a particular into a representative character is the jejune, hyperactive adolescent George. The novel dramatises George's futile attempts to mythicise her and Conrad's folly in trying to transform idiosyncracies into archetypal qualities. Take the following remark from the climactic scene in Therese's house: 'You don't think that I dealt with you sentimentally enough perhaps? But the sentiment was there; as clear a flame as ever burned on earth from the most remote ages before that eternal thing which is in you, which is your heirloom' (p. 299). The crudity of *dealt* undermines any pretensions Conrad might have about George's sensitivity or perspicacity. Conrad is immersed in George's emotions to the point where discrimination is usually impossible.

Despite the plethora of descriptions, Rita remains vague. Conrad does not discover the objective correlative to present her. George's recollection of his first view of Rita is typical:

> The white stairs, the deep crimson of the carpet, and the light blue of the dress made an effective combination of colour to set off the delicate carnation of that face, which, after the first

glance given to the whole person, drew irresistibly your gaze
to itself by an indefinable quality of charm beyond all analysis
and made you think of remote races, of strange generations, of
the faces of women sculptured on immemorial monuments and
of those lying unsung in their tombs.   (p. 66)

Conrad's efforts to magnify Rita's significance by allusions are
undermined by her fundamental lack of stature. In a pathetic
moment, she tells George that all Ortega's ravings are true, including,
presumably, the most egregious one: 'And what is she, after all, but a
Parisian woman with innumerable lovers, as I have been told'
(p. 269).

Nor are Conrad's symbols effective. The arrow is supposed, I
suspect, to represent the intensity and sexuality of George's and Rita's
passionate love, and supposed to contrast with the headless dummy
which represents the sterile aestheticism of Henry Allègre's world,
whose inhabitants seek a magic circle to enclose devotees of art. In the
former studio that serves as Blunt's room, the dummy 'lay there
prostrate, handless, without its head, pathetic, like the mangled
victim of a crime' (p. 189). But the phallic arrow seems ostentatious
and ultimately foolish.[11] And, because Rita never becomes more
than a shallow icon for George to worship, she is unintentionally
parodied by that headless statue of an empress for which she
modelled.

In *The Arrow of Gold* Conrad continues his satire of European
civilisation. George detests the fashionable world even though he
reserves a table in one of its cafés. Like Heyst, he chooses to define his
identity in response to social conventions he despises and to which he
is still drawn. After losing his ship, he visits the *petit salon*, where his
hat and stick make him perfectly at home; but once there he asks
himself, 'What had I to do with them, this elegant dust, these moulds
of provincial fashion?' (p. 167). The aristocrats exploit whom they
need; they destroy the innocence of Rita, whose wealth and influence
they require. With her apparent approval, they enlist George because
he will be useful; he in turn enlists Dominic. The aristocrats' political
activity is based on using people. The wealthy and influential seem to
risk very little on behalf of the Pretender.

Allègre represents to Conrad the kind of dilettantism presented in
'Il Conde' and 'The Informer'; in his studio 'every hard truth had
been cracked and every belief had been worried into shreds' (p. 56).
Conrad despised those who made a fetish or religion of art. In 1918 he

may have had in mind any number of targets, including Bloomsbury and various groups in Europe, in particular the Stein salon. Allègre admitted people to his company who would 'feed and amuse [his] scorn of the world, which was insatiable' (p. 95). At the age of seventeen Rita has been educated at the school of his cynicism, where all values seem like the Emperor's new clothes: 'If ever anybody saw mankind stripped of its clothes as the child sees the king in the German fairy tale, it's I!' (p. 96). Shaped by this training, she withholds something of herself in relationships with men. In a sense, she is a dilettante of emotions and a collector of an odd assortment of admirers, voyeurs and lovers. She cannot give herself entirely to one man; once the subject of attention is out of sight, she turns her attention to another subject of interest. But Allègre's world is no worse than the conventions and forms of the aristocrats as represented by Blunt, who, according to Rita, speaks 'parrot language . . . the words of tradition and morality as understood by the members of the exclusive club to which he belongs' (p. 208). Of Blunt she says, 'His conventions, will always stand in the way of his nature' (p. 210). Blunt has reduced himself to a handful of shibboleths, such as '*Je suis Américain, catholique et gentilhomme*' (p. 18) and 'I live by my sword' (p. 14). Beneath Blunt's 'air of good breeding' is a pathologically jealous man who will kill another man in a duel (p. 174). And his civilised mother—a woman of 'infinite style' 'refinement' and 'subtlety'—plots an alliance with Rita to gain the fortune Henry Allègre left her. As in *Victory*, perfect manners do not inhibit the human impulses to greed, passion and self-interest.

Rita perceives herself as a victim of her social milieu and her *Zeitgeist*; she speaks of George and herself as 'Simple people, in this world which is eaten up with charlatanism of all sorts so that we, the simple, don't know any longer how to trust each other' (p. 199). She knows that the Legitimist movement is an extension of the artificial world in which she has lived: she complains that she continuously listens to lies, 'empty words' and 'false protestations'. Nor can she free herself from Allègre's tutelage. Rita's own commitment to the Carlists is a reaction to Allègre's cynicism. Her response to Blunt in aesthetic terms suggests that her response to George may also have an aesthetic ingredient.

You have no idea of the charm and the distinction of his pose. I couldn't help admiring him: the expression, the grace, the fatal suggestion of his immobility. Oh, yes, I am sensible to

aesthetic impressions, I have been educated to believe that there
is a soul in them. . . . His self-command is the most admirable
worldly thing I have ever seen. What made it beautiful was.
that one could feel in it a tragic suggestion as in a great work
of art.   (p. 211)

She responds to George as to an aesthetic concept that she has created
in her mind, rather than to his character as it reveals itself in the
novel's dramatic scenes. But Conrad's efforts to dramatise a world in
which people perceive in artificial aesthetic terms sometimes become
confused with his efforts to use aesthetic images to magnify the stature
of characters and to imply archetypal significance. Thus, George, the
proposed man of action and the supposedly passionate figure, also
perceives in artistic terms: 'She paused with an inscrutable smile that a
painter might have put on the face of some symbolic figure for the
speculation and wonder of many generations' (p. 211). At times, the
pervasive aesthetic images almost arrest the forward progress of the
novel and give the reader the feeling of wandering from room to
room in a gallery of paintings and sculptures.

III

The Arrow of Gold, Conrad's effort to write of the European
aristocracy with its exiles and bohemians, belies the notion that
Conrad's last novels are to be thought of as allegories. It is a
commentary upon the social milieu in which the events take place and
is Conrad's most scathing indictment of the aristocracy. It is about an
aristocracy that fails to fulfil its leadership responsibilities and casts its
lot with amoral political activities. As in Nostromo and The Secret
Agent, politics subsumes the personal lives of those committed to it.
Although he wrote the novel during wartime, Conrad eschews
patriotic commitment. Conrad had neither the energy nor the desire to
write about politics in 1917–18. Moreover, political motives are
revealed as private pique. Ortega is motivated by his obsession for
Rita and has no real interest in the Legitimist cause; indeed, he wishes
for a 'red' revolution so that he can settle private accounts. The
Carlists are unconcerned with the welfare of the people. George is a
gun-runner for a cause in which he has no interest. George and Blunt
are fighting to win the favour of Rita, whose support for the Prince is
a kind of consolation prize, since she has refused to be the latter's

mistress. That George's commitment to Rita is chivalric not ideological tells us something about Conrad's concept of love in 1918 as well as his disinterest in politics: 'All the others might have been merged in the idea, but I, the latest recruit, I would not be merged in the Legitimist Principle. Mine was an act of independent assertion. Never before had I felt so intensely aware of my personality' (p. 89).

The novel asks whether passion itself can be genuine within a world that is insincere and artificial. It may be Conrad's response to Lawrence, who was arguing for the primacy of the passions. In this fundamentally pessimistic novel, emotions do not really provide an island, despite the lovers' six-month retreat, which is presented as a bare summary in the second note. For this retreat is not part of the dramatised world of the novel and hence does little to qualify the emotional inefficiency and the failure of personal relationships within the novel. Does George really preserve his innocence within a corrupt world? After all, he learns to scorn his fellows and seriously contemplates murder. To an extent, he recapitulates Rita's education, an education that leaves each man as an isolated cynical fragment. Mills, the mysterious but widely praised man of books, has retreated from the world of action at the end; indeed, if he finds any solace in human relationships or ideas we are never told of them. Nor does this 'solitary man of books' who has 'a secret taste for adventure' ever risk much (p. 83). His reappearance in the second note, like that of the editor narrator, represents a return of the normal and becomes an implicit ironic comment on the escalating hyperbole and even hysteria of George's narration. Mills's final poignant and ironic comment merges with the regretful voice of the sixty-year-old author who must return from the 1870s to the present: 'You know that this world is not a world for lovers, not even for such lovers as you two who have nothing to do with the world as it is. No, a world of lovers would be impossible. It would be a mere ruin of lives which seem to be meant for something else' (p. 350). Notwithstanding his nostalgic sympathy for George's emotions in 1917-18 as he felt himself ageing and the world war continued, Conrad felt that human fulfilment in this amoral world, even in the form of passionate love, was unlikely if not impossible.

NOTES

1. Palmer, *Conrad's Fiction* (Ithaca, NY: Cornell University Press, 1968), p. 249.

2. Baines, *Conrad: A Critical Biography* (New York: McGraw-Hill, 1960), p. 45, and Karl, *Conrad: The Three Lives* (New York: Farrar, Straus and Giroux, 1979), p. 130.

3. See Baines, *Conrad: A Critical Biography*, p. 50.

4. Jean-Aubry provides no further date.

5. In *Joseph Conrad: The Three Lives*, pp. 159–72. Karl convincingly argues that, despite the resemblances between Conrad and George, the novel should not be taken as biography. Karl speculates that 'Conrad's 1916 meeting with Jane Anderson . . . apparently set off his memories of the youthful romance of George and Rita' (*Conrad: The Three Lives*, p. 162).

6. See Zdzislaw Najder, *Conrad's Polish Backgound: Letters to and from Polish Friends* (London: Oxford University Press, 1964).

7. In *Language and Being: Joseph Conrad and the Literature of Personality* (New York and London: Columbia University Press, 1976), p. 33, Peter J. Glassman speculates on Conrad's suicide attempt: 'In 1878 Conrad acted not only to destroy [what Meyer has called] "the desperate and chaotic condition of his immediate situation" in Marseilles, but to engage and to obliterate his entire experience of being; . . . Conrad wished in firing his pistol not to evade a particular accumulation of circumstances but to annihilate himself and his whole vile history.' See Meyer, *Conrad: A Psychoanalytic Biography* (Princeton, NJ: Princeton University Press, 1967), pp. 35 – 57.

8. Karl, *Conrad: The Three Lives*, p. 161n. See Karl's discussion of the novel's parallels with *The Sisters*, the fragment Conrad abandoned in 1896 (ibid., pp. 168–9).

9. Moser, *Conrad: Achievement and Decline* (Cambridge, Mass.: Harvard University Press, 1957), p. 185.

10. Guerard, *Conrad the Novelist* (Cambridge, Mass.: Harvard University Press, 1958), p. 281.

11. Karl finds the arrow symbol more convincing. For his interesting discussion, see his *Conrad: The Three Lives*, p. 167.

9 *The Rover*: Conrad's fictional testament

I

Throughout Conrad's career, he spoke of the search for solidarity with his kind, and made clear that he did not want to write for a coterie. In the 1920 Author's Note to *Chance* he defines this position: 'I have never sinned against the basic feelings and elementary convictions which make life possible to the mass of mankind and, by establishing a standard of judgment, set their idealism free to look for plainer ways, for higher feelings, for deeper purposes' (p. x). The last novel Conrad completed, *The Rover* (1923), was written with the idea of reaching that part of the mass of mankind which was literate. In important respects, it is a synopsis of a number of major themes in his previous work. Peyrol, the rover, is an heroic version of the kind of man Conrad sought to reach. Every aspect of the novel—the style, voice and structure—reflects his attempt to reach beyond a limited audience to those who would recognise a kinship with a forceful, competent, shrewd but not intellectual hero. Conrad's artistic economy is appropriate for the barely verbal and unself-conscious characters of *The Rover*. For example, the voice sometimes seems to be an articulate version of Peyrol; the style deliberately eschews the elaborate syntax of Marlow's meditative, introspective style or the hyperbole and imprecision of such later works as 'The Planter of Malata' and *The Arrow of Gold*; the structure avoids disrupted chronology and elaborate narrative technique. *The Rover* is a spare, bold minor masterpiece even if it does not integrate plot, character and historical context with the subtlety and intensity of *The Secret Agent* and 'Heart of Darkness'.

Conrad's quest for purity of design and clarity of conception is indicated by one of his last letters to Edward Garnett; he speaks of his 'secret desire to achieve a feat of artistic brevity, once at least, before I died' (4 Dec 1923, *LL*, ii, p. 327). Certainly, part of the simplicity of design has to do with the novel's being written by dictation, but, as *The Arrow of Gold* shows, neither dictation nor the simplified plot that results when Conrad used that method ensures the intensity, coherence and efficiency of a novel's structure and texture. The decisive ending also owes something to Conrad's frustration with *Suspense*, a Napoleonic novel that he never completed, and to his fear that he did not have much time left. Speaking in the same letter of why he did not add a scene between Catherine and Scevola, he adds, 'I was feeling a little bit heartsick then, too, and anxious also to demonstrate to myself as soon as possible that I could finish a piece of work. . . . Here you have, my dear Edward, the confession of my weaknesses in connection with the secret history of *The Rover*.' Beginning with *The Nigger of the 'Narcissus'*, Conrad used the voyage as a means of ordering his own writing process.[1] Imagining the completion of a quest or a voyage released Conrad from the agonies of writing. In *The Rover* the small number of individuals in an isolated setting enables Conrad to insulate the characters from outside factors and to limit tangential interactions. In this way, the novel's fictional materials resemble the voyage experience with which as an artist he felt most comfortable.

Rarely, if ever, does Conrad allow one character to dominate the space of a novel. Yet, in this novel, every other character revolves around Peyrol's presence. *The Rover* is like a pre-Renaissance painting in which Christ and the Holy Family are several times the size of the other characters. Peyrol's boldness, ingenuity, intelligence, courage and self-confidence contrast to the tentativeness, introspection and parochial political commitments of most of the other characters. Aspects of Peyrol recur in every character. Virtually every male character, including the inarticulate, compulsive fanatic Scevola, embody and objectify one aspect of the principal character: Symons is the man he once was; Captain Vincent is a kind of English counterpart to his patriotic present self; and the aging but tenacious admiral Nelson echoes important characteristics of Peyrol.

The Rover is a fairy-tale that Conrad tells to himself. He magnifies the stature of Peyrol by means of epic allusions.[2] For example, he draws a parallel between Peyrol and Ulysses, another rover and wanderer: 'On that sea ruled by the gods of Olympus he might have been a pagan mariner subject to Jupiter's caprices; but like a defiant pagan he shook his fist vaguely at space which answered him by a short and threatening mutter' (p. 237). Conrad may be deliberately suggesting Tennyson's 'Ulysses', particularly the closing lines, which could be an epigraph for *The Rover*:

> We are not now that strength which in old days
> Moved earth and heaven; that which we are, we are;
> One equal temper of heroic hearts,
> Made weak by time and fate, but strong in will
> To strive, to seek, to find, and not to yield.

Like Tennyson's ageing hero, Peyrol knowingly undertakes a last desperate mission after an arduous return home. For Conrad, life at sea was romance and epic, and the successful completion of a voyage such as Peyrol's climactic one can be equivalent to asserting or regaining identity. *The Rover* is not only a version of the Ulysses myth, but also a fictional version of *A Personal Record*; with its elegiac tone, its sense of forthcoming death, and its emphasis on returning home to discover the self that has been created abroad, Conrad's autobiographical volume anticipates major concerns of *The Rover*.

Conrad spoke of *The Rover* in terms that suggested its special importance to him: 'I have wanted for a long time to do a seaman's "return" (before my own departure)' (22 Feb 1924, *LL*, ii, p. 339). Peyrol's desire in his final voyage to merge his destiny with that of his nation may reflect Conrad's desire, as he approached death, to contribute meaningfully to Poland's destiny. His fantasy of a significant political act is embodied in Peyrol. If, like Nabokov's, Conrad's life was embodied in his imagination, he was never comfortable that he had turned his back on politics and the heritage of his father, whom he recalled as an idealistic patriot. The novel's title also refers to himself, the twice transplanted alien who finally found a home in England and no longer felt himself something of an outsider. Peyrol re-creates himself at fifty-eight when circumstances connive with his own weariness to deprive him of his past; he creates a new identity just as surely as a younger Conrad did when he left Poland to go to sea and, later, when he turned from the sea to a writing career.

The Rover combines Conrad's fantasy of retreat with his lifelong fantasy of an heroic return home. (Neither his first visit to Poland in 1890, nor his second at the outbreak of the war, quite fulfilled this fantasy.) *The Rover* associates Peyrol's return with Conrad's own romantic desire to return to his past. In *A Personal Record*, writing of his first return to Poland, Conrad wrote how the faces 'were as familiar to me as though I had known them from childhood, and my childhood

were a matter of the day before yesterday' (p. 27). Upon arriving in
France, Peyrol is struck by the parallel between himself and the
people he encounters, including even the cripple:

> Any woman, lean and old enough, might have been his
> mother; he might have been any Frenchman of them all, even
> one of those he pitied, even one of those he despised. He felt
> the grip of his origins from the crown of his head to the soles
> of his feet while he clambered on board the tartane as if for a
> long and distant voyage.   (p. 98)

Gradually he feels that he belongs to France, represented in his mind
by the tiny coastal hamlet in which he lives and the people he knows
there:

> The disinherited soul of that rover ranging for so many years a
> lawless ocean . . . had come back to its crag, circling like a
> great sea bird in the dusk and longing for a great sea victory
> for its people: that inland multitude of which Peyrol knew
> nothing except the few individuals on that peninsula cut off
> from the rest of the land by the dead water of a salt
> lagoon.   (p. 142)

Peyrold embodies Conrad's lifelong relationship with the country he
had left and his desire to return to the land of the parents who had died
while he was a young child.

Peyrol is the obverse of Conrad's meditative, introspective aspect,
the aspect dramatised by Marlow. Rather he represents Conrad the
man of action, the man who, even while mistrusting democracy,
sought solidarity with the rest of mankind: Peyrol is also a surrogate
for the ageing Conrad. He retires after success as a man of action and
misses the life he has left behind. He finds difficulty finding a
comfortable niche in his new life and, like Conrad, sustains himself
with the dream of resuming his sea life. Despite formal omniscience,
the distance between Conrad and Peyrol often dissolves, because
Peyrol is the fictional counterpart for Conrad's fantasies of a
significant death to climax an heroic old age. Conrad's sympathies
move back and forth from narrator to character, from his observer to
his subject. His analysis of Peyrol often oversimplifies his behaviour to
the point of distorting it; that is, his comments do not do justice to the
subtlety of his character. In a sense, Conrad is trying to write

an adventure story in the Kipling and Stevenson tradition, but in the final scene his moral imagination resists the necessary structural simplicity, partly because he cannot fully separate himself from his protagonist. Peyrol need not have committed suicide to be captured; by having Peyrol take his loyal followers Michel and Scevola to their death, Conrad shows once again the ambiguity of decisive action.

Conrad suspends his own moral fastidiousness when treating Peyrol's plunder, not only because he despised the bloodthirsty revolutionaries who were to receive the plunder, but also because Peyrol is Conrad's version of the pastoral, is his own romance. Like Nostromo, Peyrol might have been burdened by an illegally procured treasure. But, because Peyrol is an enactment of Conrad's fantasies of material comfort and escape from the world of responsibilities, the treasure enables Peyrol to retire to his native land in leisure. Peyrol, who after all has in a sense betrayed his country by absconding with the plunder, movingly illustrates Conrad's poignant statement in *A Personal Record* about the different faces loyalty and patriotism wear:

> No charge of faithlessness ought to be lightly uttered. The appearances of this perishable life are deceptive like everything that falls under the judgment of our imperfect senses. The inner voice may remain true enough in its secret counsel. The fidelity to a special tradition may last through the events of an unrelated existence, following faithfully, too, the traced way of an inexplicable impulse.   (pp. 35 – 6)

In *A Personal Record* Conrad used terms such as 'betrayal', faithlessness' and 'desertion'—terms that might have been applicable to Peyrol's departure from the Revolutionary navy—to describe his departure from Poland: 'It would take too long to explain the intimate alliance of contradictions in human nature which makes love itself wear at times the desperate shape of betrayal' (p. 36). Peyrol's increasing stature as he triumphs on personal and national terms acts out Conrad's own desire to be honoured in the land he left.

Like his creator, Peyrol has 'secret contempt' for 'revolutionary jargon' and is indifferent to political ideology. Conrad wrote in 'A Familiar Preface' to *A Personal Record*, 'The revolutionary spirit is mighty convenient in this, that it frees one from all scruples as regards ideas. Its hard, absolute optimism is repulsive to my mind by the menace of fanaticism and intolerance it contains. . . . All claim to

special righteousness awakens in me that scorn and anger from which
a philosophical mind should be free' (pp. xxi–xxii). Peyrol's version
of Revolutionary principles is parodic: 'Liberty—to hold your own
in the world if you could. Equality—yes! But no body of men ever
accomplished anything without a chief. All this was worth what it
was worth. He regarded fraternity somewhat differently. . . . In his
view the claim of the Brotherhood was a claim for help against the
outside world' (p. 132). This reductive credo is more a justification
for the solidarity of a crew on board ship, or even for a band of
brigands, than for a nation.

Scevola's fanaticism is an example of intemperate political commitment that subsumes personal identity and prevents the growth of
private relationships. The fanatic terrorist is obsessed with purifying
France of monarchists and priests. Just like the anarchists in *The Secret
Agent*, he represents a threat to morality and civilisation. The
characterisation of Scevola undermines Fleishman's contention that
Conrad identifies 'a political movement, the French Revolution with
the spirit of the people, the general will'.[3] On the contrary, Conrad's
bitter satire of the Revolutionists in general and Scevola in particular
affirms his mistrust of political movements. Peyrol knows that, 'by
himself, [Scevola] was nothing. He had never been anything but a
creature of the universal blood lust of the time' (p. 48). Scevola has no
identity other than as part of a mob. He even expresses his own
sexual jealousy in political terms. As he goes with a pitchfork to stab
Réal, the man he correctly suspects has won Arlette's attentions, he
thinks that he 'was going to act in the cause of virtue and justice. It was
not to be a matter of personal contest at all' (p. 187). On board the
tartane, he can only speak in the formulas of the Revolution; he is so
locked into his own language and epistemology that he is unable to
evaluate the intentions of others.

II

The Rover is Conrad's *Death in Venice*. Every element combines to
provide the orchestration for Peyrol's death. As in *Death in Venice*, the
narrator's distance from his protagonist fluctuates, but, as Mann did
with Aschenbach, Conrad is objectifying part of himself in the
character of Peyrol. He is the inarticulate, courageous man of action
that Conrad might have become. Motivated not by commitment to

political dogma, but by love of country, he is the man who finally makes a difference in the affairs of his nation. *The Rover* is about coming to terms with age and dying. Peyrol fulfils Conrad's fantasy of an elegant death in an heroic action. When Conrad writes about Peyrol's ageing, we feel an immediacy and intensity that belie the expected distance between author and character. Shaving for the last time, even before he knows that he is to sail out to die, Peyrol realises that 'life was a dream less substantial than the vision of Ceylon lying like a cloud on the sea' (p. 233). To fulfil himself, he *needs* to die in action. The presence of Réal nullifies his fantasies of playing anything but a paternal role to Arlette. Virtually his last words on shore are 'I am tired', but unlike Aschenbach he does not slip into rest, but sculpts his last hours into an heroic death.

Conrad, himself sixty-four when he completed the novel, in June 1922, identifies with his sixty-six-year-old hero's death. If at fifty-eight Peyrol's 'instinct for rest' mirrors one aspect of Conrad's mood in his seventh decade, the desire of Peyrol at sixty-six for one last triumph mirrors another aspect. Conrad's triumph is the novel that contains Peyrol; Peyrol's is the suicidal voyage at the behest not only of his patriotism, but also of his generous desire to give his beloved Arlette, his surrogate daughter and his fantasy mistress, the ultimate present: the man whom she loves and whom Peyrol realises, despite his jealousy, is a man of quality. As he dies, 'he beheld in a flash the days of his manhood, of strength and adventure' (p. 269). His death has the kind of significance to others that Conrad hoped his own would have.

Since Conrad would have expected us to remember that France lost the Napoleonic Wars, Peyrol's efficacy must be measured in other than political or military results.[4] In Peyrol's death lie the seeds of renewed life. Even while Peyrol dies, Réal and Arlette are reborn. In his death, 'he had left them to themselves on a sudden impulse of scorn, of magnanimity, of a passion weary of itself' (p. 260). In giving up his life for Arlette and Réal, Peyrol completely surrenders himself to sentiment, after he had disparaged it earlier. But this change of attitude mimes Conrad's own gradual modification during his years on land. For the graph of his career from *The Nigger of the 'Narcissus'* to his later works shows how he had come to appreciate the values of private relationships and attachments based on sentiment—his somewhat disparaging term for generous human feelings, which are often contrary to one's self-interest. Arlette's and Réal's happy

marriage derives from Peyrol's generosity. Catherine has renewed
pride and vigour as the family homestead is re-established on proper
principles. Peyrol not only brings 'triumphant life' to Arlette and
Réal, but also triumphs himself in Vincent's recognition of his success
and in the memories of those who survive him at the Escampobar
farm (p. 260). That Vincent praises him for 'courage' and 'determination' and that Nelson compares himself to the legend of 'that
white-headed man' provides reinforcement to his triumph (pp. 275 –
6). Vincent is the better for his perception of 'the whole episode that
suggested a more than common devotion to duty and a spirit of
daring defiance' (p. 277). His *reading* of the episode is a model for ours;
his insistence on honouring his rival contributes to the lyrical ending,
which urges us to suspend our judgements of Peyrol's suicide and
homicides.

Because Conrad's imagination was obsessed with death while he
wrote *The Rover*, death is a continuous presence. The persistence of
death in conversations, interior monologues and the omniscient
narrator's descriptions arouses our expectations of death as a
structural ingredient of the story as much as the prevalence of old
characters such as Peyrol, Catherine, Nelson, Symons and Michel.
As in Joyce's 'The Dead', the reader's mind becomes imbued with
suggestions of death, until, without his realising quite why, Peyrol's
death comes as an inevitable fulfilment of an expected pattern. When
Peyrol retires from the sea to his homeland, the setting is described in
terms which suggest the stasis of death and the evanescence of life:
'The immobility of all things seemed poised in the air like a gay
mirage. . . . Yes, this was the place for him; not because expediency
dictated, but simply because his instinct of rest had found its home at
last' (p. 31). But in his last home his life reaches completion. He
discovers the family relationship he lacks; he becomes a surrogate
father to Arlette and a substitute if asexual husband to Catherine.
Rereading, we realise that the tartane is the boat that will take the
wanderer across Styx to death, and the non-verbal Michel is a kind of
Charon figure. Gradually, in the last twenty-four hours that comprise
the action of the novel, after the three chapter prologue when he
returns to his homeland, Peyrol comes to terms with his
entire life.[5] Symons represents his earlier outlaw self that felt no
national commitment but formed ties on the basis of personal and
tribal relationships. When Symons returns to his boat, Peyrol 'had a
strange notion that those English boats had carried off something

belonging to him, not a man but a part of his own life, the sensation of a regained touch with the far-off days in the Indian Ocean' (p. 201).

Réal, another outsider who arouses and loves Arlette, recapitulates Peyrol's return eight years earlier. Clearly, had Peyrol not aroused her dormant emotions, she would never have responded to Réal. The narrator stresses the parallels between these two men who do not really trust one another: 'The moon . . . seemed to shine on two friends so identical in thought and feeling that they could commune with each other without words' (p. 203). At first this seems a facile comparison of dissimilar characters. After all, the naval officer is not living the kind of pirate life that the rover, the adventurer, had lived, but gradually we realise that Réal is another version of Peyrol: 'Honour, decency, every principle forbade him to trifle with the feelings of a poor creature with her mind darkened by a very terrifying, atrocious, and, as it were guilty, experience. . . . Taciturn and guarded, he had formed no intimacies. Relations he had none. He had kept clear of social connections' (pp. 208–9). Réal and Peyrol have much in common despite their distrust. They are both independent, impulsive, courageous and passionate.

At some level, Peyrol understands that Réal is a younger version of himself. They understand one another because they resemble one another: 'A mute, strangely suspicious, defiant understanding had established itself imperceptibly between [Réal] and that lawless old man' (pp. 71–2). Réal's service to the navy has the same personal motive as Peyrol's to the Brotherhood. Both seek to compensate for the lack of family ties by mythicising the quiet Arlette into the sympathetic other self that they seek; both ironically create her as a secret sharer even though Arlette is barely responsive to either of them, until Réal kisses her, at which point he becomes his fantasy lover. Réal's movement from action to retirement recapitulates the movement of Peyrol at the outset of the novel. The fantasy of quiet retreat from responsibility fulfils Conrad's own dream. Both Peyrol and Réal wish to escape the mesh of public events. As in *Nostromo*, *The Secret Agent* and *Under Western Eyes*, political partisanship is the enemy of human relationships; even Peyrol's patriotic suicide illustrates this.

While Peyrol is a romanticised version of the ageing Conrad, Réal is an image of a younger Conrad who at times sought a refuge from permanent emotional commitment in his work. If Peyrol is the instinctive, passionate side of Conrad, Réal is the moody introspective self that haunted him throughout his life. Conrad felt throughout his career that politics blights innocent lives and leaves human wreckage. Arlette and, to a lesser extent, Réal spend their lives recovering from the scars of the Revolution. The very night after he kisses her and fulfils her need for love, she dreams of 'Réal set upon by a mob of men and women, all dripping with blood' (p. 245). Owing to his parents' losing their heads on a scaffold, Réal becomes 'very self-contained', and cannot love Arlette without feeling guilt and anxiety. He is a moral absolutist, who will not compromise with his emotions: 'On emerging from boyhood, [Réal] had laid himself a rigidly straight line of conduct amongst the unbridled passions and the clamouring falsehoods of revolution which seemed to have destroyed in him all capacity for the softer emotions' (p. 209). Of aristocratic parents, Réal is both an actual and political orphan. Without any help or favours, he had become an officer on merit. Like Peyrol, he is accustomed to relying on his own resources, and sceptical if not cynical about human nature.

Réal, like Peyrol, seeks in Escampobar a pastoral retreat from his diurnal life. But he withdraws only to discover that he has needs he has not recognised. Just like Heyst, Peyrol and Réal are awakened from indifference to acknowledge emotions and needs that they have repressed. Arlette 'produced on [Peyrol] the effect of a child, aroused a kind of intimate emotion which he had not known before to exist by itself in a man' (p. 88). Ironically, he equates sentiment with ageing: 'Is it that I am getting old?' (p. 88). Underneath the surrogate father – daughter relationship there are nuances of sexual playfulness, as when she says to him, 'You used to love me Peyrol', after begging him, as if he had magic powers, to return Réal to her (p. 248), or when she presses Peyrol's hand to her breast to feel how her heart responds to Réal's love. Arlette regards Peyrol as a man of immense force, as 'the man of mystery and power' who can make things happen according to his desires. Yet she instinctively plays upon his sexual attraction to her, because that is the only resource she knows (and the one that saved her life during the reign of terror). Peyrol clearly perceives Arlette in sexual terms as well: 'The way she had taken to dressing her hair in a plait with a broad black velvet ribbon and an Arlesian cap was very becoming' (p. 103). He is extremely jealous that Réal plays the role that he had fantasised for himself (the same role ironically, that Scevola imagined for himself). Because he suspects Réal as a rival, he is a reluctant surrogate father to him. Réal understands even more clearly than Peyrol that their mutual attraction to Arlette is the grounds for the hostility that punctuates the intimacy between the two men. (It is possible that Peyrol's ambiguous relationship to Arlette reflects Conrad's relationship to Jane Anderson, who was originally Borys's friend before Conrad became interested in her.[6])

Réal, another orphan and a younger version of Peyrol, is emotionally awakened by the same woman. Like Heyst, Réal is drawn to a social-inferior to compensate for a lack of sexual confidence. Réal is attracted to Arlette, as the captain in 'The Smile of Fortune' is attracted to Alice, *because* of her vulnerability. Because of Arlette's plight as a sexual victim of the Revolution, she enables him to fulfil his need for a social inferior. In each of the later novels, except *The Shadow-Line* and *The Rescue*, which was conceived in the 1890s, a strong male figure rescues a helpless female. Lena, Alice, Rita and Arlette are all either socially or sexually compromised. Rescuing Arlette assuages the inevitable guilt he feels for not being able to prevent his parents' death at the hands of Revolutionaries. That Conrad presents through the characterisation of Arlette and Réal the effects of being orphaned and of being prematurely introduced to violence gives the novel part of its compelling personal urgency as Conrad's last testament.

Conrad realised that he had not made Réal 'a great figure worthy of Peyrol' and that Peyrol dominated his canvas (4 Dec 1923, *LL*, ii, p. 327). Réal's moral fastidiousness, recalling that of Captain Anthony's, causes him to regard his love as 'an unworthy passion'. This feeling derives from the ambiguous state of Arlette's relationship with Scevola and from her emotional and intellectual vulnerability. Yet Réal never really regards her as distracted, and his suicidal impulse seems to be disproportionate to any reason that Conrad gives. Réal's death wish reflects Conrad's recurring sexual puritanism, which is perhaps a vestige of his Roman Catholicism. Réal's sexual desires are displaced by guilt, ennui, and morbidity.

The possibility of death is continually proposed by the texture, but a first reader cannot be sure whether it applies to Réal or Peyrol. Peyrol remarks, 'Well, perhaps old Peyrol is dead. At any rate he has buried himself here' (pp. 106–7). And, in an ironic prolepsis, Réal responds, 'I don't want to disturb the dead. . . . I want to talk to the gunner Peyrol' (p. 107). But Réal's conscience raises the spectre of death as a proper reward for illicitly and irresponsibly loving Arlette: 'He had been growing sick of his work. He had no place in the world to go to, and no one either' (p. 71). Moreover, the plot posits and discards the possibility of Réal's death. It is Réal who is visited by Catherine in the guise of Death: 'At the foot of his bed stood a figure in dark garments with a dark shawl over its head, with a fleshless predatory face and dark hollows for its eyes, silent, expectant, implacable' (p. 225). Because he has violated his own standards by loving a woman who may be bereft of her senses and who, in some peculiar way, seems to belong to another man, he contemplates suicide, and then opts on personal grounds for the mission to deceive the British navy by being captured with false documents. His passionate embrace of Arlette raises the spectre of death: 'He felt like a man chained to the wall and dying of thirst, from whom a cold drink is snatched away' (p. 224). An unsuspecting reader might think that the foreshadowing was in anticipation of Réal's death. After all, Réal receives in the person of Catherine's intimidating visitation the sign from death of which she had spoken.

Gradually, as the novel intensifies, Peyrol becomes more and more conscious of his own mortality and of his own limitations. He makes up his mind to undertake the mission on Réal's behalf because gradually he loses interest in the affairs of life. Thinking morbidly of how men receive the sign of death, Peyrol felt an 'intimate inward sense of the vanity of all things, that doubt of the power within himself' (p. 173). At first, he represses the flickering awareness of his own inevitable deterioration, which encroaches on his 'whole robust personality' not only in the shape of diminishing powers but also in the shape of diminishing possibilities: 'I am not sick of life. I am disparu and that's good enough. There's no need for me to die' (p. 116). A few minutes later, 'an uneasiness came over the old rover, a sense of the endangered stability of things, which was anything but welcome. He wondered at it and the thought "I am growing old" intruded on him again' (pp. 121-2). Réal thinks that, in contrast to his own preoccupation with death, Peyrol is oblivious to the possibility, but ageing is the one subject about which Peyrol is self-conscious. He ironically imagines that the younger Captain Vincent is a reflection of himself and is an ageing adversary, 'Long-faced, with yellow teeth and a wig' (p. 234). Peyrol's self-consciousness about ageing intensifies as the climactic twenty-four hours progress and is a major reason for his final sacrifice.

III

Peyrol's sacrifice for Réal is Conrad's final version of the recurring moral dilemma that a man faces when he must choose either self-interest or self-abnegation. As we saw in our discussion of 'The Secret Sharer', Conrad uses the Cain—Abel myth as a paradigm for this conflict. Peyrol illustrates true fraternity, as Conrad would have understood it; he responds sympathetically to the deepest needs not only of Arlette, but also those of his rival. Conrad had written to Cunninghame Graham in 1899, 'There is already as much fraternity as there can be,—and that's very little and that very little is no good. What does fraternity mean? Abnegation,—self-sacrifice means something. Fraternity means nothing unless the Cain Abel business. That's your true fraternity' (8 Feb 1899, *LL*, i, p. 269). For Conrad, except in extraordinary circumstances, fraternity means competitiveness and self-interest, as represented in the radical metaphor of the biblical fratricide. But those rare instances of another, humane kind of fraternity, when one man might respond to the needs of another, interested Conrad throughout his career. By his heroic act, Peyrol shows the meaning of fraternity as self-sacrifice with a purity and clarity that few Conradian deeds permit. Yet even here we see that self-sacrifice has consequences to Michel and Scevola that undermine the quality of his heroism for us, if not for Conrad.

Readying the boat gives Peyrol the same sense of purpose that writing gave Conrad, who, we recall, not only often needed to think of writing as an action, but also in his mind equated his progress on a work of fiction with sailing a ship toward its destination: Peyrol 'welcomed something to do; this congenial task had all the air of preparation for a voyage, which was a pleasing dream, and it brought every evening the satisfaction of something achieved to that illusory end' (pp. 87—8). Working on the boat provides Peyrol with the psychologically necessary feeling that he can depart if he wants. Yet Peyrol has already become ambivalent about leaving the farm: 'His desire to have something of his own that could float was no longer associated with any desire to wander' (p. 97). We recall that Conrad sustained himself for years with the fiction that writing was a temporary respite from the sea, to which he would soon return.

The novel commends Peyrol's suicidal generosity for Arlette and France. In the three-chapter prologue, Peyrol is given essential qualities that prepare the reader for the possibility of such behaviour. He is patient and has 'a fund of self-command amounting to placidity'

(p. 33); his soul contains 'a drop of universal scorn, a wonderful sedative' (p. 25). Peyrol is in the first three chapters completely detached from family and nation but the novel redefines him in terms of personal and national commitment. As the climactic twenty-four hours progress, we see that beneath his surface lies passion, self-confidence and national pride. The eight years on land have softened, matured, and developed his character. Peyrol, in fact, resembles Lingard of *The Rescue*, another self-contained egoistic hero who at first defines his own morality in opposition to accepted standards and codes. But human relationships intrude upon both of them and make them redefine their self-contained iconoclasm. By a careful dialectical process which modifies his own scorn for politics, the polarity between personal life and politics is reformulated in terms of patriotic love of country based upon familiarity and deep affection for the inhabitants. Gradually Peyrol comes to love not only Arlette, but also Catherine, Michel and even the hunchback. What makes Peyrol heroic to Conrad in part is the evolution of his humanism and empathy, an evolution that recalls the far more limited understated heroism of the speaker in *Under Western Eyes*. Peyrol's patriotism springs not from rhetorical abstractions but from his fidelity to individuals whom he loves and appreciates as individuals. Peyrol dies from a desire to fulfil the life of his surrogate daughter and to leave his life in a manner befitting his life of action; yet he is also the incarnation of a national spirit that transcends politics.

IV

The Rover is Conrad's artistic epitaph not only because it is a synopsis of major themes, but also because it is his final response to desperation, self-doubt, loneliness and suicidal impulses which plagued him throughout his life. The novel is an attempt by the aging writer to use his fiction to work out the recurring concerns of his psyche. Conrad's letter to Garnett about *The Rover* contains a characteristic reaching out toward his alter ego to authenticate both his work and himself:

Every word of your commendation has electrified the dulled fibres of my being. My absolute belief in your sincerity in questions of literary art has relieved me of that load of weary doubt which I have not been able to shake off before. It relieved me thoroughly, because the belief in the absolute

unflawed honesty of your judgment has been one of the
mainstays of my literary life. (4 Dec 1923, *LL*, ii, p. 325)

Imagining decisive action freed Conrad from the paralysing writer's
block that beset him, a block which he so frequently defined in terms
of physical illness. The successful outcome of Peyrol's plotting, the
triumph of his fantasy self, gave Conrad great satisfaction. The
language the narrator uses as he dies is unusually precise for Conrad
when he is penetrating the consciousness of one of his major figures.
He wished to emphasise that Peyrol dies without uncertainty or
anxiety:

A feeling of peace sank into him, not unmingled with pride.
Everything he had planned had come to pass. He had meant to
play that man a trick, and now that trick had been played.
Played by him better than by any other old man on whom age
had stolen, unnoticed, till the veil of peace was torn down by
the touch of sentiment unexpected like an intruder and cruel
like an enemy. (pp. 267–8)

For Peyrol's suicidal mission on behalf of Arlette is not only an act of
heroism and integrity, but also, for Conrad the artist and the man, the
fulfilment of his vision of a significant death. Perhaps at some level
Conrad felt that suicide—plotting and directing one's own death—is
the ultimate metaphor for merging life and art. Peyrol's final delight
is an aesthetic one as he and his creator merge to admire the
completion of Peyrol's mission.

NOTES

1. See Schwarz, *Conrad: 'Almayer's Folly' to 'Under Western Eyes'* (London:
   Macmillan; Ithaca, NY: Cornell University Press, 1980).
2. See Elizabeth Cox Wright, 'The Defining Function of Vocabulary in Conrad's
   The Rover', *South Atlantic Quarterly*, vol. 59 (Spring 1960), pp. 265–77.
3. Avrom Fleishman, *Conrad's Politics: Community and Anarchy in the Fiction of
   Joseph Conrad* (Baltimore: Johns Hopkins Press, 1967), p. 54.
4. In 'Autocracy and War' Conrad had written, 'The subtle and manifold influence
   for evil of the Napoleonic episode as a school of violence, as a sower of national
   hatreds, as the direct provocator of obscurantism and reaction, of political
   tyranny and injustice, cannot well be exaggerated' (*NLL*, p. 86).
5. In his *Conrad: The Three Lives*, p. 865, Karl writes, 'The Rover . . . was, in a real
   sense, a statement about values: connected as it was to the sea as a method of

resolving tensions which on land are irresolvable. One must achieve personal mastery, one must demonstrate individual skill, by taking control of the ship oneself and directing the rudder.'

6. In 1916 Conrad had been fascinated with a younger woman, Jane Anderson, who like Arlette seemed to have a nominal husband. Interestingly, while Peyrol competes with his surrogate son, Conrad's rival may have been his own son, Borys (see Baines, *Conrad: A Critical Biography* (New York: McGraw-Hill, 1960), p. 408, and Karl, *Conrad: The Three Lives* (New York: Farrar, Straus and Giroux, 1979), pp. 162–3, 784–5, 790–1.

Conclusion

When Conrad died in 1924, he left a large fragment entitled *Suspense*. Although had he lived he would undoubtedly have edited the manuscript, it runs to about 75,000 words. Since 1904, if not before, he had planned a large novel of the Napoleonic period and had been working on it intermittently. 'Suspense' refers to the period when Napoleon was exiled to Elba in 1814–15 and Europe was awaiting with great anticipation for the Congress of Vienna to reverse his actions. But in the incomplete novel we see Conrad probing in several directions for his subject. While he completed and revised *The Rover* in only seven months, he was having characteristic difficulty making progress on the far more ambitiously conceived *Suspense*, in part because of his age and ill health, but more because he had trouble deciding what kind of novel to write.

Had it been completed, *Suspense* would certainly have been an artistic recapitulation of Conrad's career rather than a bold foray into new territory. *Suspense* is conceived as an epic novel on the order of *Nostromo* and has the scrambled chronology and large canvas of that novel. Conrad places the lives of individuals in the context of historical events and, as in his political novels, implies that man is partly shaped by historical forces beyond his control. Another reason why he may have had trouble finishing it is that he has created a young English nobleman completely different from himself in age, class and background. By this time in his life, Conrad needed some grounds of identification with a major character to write successfully, and seems to have had trouble imagining the emotional life of his young protagonist Cosmo. Conrad is preoccupied with Cosmo's passion for Adèle, who, unbeknown to him, is his half-sister; that preoccupation deflects him from the intended historical perspective.

Posing as an historical novel, *Suspense* is in part a novel of manners. Napoleon is regarded by Talleyrand as 'the born enemy of good taste' (p. 181). The only time Napoleon speaks to Adèle, who has an unfortunate marriage to the aging and crass Count de Montevesso, his advice is crude and immoral: 'You should try to make some other arrangement' (p. 146). The Count, a successful soldier of fortune, who has been rewarded for his services with a title, cannot disguise his heritage by living in sumptuous style. Of their marriage Adèle tells Cosmo, 'I was being constantly surprised and shocked by the display of evil passions and his fits of ridiculous jealousy which were expressed in such a coarse manner that they could only arouse my resentment and contempt' (p. 137). His materialistic philosophy represents an attitude that Conrad detested. Alternatively lavish and parsimonious, he extinguishes every light in the palace because, in his words, he 'detest[s] waste of all kinds' (p. 154).

Suspense also seems to be an initiation tale on the lines of 'Youth', 'Heart of Darkness', 'The Secret Sharer' and *The Shadow-Line*. We are told that Cosmo, the protagonist, 'lacked that assurance of manner which his good looks and his social status ought to have given him' (p. 76). His inexperience in love before meeting Adèle recalls that of George in *The Arrow of Gold*; socially superior, victimised by an older man, and prematurely experienced, Adèle is another version of Rita. Like Rita, Adèle has learned to live in a hostile world; 'I learned early to suppress every expression of feeling' (p. 150). Adèle needs a responsive consciousness with whom to share her burden. But George, surrounded by intrigue and mystery, is also in need of someone whom he can trust. A pivotal moment in *Suspense* is the confession scene in which Adèle explains herself to Cosmo. Clelia, the emotional invalid, recalls Alice in 'A Smile of Fortune'. *Suspense* even has a version of the 'secret sharer' motif in the form of the relationship between the lower-class man of action, Attilio, and the more self-conscious and contemplative son of English nobility, Cosmo.

Conrad's later works demonstrate the continuity of his career. Throughout his career, his works are expressions of his quest for values and self-definition. Continuing the focus of the novels about politics (*Nostromo*, *The Secret Agent* and *Under Western Eyes*), Conrad's later works are more concerned with family and personal relationships than are his prior works. Except for 'The Secret Sharer' and *The Shadow-Line*, the works discussed in this study are concerned with how and why people love one another. But they also address how historical and social forces limit and define the possibilities for love and action. Conrad never puts behind him the conviction that man is caught in a web of circumstances beyond his control. But he also believes in man's capacity to grow, to love, and to know himself. Conrad believes that, within an indifferent if not hostile universe, man's indomitable will enables him to survive despite setbacks and individual failures. Thus he is not the nihilist and the prophet of darkness that he has been depicted in much recent criticism.

Conrad's later work contains qualities that typify the work of many older artists: the revival of forms and themes of past artistic successes, references to earlier works, nostalgia for an earlier period of life, emphases on turning-points in life, and intermittent sensuality. But what is lacking in Conrad's later work is the creative rage of the older Yeats, the aging Monet's willingness to take a chance, the bold disregard for precedents of the Joyce who wrote *Finnegans Wake*, and the Olympian turning away from mere nominalistic details to focus on essential truths that characterises the later work of Matisse.

Yet, were Conrad to have written only the works discussed in this study, his place within English fiction would be secure, and he would rank as a major twentieth-century figure behind Lawrence, Joyce and maybe Woolf. 'The Secret Sharer' is one of the great novellas in English literature; *The Shadow-Line* is a beautiful, intense short novel which, like 'The Secret Sharer', is concerned with a young captain's discovery of his own abilities. Despite their flaws, *Victory*, *Chance* and *The Rover* are important and challenging works. While *Victory* and *Chance* offer profound analyses of human failings and intricate personal relationships, *The Rover* is a lyrical novel about mutability and the rhythms of human existence in which one man confronts mortality in order to create the possibility of life and love for others.

However, it is on the work of his entire career that Conrad's importance must be considered. On the basis of his novels about politics and his analysis of the human psyche, he is a major figure in creating literary and intellectual modernism. His innovative use of the meditative voice probing crucial past experience, and his organisation of a narrative by juxtaposition of morally and psychologically significant incidents rather than by chronologically consecutive incidents, have had a profound effect upon the techniques of modern fiction. Furthermore, Conrad invented a means—not only a vocabulary, but also the narrative and rhetorical methods—for speaking about the interior self. By dramatising doubles of his characters and himself, he taught us how to think about the ambiguity of our identities and made us aware of that other self that we can neither quite know nor evade.

Conrad was a pioneer in discovering for us the imaginative and intellectual mind-scape in which we, sometimes to our dismay, now live. Coming to terms with his own psyche and his own past enabled Conrad to understand his era. As an exile, the orphan child of political revolutionaries, a man who felt himself an outsider until his final years and who was beset by anxiety and self-doubt, Conrad represents his—and our—historical period. His work reflects his personal history. But, as Stephen Dedalus says of Shakespeare in *Ulysses*, 'He found in the world without as actual what was in his own world within as possible.' Conrad is concerned with the obsessions and fixations that shape man's behaviour. He understands that man's moral behaviour is often a disguise for his psychological needs. Yet he sees the importance also of defining man's moral behaviour as a result of his *Zeitgeist*.

In many ways Conrad anticipated our perception of ourselves. He sees the limitations of political solutions and the ambiguity of political behaviour. He insists upon psychological explanations for social behaviour and understands the fragility of man's moral existence in an amoral cosmos. He realises that man must find his own salvation just as he must discover his own values. That Conrad recognises man's potential and his folly, his creativity and his impotence, his energy and his irrational impulses, his need to be understood and his primitive selfishness, makes the present-day reader feel that Conrad is one of us.

NOTE

1. See Karl, *Conrad: The Three Lives* (New York: Farrar, Straus and Giroux, 1979), pp. 863, 873.

Appendix

Story and volume	Date of completion	Year of first publication, in serial form or in a collection
Tales of Unrest (1898)		
'The Idiots'	May 1896	1896
'An Outpost of Progress'	July 1896	1897
'The Lagoon'	Aug 1896	1897
'Karain'	Apr 1897	1897
'The Return'	Sep 1897	1898
Youth (1902)		
'Youth'	June 1898	1898
'Heart of Darkness'	Feb 1899	1899
'The End of the Tether'	Oct 1902	1902
Typhoon (1903)		
'Typhoon'	Jan 1901	1902
'Falk: A Reminiscence'	May 1901	1903
'Amy Foster'	June 1901	1901
'Tomorrow'	Jan 1902	1902
A Set of Six (1908)		
'Gaspar Ruiz'	Nov 1905	1906
'The Brute'	*c.* Dec 1905	1906
'An Anarchist'	Nov–Dec 1905	1906
'The Informer'	Dec 1905–Jan 1906	1906
'Il Conde'	Dec 1906	1908
'The Duel'	Apr 1907	1908
'Twixt Land and Sea (1912)		
'The Secret Sharer'	Dec 1909	1910

Story and volume	Date of completion	Year of first publication, in serial form or in a collection
'A Smile of Fortune'	Aug 1910	1911
'Freya of the Seven Isles'	Feb 1911	1912
Within the Tides (1915)		
'The Partner'	Oct–Nov 1910	1911
'The Inn of the Two Witches'	Dec 1912	1913
'The Planter of Malata'	Dec 1913	1914
'Because of the Dollars'	Dec 1913 or Jan 1914	1914
Tales of Hearsay (1925)		
'The Black Mate'	*c.* 1886 (possibly revised 1908)	1908
'Prince Roman'	Sep–Oct 1910	1910
'The Warrior's Soul'	Mar 1916	1917
'The Tale'	Oct 1916	1917

Novel	Date of completion	Year of first publication, in serial or bound form
Almayer's Folly	Mar 1894	1895
An Outcast of the Islands	Sep 1895	1896
The Nigger of the 'Narcissus'	Jan 1897	1897
Lord Jim	July 1900	1899–1900
Nostromo	Aug 1904	1904
The Secret Agent	Nov 1906	1906–7
Under Western Eyes	Dec 1909	1910–11
Chance	Mar 1912	1912
Victory	June 1914	1915

Novel	Date of completion	Year of first publication, in serial or bound form
The Shadow-Line	Dec 1915	1916
The Arrow of Gold	June 1918	1919
The Rescue	May 1919	1919
The Rover	June 1922	1923

Selected Bibliography

The following list includes all critical and scholarly studies cited in the notes plus a number of items that have been particularly significant to the growth of this study.

Auerbach, Erich, *Mimesis: The Representation of Reality in Western Literature*, trans. Willard Trask (Princeton, NJ: Princeton University Press, 1953 [orig. ed. 1946]).

Baines, Jocelyn, *Joseph Conrad: A Critical Biography* (New York: McGraw-Hill, 1960).

Beach, Joseph Warren, 'Impressionism: Conrad', in his *The Twentieth Century Novel: Studies in Technique* (New York: Appleton-Century, 1932), pp. 337–65.

Blackburn, William (ed.), *Joseph Conrad: Letters to William Blackwood and David S. Meldrum* (Durham, NC: Duke University Press, 1958).

Blackmur, R. P., *Eleven Essays in the European Novel* (New York: Harbinger Books, 1954).

Booth, Wayne C., *The Rhetoric of Fiction* (Chicago: University of Chicago Press, 1961).

Bradbrook, Muriel C., *Joseph Conrad: Poland's English Genius* (Cambridge: Cambridge University Press, 1941).

Burke, Kenneth, *The Philosophy of Literary Form*, rev. edn (New York: Vintage Books, 1957).

Cassirer, Ernst, *The Logic of the Humanities*, trans. Clarence Smith Howe (New Haven, Conn.: Yale University Press, 1961).

Conrad, Joseph, *Complete Works*, Kent edn, 26 vols (Garden City, NY: Doubleday, 1926).

Cox, C. B., *Joseph Conrad: The Modern Imagination* (London: J. M. Dent, 1974).

Crews, Frederick, 'The Power of Darkness', *Partisan Review*, vol. XXXIV (Autumn 1967), pp. 507–25.

Curle, Richard, *The Last Twelve Years of Joseph Conrad* (London: Sampson, Low, Marston, 1928).

—— (ed.), *Conrad to a Friend, 150 Selected Letters from Joseph Conrad to Richard Curle* (New York: Doubleday, Doran, 1928).

Daleski, H. M., *Joseph Conrad: The Way of Dispossession* (New York: Holmes and Meier, 1976).

Dangerfield, George, *The Strange Death of Liberal England 1910–1914* (New York: Capricorn, 1961 [orig. ed. London, 1935]).

Dike, Donald, 'The Tempest of Axel Heyst', *Nineteenth Century Fiction*, vol. XVII (Sep 1962), pp. 95–113.

Ellmann, Richard and Feidelson, Charles, Jr (eds), *The Modern Tradition* (New York: Oxford University Press, 1965).

Fernando, Lloyd, 'Conrad's Eastern Expatriates: A New Version of His Outcast', *PMLA*, vol. XCI (1976), pp. 78–90.

Fleishman, Avrom, *Conrad's Politics: Community and Anarchy in the Fiction of Joseph Conrad* (Baltimore: Johns Hopkins Press, 1967).

Ford, Ford Madox, *Joseph Conrad: A Personal Remembrance* (Boston, Mass.: Little, Brown, 1924).

Garnett, Edward, *Letters from Joseph Conrad, 1895–1924* (Indianapolis: Bobbs-Merrill, 1928).

Gee, John A., and Sturm, Paul J., *Letters of Joseph Conrad to Marguerite Poradowska, 1890–1920* (New Haven, Conn.: Yale University Press, 1940).

Gillon, Adam, *The Eternal Solitary* (New York: Bookman Associates, 1960).

Glassman, Peter J., *Language and Being: Joseph Conrad and the Literature of Personality* (New York and London: Columbia University Press, 1976).

Graver, Lawrence, *Conrad's Short Fiction* (Berkeley and Los Angeles, Calif.: University of California Press, 1969).

——, 'Conrad's First Story', *Studies in Short Fiction*, vol. II (Winter 1965), pp. 164–9.

Guerard, Albert J., *Conrad the Novelist* (Cambridge, Mass.: Harvard University Press, 1958).

Guetti, James, ' "Heart of Darkness": The Failure of Imagination', in his *The Limits of Metaphor: A Study of Melville, Conrad, and Faulkner* (Ithaca, NY: Cornell University Press, 1967), pp. 46–68.

Gurko, Leo, *Joseph Conrad: Giant in Exile* (New York: Macmillan, 1962).

Harkness, Bruce (ed.), *Conrad's 'The Secret Sharer' and The Critics* (Belmont, Calif.: Wadsworth, 1962).

Haugh, Robert F., *Joseph Conrad: Discovery in Design* (Norman, Okla.: University of Oklahoma Press, 1957).

Hay, Eloise Knapp, *The Political Novels of Joseph Conrad* (Chicago: University of Chicago Press, 1963).

Hewitt, Douglas, *Conrad: A Reassessment* (Cambridge: Bowes and Bowes, 1952).

Howe, Irving, 'Conrad: Order and Anarchy', in his *Politics and the Novel* (New York: Horizon Press and Meridian Books, 1957), pp. 76–113. Reprinted from *Kenyon Review*, vol. xv (Autumn 1953), pp. 505–21, and, vol. xvi (Winter 1954), pp. 1–19.

Hynes, Samuel, *The Edwardian Turn of Mind* (Princeton, NJ: Princeton University Press, 1968).

James, Henry, *Notes on Novelists* (New York: Charles Scribner's Sons, 1914).

Jean-Aubry, G., *Joseph Conrad: Life and Letters*, 2 vols (Garden City, NY: Doubleday, Page, 1927).

Johnson, Bruce M., *Conrad's Models of Mind* (Minneapolis: University of Minnesota Press, 1971).

Karl, Frederick R., *A Reader's Guide to Joseph Conrad* (New York: Noonday Press, 1960).

——, *Joseph Conrad: The Three Lives* (New York: Farrar, Straus and Giroux, 1979).

Kirschner, Paul, 'Conrad and Maupassant: Moral Solitude and "A Smile of Fortune"', *Review of English Studies*, vol. 7 (1966), pp. 62–77.

Laing, R. D., *The Divided Self: An Existential Study in Sanity and Madness* (Baltimore: Penguin Books, 1965).

Langbaum, Robert, *The Poetry of Experience* (New York: Norton, 1963 [orig. ed. 1957]).

——, *The Modern Spirit: Essays on the Continuity of Nineteenth and Twentieth Century Literature* (New York: Oxford University Press, 1970).

Langer, Susanne K., *Feeling and Form* (New York: Charles Scribner's, 1953).

Leavis, F. R., *The Great Tradition: George Eliot, Henry James, Joseph Conrad* (London: Chatto and Windus, 1948).

Lester, John A., Jr, *Journey Through Despair 1880–1914: Transformations in British Literary Culture* (Princeton, NJ: Princeton University Press, 1968).

McCall, Dan, 'The Meaning in Darkness: a Response to a Psychoanalytical Study of Conrad', *College English*, vol. xxix (May 1968), pp. 620–7.

Martz, Louis L., *The Poetry of Meditation*, 2nd ed. (New Haven, Conn.: Yale University Press, 1962 [orig. ed. 1954]).

Meyer, Bernard C., MD, *Joseph Conrad: A Psychoanalytic Biography* (Princeton, NJ: Princeton University Press, 1967).

Miller, J. Hillis, *The Disappearance of God* (Cambridge, Mass.: Belknap Press of Harvard University Press, 1963).

——, *Poets of Reality: Six Twentieth Century Writers* (Cambridge, Mass.: Belknap Press of Harvard University Press, 1965).

Moser, Thomas, *Joseph Conrad: Achievement and Decline* (Cambridge, Mass.: Harvard University Press, 1957).

——, 'Conrad, Ford, and the Sources of *Chance*', *Conradiana*, vol. VII (1976), pp. 207–24.

—— (ed.), *Lord Jim*, Norton Critical edition (New York: Norton, 1968).

——, 'The "Rescuer" Manuscript: A Key to Conrad's Development—and Decline', *Harvard Library Bulletin*, vol. X (1956), pp. 325–55.

Najder, Zdzislaw, *Conrad's Polish Background: Letters to and from Polish Friends* (London: Oxford University Press, 1964).

Palmer, John A., *Joseph Conrad's Fiction: A Study in Literary Growth* (Ithaca, NY: Cornell University Press, 1968).

Perry, John Oliver, 'Action, Vision, or Voice: The Moral Dilemmas in Conrad's Tale-telling', *Modern Fiction Studies*, vol. X (Spring 1964), pp. 3–14.

Rosenfield, Claire, *Paradise of Snakes: An Archetypal Analysis of Conrad's Political Novels* (Chicago: University of Chicago Press, 1967).

Roussel, Royal, *The Metaphysics of Darkness: A Study in the Unity and Development of Conrad's Fiction* (Baltimore and London: The Johns Hopkins Press, 1971).

Said, Edward W., *Joseph Conrad and the Fiction of Autobiography* (Cambridge, Mass.: Harvard University Press, 1966).

Scholes, Robert, and Kellogg, Robert, *The Nature of Narrative* (London: Oxford University Press, 1966).

Schwarz, Daniel R., *Conrad: 'Almayer's Folly' to 'Under Western Eyes'* (London: Macmillan; Ithaca, NY: Cornell University Press, 1980).

Secor, Robert, *The Rhetoric of Shifting Perspectives: Conrad's 'Victory'*, Pennsylvania State University Studies, no. 32 (University Park, Pa., 1971).

Sherry, Norman, *Conrad's Eastern World* (Cambridge: Cambridge University Press, 1966).

——, *Conrad's Western World* (Cambridge: Cambridge University Press, 1971).

Stallman, Robert W. (ed.), *The Art of Joseph Conrad: A Critical Symposium* (East Lansing, Mich.: Michigan State University Press, 1960).

Tindall, W. Y., 'Apology for Marlow', in R. C. Rathburn and M. Steinmann, Jr (eds), *From Jane Austen to Joseph Conrad* (Minneapolis: University of Minnesota Press, 1959).

Van Ghent, Dorothy, *The English Novel: Form and Function* (New York: Harper Torch Books, 1961 [orig. ed. 1953]).

Warren, Robert Penn, Introduction to *Nostromo* (New York: Modern Library, 1951). Reprinted from *Sewanee Review*, vol. LIX (Summer 1951), pp. 363–91.

Watt, Ian, 'Conrad, James, and *Chance*', in Maynard Mack and Ian Gregor (eds), *Imagined Worlds: Essays in Honour of John Butt* (London: Methuen, 1968), pp. 301–22.

——, 'Story and Idea in Conrad's *The Shadow-Line*', *Critical Quarterly*, vol. II (Summer 1960), pp. 133–48.

Watts, C. T. (ed.), *Joseph Conrad's Letters to R. B. Cunninghame Graham* (Cambridge: Cambridge University Press, 1969).

Wiley, Paul L., *Conrad's Measure of Man* (Madison: University of Wisconsin Press; Toronto: Burns and MacEachern, 1954).

Williams, Porter, Jr, 'Story and Frame in Conrad's "The Tale" ', *Studies in Short Fiction*, vol. V (1968), pp. 179–85.

Wright, Elizabeth Cox, 'The Defining Function of Vocabulary in Conrad's *The Rover*', *South Atlantic Quarterly*, vol. LIX (Spring 1960), pp. 265–77.

Wright, Walter F., *Romance and Tragedy in Joseph Conrad* (Lincoln, Nebr.: University of Nebraska Press, 1949).

Zabel, Morton Dauwen, 'Conrad', in his *Craft and Character in Modern Fiction* (New York: Viking, 1957), pp. 147–227. Includes revised verson of 'Joseph Conrad: Chance and Recognition', *Sewanee Review*, LIII (Winter 1945), pp. 1–22.

——, Introduction to *The Portable Conrad*, ed. Zabel (New York: Viking, 1947), pp. 1–47.

——, Introduction to '*The Shadow-Line*', '*Typhoon*', and '*The Secret Sharer*' (Garden City, NY: Doubleday, 1959), pp. 1–27.

Zuckerman, Jerome, ' "A Smile of Fortune": Conrad's Interesting Failure', *Studies in Short Fiction*, vol. I (Winter 1964), pp. 99–102.

——, 'Architecture of *The Shadow-Line*', *Conradiana*, vol. III (1971–2), pp. 87–92.

Index